HENRY MANCINI SERIES on the Arts

EXPLORING MUSICAL STRUCTURE

William Perkins

MUSIC

Henry Mancini Series on the Arts: Exploring Musical Structure

ISBN-13: 978-0692534229
ISBN-10: 0692534229

Published by Prodigy Books a division of Sentient Enterprises, Inc. Pittsburgh, PA. Copyright © 2015 by Sentient Enterprises, Inc. All rights reserved.

Permission in writing must be obtained from the publisher before any part of this work may be reproduced or transmitted in any form or by any means, electronic or mechanical, including photocopying and recording, or by any information storage or retrieval system. All trademarks, service marks, registered trademarks, and registered service marks are the property of their respective owners and are used herein for identification purposes only.

Printed in the United States of America
10 9 8 7 6 5 4 3 2 1

Cover design by Scott Sheariss

Anna's Theme
from *The Red Violin*
By John Corigliano
Copyright (c) 1999 Sony/ATV Music Publishing LLC
All Rights Administered by Sony/ATV Music Publishing LLC,
8 Music Square West, Nashville, TN 37203
International Copyright Secured All Rights Reserved

PREFACE

WHY STUDY MUSICAL STRUCTURE?

Many music lovers are curious about how a composition is structured, about its musical architecture. By studying its structure, the music enthusiast can unlock keys to how a musical piece "works". The contents of this book can help prepare the student for further courses in music. Musical structure is like the trunk of a tree with many branches. Students need to understand the structure of music as prerequisite for later courses in such subjects as orchestration, counterpoint (how lines in music move against one another), or arranging and composing. Even an obviously performance-based course like Improvisation will require the basics of musical structure. Some readers study the structure of music because they want to understand more about some specific area of music. For example, a guitar or keyboard player would learn about chords and harmony by studying those topics in this book.

WHAT CAN THE READER LEARN IN EXPLORING MUSICAL STRUCTURE?

This can be an intriguing and fun study because it helps develop or improve musicianship skills and helps solve many mysteries of musical structures and sounds. This book presents the basics of musical sound (pitch, melody, rhythm, harmony, etc.) and how they appear in music. The student will also be guided through elements and exercises in reading and interpreting standard musical notation and will be given exercises to acquire and sharpen such skills. Studies in musical structure will reveal how melodies, harmonies, and rhythms are formed and work together. Later in the book, the reader will apply presented principles in a very interesting exercise in writing harmony for a given melody. The later chapters in the book expand theoretical knowledge into some very practical applications in such areas as writing for different instruments, the very interesting sounds of jazz harmonies, changing keys in the middle of a piece, and examining and understanding some musical forms that organize whole works.

This treatment of music contains material for enthusiasts at different levels and abilities. For the reader wanting some content of special interest or additional challenge, there are brief sections called "**Something extra**", such as that following the topic on perfect intervals. Yet the approach "leaves no stone unturned" in taking the reader step-by-step from the most fundamental issues on through exploring the nature of harmonic flow and musical forms.

What approach is used in this book?

The educational approach is one that is necessitated by the multidimensional nature of the field of music. The approach used in this book is a kind of "simple to complex", step-by-step method. Such method makes it possible to utilize more interesting examples than would have been the case if certain topics had been presented comprehensively before moving on to other topics. For example, the topic of musical intervals is treated in stages. Introducing seconds and the octave in the early chapters on intervals allows us to cover the topic of scales. Then, after covering topics on the notation of pitch and some rhythmic elements, the author is able to use more interesting examples from musical literature when the content moves on to the second treatment of intervals. Additionally, the author uses a "just in time" approach in introducing the perfect fifth interval within the sections on key signatures so that the "circle of fifths" can be used as a visual tool in understanding and remembering key signatures. The reader may sometimes notice a bit of repetition. This is done on purpose. When returning to a topic that has not been treated for a while, some review helps facilitate recall. This gentle, "one level at a time" approach should help the reader move smoothly and successfully through the content.

Wherever practical, the author has used examples from known masters of composition. In some situations, the author has found it expeditious to invent short examples rather than draw from literature. Because of the close attention paid to selecting and composing examples, it is strongly suggested that the material be read in the order in which it appears in the book.

How can the reader best navigate through the content?

Those who do not yet read conventional musical notation should start at the beginning and not skip around (each chapter builds upon the previous). Those who already read musical scores and play an instrument or sing from score could begin at Chapter 13, Non-Diatonic Scales. (Still skim earlier chapters to make sure you don't miss unfamiliar content).

Audio Files That Accompany This Book

The reader will notice that many of the musical figures and examples have a small "musical notes" icon (♪) printed beside them. For these, the reader will find accompanying sound files at the following web address: www.manciniarts.com.

I wish you a rewarding and fascinating journey as you explore musical structure,

Bill Perkins

TABLE OF CONTENTS

Chapter 1	♦ Music Elements	2
Chapter 2	♦ Time Values	7
Chapter 3	♦ Clefs and Staves	12
Chapter 4	♦ Meter	24
Chapter 5	♦ Intervals: Part 1	32
Chapter 6	♦ Accidentals	42
Chapter 7	♦ The Major Scale	49
Chapter 8	♦ Key Signatures	57
Chapter 9	♦ Altering Time Values; Articulations	64
Chapter 10	♦ Intervals: Part 2	74
Chapter 11	♦ Minor Scales and Keys	89
Chapter 12	♦ Compound Meter, Tuplets, and Ornaments	98
Chapter 13	♦ Non-Diatonic Scales	107
Chapter 14	♦ Chords: Part 1	115
Chapter 15	♦ Chords: Part 2	123
Chapter 16	♦ Functional Harmony: Part 1	133
Chapter 17	♦ Functional Harmony: Part 2	143
Chapter 18	♦ Functional Harmony: Part 3	151
Chapter 19	♦ Extended Metric and Rhythmic Practices	159
Chapter 20	♦ Modal and Non-Western Scales	170

Chapter 21	♦	Non-Harmonic Notes	181
Chapter 22	♦	Voice leading: Two Voices	197
Chapter 23	♦	Voice leading: Four Voices	208
Chapter 24	♦	Functional Harmony: Part 4	223
Chapter 25	♦	Identifying Chord Function	233
Chapter 26	♦	Melodic Structure	244
Chapter 27	♦	Harmonizing a Melody	258
Chapter 28	♦	Four-Voice Writing	269
Chapter 29	♦	Transposition and Instrumentation	287
Chapter 30	♦	Jazz Harmony	299
Chapter 31	♦	Modulation: Part 1	311
Chapter 32	♦	Modulation: Part 2	320
Chapter 33	♦	Musical Forms 1	329
Chapter 34	♦	Musical Forms 2	348
Chapter 35	♦	Musical Forms 3	358
Chapter 36	♦	Beyond Traditional Tonality	371

APPENDICES

Appendix A	♦	Recommended Listening Exercises	390
Appendix B	♦	Instrument Transpositions and Ranges	394
Appendix C	♦	Quiz Answer Keys	400

EXPLORING
MUSICAL STRUCTURE

CHAPTER 1: MUSIC ELEMENTS

Objectives:

1. Describe basic concepts for the elements of music presented in this chapter, or recognize and distinguish among their definitions. Basic concepts include the following: music theory, musical dynamics (loudness), pitch, duration, tone, note, rest, score, accent, beat, tempo, and rhythm.
2. Identify symbols for musical dynamics.

What Is "Musical Structure"?

Musical Structure is the study of the structure of constructed music whether the "constructing" is done with symbols on pages or it is "constructed" by assembling sounds via a computer music system (without first notating it). The principles are the same regardless of the tools used to put the music together. Practicing musicians still follow directions on conventionally written scores to know how to produce the sounds to be made. This book will pursue the study of musical structuring by studying musical examples that use conventional notation.

Though the history of music is an interesting and scholarly subject, this book limits discussion to the basic theoretical facts, concepts, principles and relations that are evident in the musical compositions since the middle ages (since about the 14th century) and still being performed in today's concerts.

Basic Concepts

The study of music is one that builds progressively from basic principles and concepts. Following are the basic concepts that must be attained before moving on. Even if the reader already knows these because of his/her interest and practice in music, it is important to start with a solid understanding of the foundational principles.

Musical dynamics (loudness)

Music is made up of successions of sounds and silences. Some sounds can barely be heard; others may be so loud that they hurt your ears. **Loudness**, also called **volume**, is how loud or how soft a sound is. Levels of loudness in music are called dynamics. Sound can be heard only if it travels to the ear through a physical, elastic medium, such as air or water. The sound is carried through this medium by way of pressure waves that cause the ear drum to move back and forth. The degree of loudness is proportional to the amplitude of these pressure variations. Perhaps you can recall science fiction movies in which there are these big explosions in space with consequent loud blasts of sound.

Actually, this can't happen. In space, there is no elastic medium capable of transporting pressure variations. If you saw the movie 2001: A Space Odyssey, you may recall that when the access door to space was blown, the sound ceased. The author of the text and technical consultant for the movie was Arthur C. Clark, who is a famous engineer as well as science fiction novelist, and he made sure that the movie contained such technical accuracies.

Another very practical fact that you should know about loudness is that it is possible for sound to be so loud that it can permanently damage your hearing. Therefore, when at a concert containing very loud music, do not sit close to and directly in front of the speakers. Resulting damage to the hearing cannot (yet) be reversed. (It actually rips out the tiny hair cells that connect the inner ear to the brain!) Loudness levels can be measured by engineers and are measured in units of the decibel. A doubling of the pressure intensity corresponds to about 3 decibels of change in loudness. A change of 1 decibel is barely perceptible by human hearing, but we have a range of perceptible changes in loudness of over 100 decibels. A practical fact to consider is that if two musical instruments play a sound, the change in loudness does NOT double! It takes about ten instruments playing the same note to double the loudness of just one playing it.

Different musical instruments can change loudness in different ways. Loudness might be raised by striking it with more force, stroking it with more pressure, or blowing into it harder.

Symbols for dynamics:

pp = pianissimo, very soft

p = piano, soft

mp = mezzo piano, medium soft

mf = mezzo forte, medium loud

f = forte, loud

ff = fortissimo, very loud

ppp means even softer than "very soft"

fff means even louder than "very loud"

⎯⎯⎯⎯ : crescendo, gradually get louder

⎯⎯⎯⎯ : decrescendo (or diminuendo), gradually get softer

Pitch

Remember that sound reaches your ear as variations in pressure. The rate at which these variations occur produces the sense of *pitch*. A "squeak" makes a very high pitch; a "groan", a low pitch. The pressure variations of musical sounds are actually quite complex. For a sound with a steady pitch, the pressure variations occur in a complicated pattern that is repeated over and over; it is the rate at which this pattern occurs, called the frequency of its fundamental, that determines the pitch of the sound. If the pattern repeats 440 times per second, the perceived pitch is that of the first A above middle C. (Letter names of notes will be reviewed in Chapter 2.) If you can recall hearing an orchestra tuning, the oboe starts out by playing this pitch. Human hearing has its limits; only frequencies between about 40 and 20,000 vibrations per second can be heard as pitches.

How can pitch be changed? Whatever is producing the vibrations must be capable of changing the rates of those vibrations. Here are a couple of examples. If a tube is producing the sound (e.g., a trombone or whistle), the pitch can be changed by changing the length of the tube (by moving the trombone's slide or opening a hole in the tube); longer tubes produce lower pitches. If it is a string that is vibrating, changing the length or tension or thickness of the string will change its pitch. A lower pitch is produced by a longer string, a thicker string, or a string with less tension. Think of a guitar: When you shorten a string by pressing a finger against a fret on the fret board, the result is a higher pitch; the thicker strings produce lower pitches than do the thinner strings; if you stretch a string tighter (by turning the thumb screw), you get a higher pitch.

Time

Events in a piece of music occur for differing durations of time. Timing is everything, whether over the long span of an entire composition or passage or just the duration of one particular sound. Here are a few important definitions. *Duration* is how long a particular sound lasts. A *tone* is a sound of a particular pitch and duration. A *note* is a notated symbol for a tone. A *rest* is a notated silence of a specified duration. A *score* is a set of written directions that tell music performers what notes and rests to play and when and how to play them. An *accent* in music is a special emphasis given to a note or expected at certain points in time in the music. The *beat* of a certain piece of music is that regular pulse to which the listener could naturally tap his or her foot while listening to the music or playing it. The person writing the music decides what time value is to be treated as a "beat", and notates time based on this duration. (Chapter 4 will cover in detail how this is notated.) The time rate at which the beats occur is called the *tempo* and is measured in beats per minute. *Rhythm* is a complicated sense of motion through time in music that is a combination of successive durations of notes and the timing of accents.

Summary

This Chapter has introduced musical structure and set the context for how it will be approached in this book. In presenting the basic concepts, each of the most basic parameters of music were defined and briefly explained: loudness, pitch, and time.

Next

In Chapter 2, we will discuss how time values are written in a score by using symbols for notes and rests.

Quiz 1

Match the following by placing the letter for the term beside the numbered definition.

1. a special emphasis given to a note: ___
2. what you hear that is due to the rate of vibrations of sound pressure levels: ___
3. a regular pulse in music, to which a listener could naturally tap his/her foot: ___
4. how long a particular sound lasts: ___
5. how loud or how soft a sound is: ___
6. the time rate at which beats occur in a piece of music: ___
7. a notation for silence of a specified duration: ___
8. a sound of a particular pitch and duration: ___
9. a set of written directions telling music performers what, when, and how to play: ___
10. a notated symbol for a tone: ___

a.	accent	g.	rest
b.	beat	h.	rhythm
c.	duration	j.	score
d.	loudness	k.	tempo
e.	note	m.	tone
f.	pitch		

Match the following symbols by supplying the letter for the correct description or name:

11. f ___

12. ff ___

13. fff ___

14. mf ___

15. mp ___

16. p ___

17. pp ___

18. ppp ___

19. > ___

20. < ___

a. gradually get louder
b. gradually get softer
c. loud
d. louder than very loud
e. medium loud
f. medium soft
g. soft
h. softer than very soft
j. very loud
k. very soft

CHAPTER 2: TIME VALUES

Objectives:

1. Identify correct labels for the symbols for notes and rests.
2. Report relative duration relationship between any two notes or any two rests.

We will deal with the handling of time in music in several chapters. For now, you will review the durations of notes and rests (sounds and silences) as indicated by the shapes of their written symbols.

Notes

Notes are written for sounds played on musical instruments or by sound files in music synthesizers (or computer music programs). No matter what kind of sound the instrument makes, the symbol for the note indicates the duration. One note value has to have a specified duration and then all the other note values are whole or fractional multiples of that value. The way the duration of the first note is supplied will be covered later in the topic on Meters.

Here are the most common relative note values used in modern musical scores:
The **whole note** has the longest duration in most modern scores (although there are double whole notes used in older scores). Here is its symbol: 𝒐 .

The **half note** is half the duration of a whole note – its symbol: ♩ or ♩. (The vertical line is called the *stem* of the note, and can go either up or down from the *note head*, as shown.)

The **quarter note** takes 1/4th the duration of a whole note, or half the duration of a half note – its symbol: ♩ or ♩. (After this, we will stop showing both stem-up and stem-down.)

The **eighth note** is 1/8th the duration of a whole note, or half the duration of a quarter note – its symbol: ♪ . (That little curvy line to the right of the stem is called a *flag* and helps to tell an eighth note from a quarter note).

The **sixteenth note** is 1/16th the duration of a whole note, or half the duration of an eighth note. Notice that its symbol contains two flags: ♬

Groups of consecutive 8th or 16th notes often have their flags combined into horizontal bars called **beams**. It is much easier to draw beams for these groups than it is to draw individual flags. Here are some beamed 8th notes: ♪♪♪♪ ; and here are some beamed 16th notes: ♬♬

Following is a chart that shows these note duration values in relation to one another:

Figure 2-1: Chart of relative note durations.

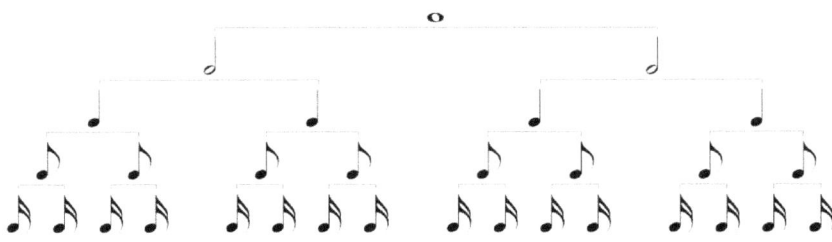

Yes, there are such things as 32nd notes ♪ and 64th notes ♪; just add more flags (or beams).

Rests

Rests are symbols that indicate silences of specified durations. A whole rest has the same duration as a whole note. Here are the names and symbols for the rests:

whole rest: ▬

half rest: ▬

Notice that while the whole rest hangs below a line, the half rest sits on top of a line.

quarter rest: 𝄽

eighth rest: 𝄾

sixteenth rest: 𝄿

Just as we showed a chart for relative note values, one can also place the rest values into such a chart:

Figure 2-2: Chart of relative durations of rests.

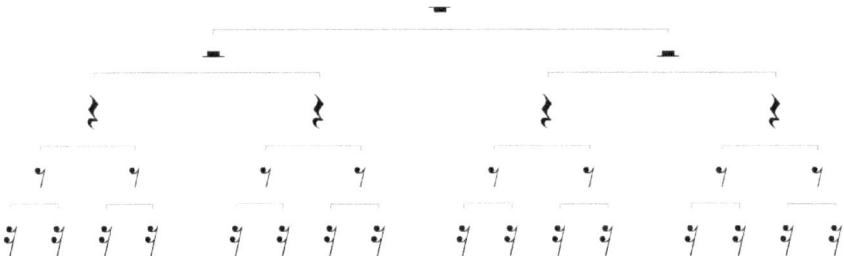

One more detail: the whole rest can be used to indicate a <u>whole measure</u> of rest, even if there are not exactly four quarter notes to a measure.

Practice Notes and Rests

If you play a musical instrument, play any pitch (high tone or low tone) you wish; only the durations matter in these exercises. You can also sing them with a neutral syllable, such as "tah", again on any pitch you choose. For a reference point, let a quarter note be any duration you choose to do the exercise comfortably (say, somewhere between a second and half second duration; or just tap your foot to a comfortable pulse and let that be one quarter note). Once you choose a duration for the quarter note, keep to that same duration. If you have never done this kind of thing before, don't worry; this is just for fun. It will be a lot easier once we deal with beats and meters in Chapter 4.

Exercise 2-1: Notes only; longer values: (Remember, half notes are twice as long as quarter notes; whole notes are 4 times as long as quarter notes; just count to 4 when you do the whole note.)

Exercise 2-2: Notes only; shorter values: (Remember that the 8th notes will go twice as fast as the quarter notes and the 16th notes will go twice as fast as the 8th notes.)

Exercise 2-3: Notes and rests:

(Hold out that last note for a duration of four quarter notes!)

> **SUMMARY**
>
> Chapter 2 reviewed duration values of notes and rests as indicated by their symbols. We ended with a bit of practice in performing durations. We will do these again in Chapter 4, where the added practices of beats and meters will help make such exercises easier.

Exploring Musical Structure

NEXT

In the next Chapter, you will study clefs and how they are used to locate pitches on the musical staff.

Quiz 2

1. This symbol, ♩, is a/an _____ note.
   a. whole
   b. half
   c. quarter
   d. eighth
   e. sixteenth

2. This symbol, ♬, is a/an _____ note.
   a. whole
   b. half
   c. quarter
   d. eighth
   e. sixteenth

3. This symbol, ♩, is a/an _____ note.
   a. whole
   b. half
   c. quarter
   d. eighth
   e. sixteenth

4. This symbol, ♪, is a/an _____ note.
   a. whole
   b. half
   c. quarter
   d. eighth
   e. sixteenth

5. This symbol, 𝄾, is a/an _____ rest.
   a. whole
   b. half
   c. quarter
   d. eighth
   e. sixteenth

6. This symbol, ▬ , is a/an _____ rest.
   a. whole
   b. half
   c. quarter
   d. eighth
   e. sixteenth

7. This symbol, 𝄾 , is a/an _____ rest.
   a. whole
   b. half
   c. quarter
   d. eighth
   e. sixteenth

8. This symbol, ▬ , is a/an _____ rest.
   a. whole
   b. half
   c. quarter
   d. eighth
   e. sixteenth

9. A half rest has the same duration as _____ quarter rests.
   a. one
   b. two
   c. three
   d. four

10. _____ eighth notes have the same duration as one half note.
    a. Two
    b. Three
    c. Four
    d. Eight

CHAPTER 3: CLEFS AND STAVES

Objectives:

1. Report the ancient, scripted letters from which the symbols for treble and bass clef were derived.
2. Given a note on a treble, bass, or grand staff, report its letter name.
3. Demonstrate beginning skill in reading note names on a staff.
4. Identify which clef is most frequently used when playing a keyboard instrument with the right hand / the left hand.

The Music Keyboard

Several different musical instruments – piano, organ, harpsichord, accordion, etc. – have a music keyboard. This keyboard consists of a number of white and black keys. On most of these instruments, the keys closer to the player are white and there are many more of them than there are black keys. The black keys occur in a pattern of groups of two and of three. Here is a picture of a music keyboard showing this pattern:

Figure 3-1: Pattern of keys on keyboard.

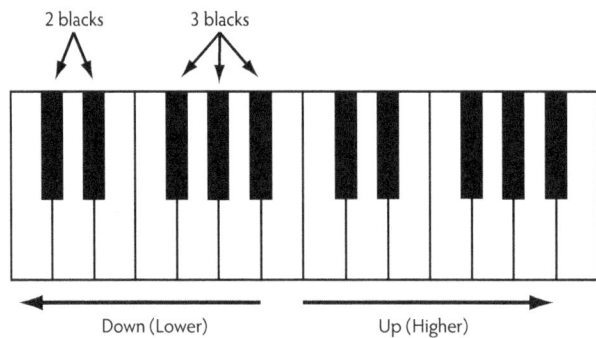

The arrows indicate the direction of higher and lower pitches for the notes (to the right - higher; to the left - lower pitches).

Just as the pattern of black keys repeats, so do the letter names of the white keys. Following is a picture of a music keyboard with some letter names of notes shown:

Figure 3-2: Letter names of white keys.

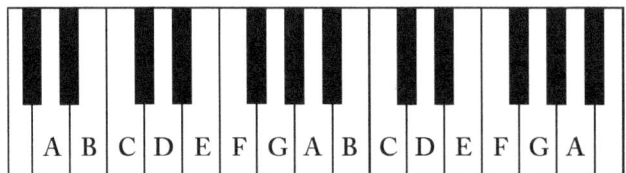

When the black-key pattern repeats, so do the letter names of the white keys. For example, notice that the note just to the left of the group of two black keys is always C.

We will get to the black keys in a later chapter. So, how are these pitches indicated in a score?

Music Staves

The conventional *staff* for pitched instruments consists of five horizontal lines. (Unpitched instruments, such as the snare drum and many other percussion instruments, use a single line instead of five lines.) On the five-line staff, both lines and spaces are used for indicating pitches. Here is a musical staff:

Figure 3-3: Musical staff.

The lines and spaces are commonly numbered from the bottom upward, like this:

Figure 3-4: Numbering lines and spaces.

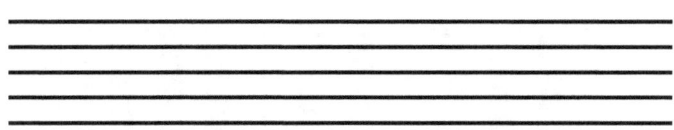

You already know that the shape of the note symbol indicates relative duration. Pitch is indicated by where the note **head** is placed on the staff. However, locating specific pitches is still not possible without providing a "clef", which shows where one particular pitch is to be located on that staff.

The Treble Clef and Staff

A musical *clef* is a symbol that identifies a reference pitch on a musical staff. Different clefs reference different pitches. This is the *treble clef*: 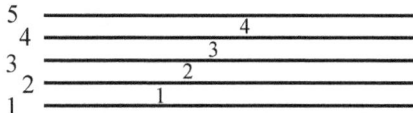 . The treble clef comes from an old scripted form of the letter "G". So, it is also called the **G clef**. The following figure shows how the G clef looks on a musical staff. This staff is called the *treble staff*.

Figure 3-5: The treble staff.

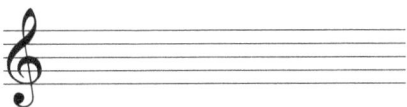

Notice that inside the clef, the line that makes up the symbol curves around the second line of the staff. This is where you find note heads for notes that have the pitch of the first G **above** middle C. The following picture shows you how to find this G on a music keyboard.

Figure 3-6: Locating G above middle C on keyboard.

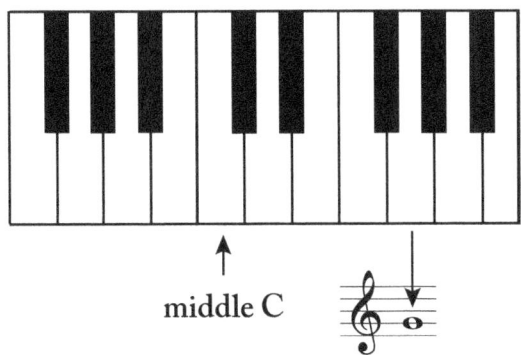

On a keyboard instrument, "middle C" is usually the C that is nearest the center of the keyboard. Once you know where this G is located, you can work out what are the other notes. When first learning the letter names of notes on a staff, it helps to have a mnemonic (a memory aid). Here is a way to recall letter names of notes on lines of the treble staff:

Figure 3-7: Notes on lines (treble staff).

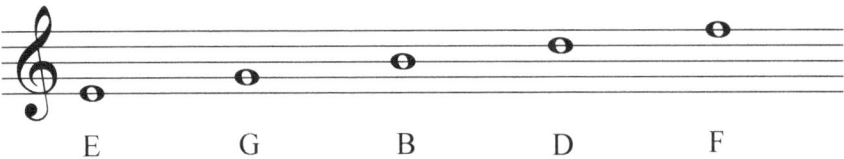

To help remember these, think of this statement: **E**very **G**ood **B**oy **D**eserves **F**udge.

To recall the letter names of notes on the spaces on the treble staff, think of the word "FACE":

Figure 3-8: Notes on spaces (treble staff)

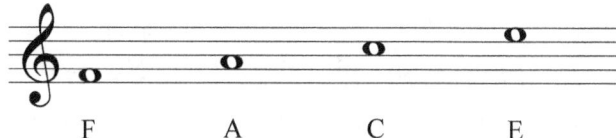

You can also write notes above and below this staff. Since the bottom line is the note E, the space just below this has the letter name D; and the line below that, C. This C is middle C.

Figure 3-9: Two notes below the treble staff.

The short line through the note head for middle C is called a **ledger line** and is used to extend the staff down or up to reach lower or higher pitches.

Likewise, since the top line is F, the next note is G and the next above that, A. Here are these notes on the treble staff:

Figure 3-10: Two notes above the treble staff.

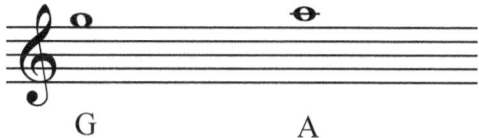

For review, following are all the notes on the treble staff, from one ledger line below through one ledger line above the staff. Notice that you go through the musical alphabet, starting over after G, so that as you go from one letter to the next, the next note is on the next line or space (from a space to the next line; from a line to the next space).

Figure 3-11: Review notes on treble staff.

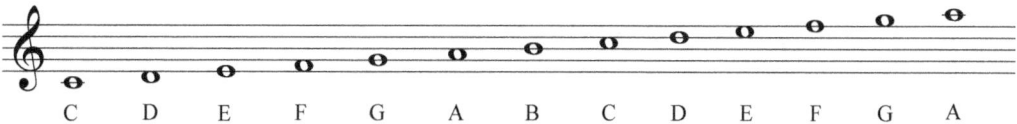

The Bass Clef and Staff

This is the symbol for the *bass clef*: 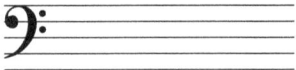 . This symbol came from an older scripted version of the letter "F", so it is also called the **F Clef**. Notice that the two dots are on either side of a line. When this special "F" appears on a musical staff, it tells the musician that the line between the two dots will be the first F below middle C. Here is how it appears on a musical staff, making it the *bass staff*:

Figure 3-12: The bass staff.

Notice that the dots appear on each side of line 4 (4th line from the bottom, 2nd line from the top). This is where you would place note heads for notes that have the pitch of the first F below middle C. The picture below shows you how to find this F on a music keyboard.

Figure 3-13: Locating F below middle C on keyboard

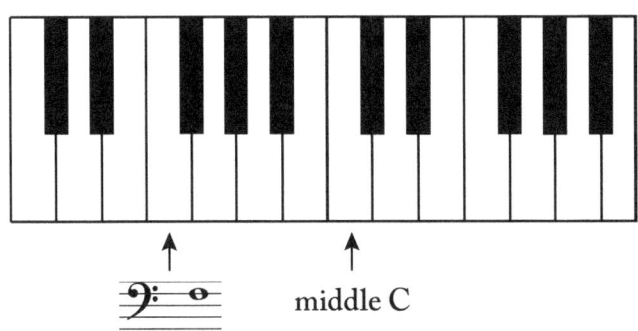

Here are notes on the <u>lines</u> of the bass staff, with a memory aid:

Figure 3-14: Lines on the bass staff.

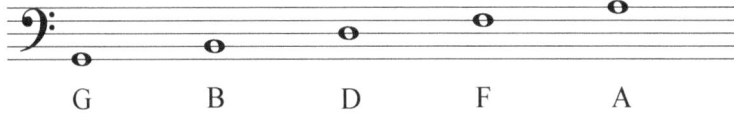

Good Boys Deserve Fudge Always

And now the notes on the spaces:

Figure 3-15: Spaces on the bass staff.

All Cows Eat Grass

As we did for the treble staff, there are some notes above and below the bass staff:

Figure 3-16: Notes above and below the bass staff.

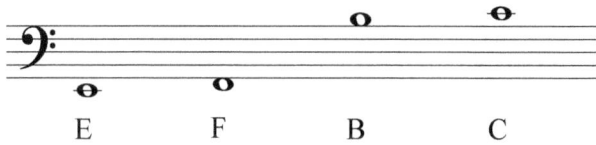

Now let's combine them all on the bass staff:

Figure 3-17: Review notes on bass staff.

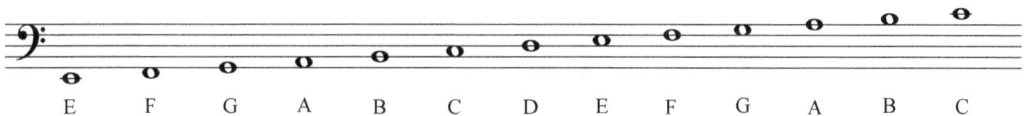

The C on the ledger line above this staff is middle C.

The Grand Staff

Notice that the note on the ledger line <u>below</u> the **treble** staff has the same pitch as the note on the ledger line <u>above</u> the **bass** staff. That is, one continues exactly where the other stopped.

Figure 3-18: Middle C, the link between treble and bass.

It is natural then to combine these staves in order to be able to notate a very wide range of pitches. This is done with the **grand** staff, which is a connection of treble and bass staves. Whenever notes on both staves are to be played by only one musician (as for a piano or vibraphones, for example), they are usually also connected with a brace.

Figure 3-19: The grand staff.

In this form, if you are playing on a standard keyboard instrument, notes on the bass staff are usually played with the left hand and those on the treble staff, with the right hand. The position of middle C has been shown on the bass and on the treble staff. When the left hand is to play middle C, it is shown on a ledger line above the bass staff; when with the right hand, it is shown on a ledger line below the treble staff.

Therefore, the following middle C would normally be played with the left hand:

Whereas this one would normally be played with the right hand:

They are the same pitch and the same key on the music keyboard.

Note: Finding middle C on a keyboard depends upon what keyboard instrument is being used. Looking at the keyboard pictures above, you can easily find a C near the middle of the keyboard. On a piano, it actually is just a bit to the left of the exact center of the keyboard; on a 61-key synthesizer, it is just to the right of the exact center. If you take lessons on a keyboard instrument, your performance teacher can help you locate which C is the one that is "middle C".

Practice Notes on Staves

A practicing musician can not take the time to go through memory aids to try to identify notes on a musical staff; the identification must come very quickly. Therefore, drilling letter names of notes on the staves is necessary practice for developing this important skill. You can use blank staff paper and randomly scatter note heads on the staff in succession. Draw a clef at the left-hand side, and then recite the letter names of the notes. Set up a steady pulse by tapping your foot, and then say the next note name each time you tap. Start out slowly and then increase the speed of the pulse slightly with each repetition. Do treble and bass clefs separately until you are somewhat comfortable with your success, then do the exercise using the grand staff. For your convenience, following are a few note naming exercises to get you started.

Exercise 3-1: *(Continue to the second line without pause!)*

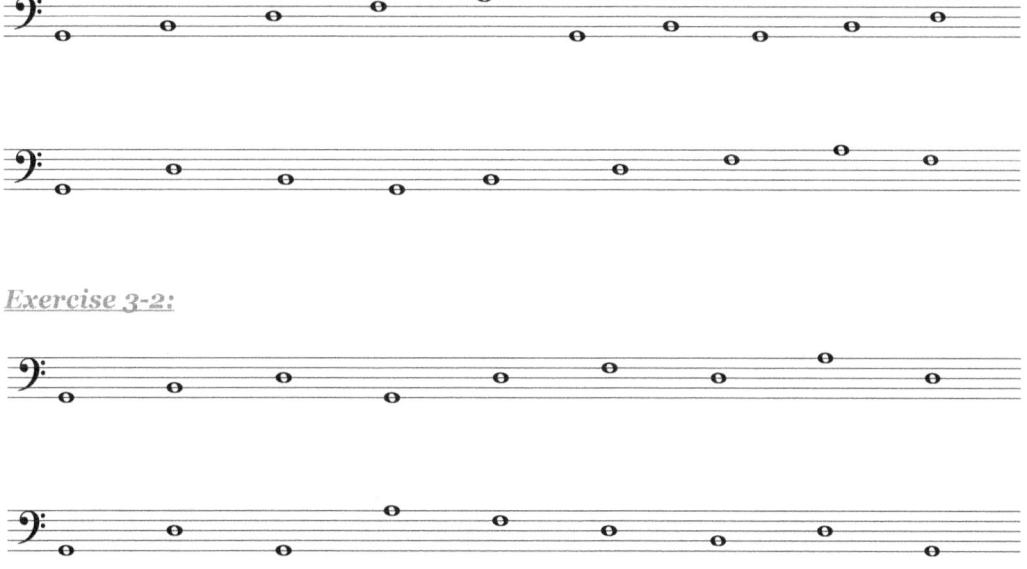

Exercise 3-2:

Exercise 3-3:

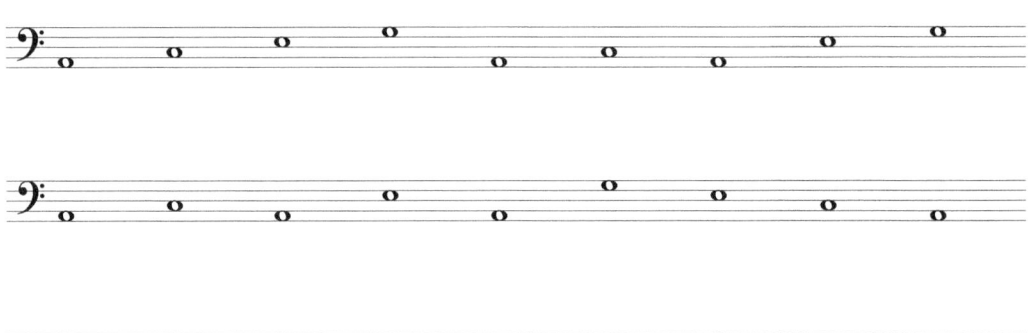

Exercise 3-4:

Exercise 3-5:

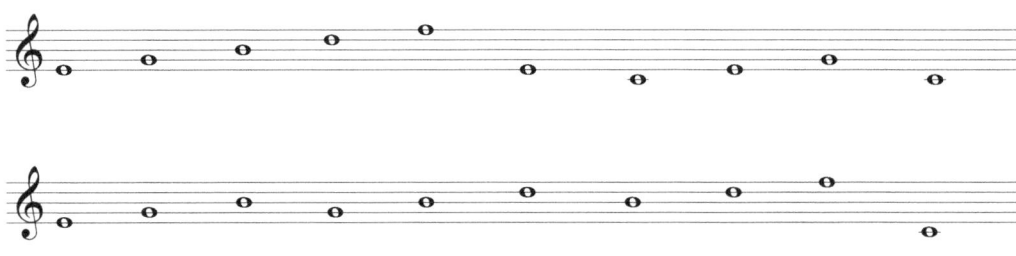

Exercise 3-6:

Exercise 3-7:

Exercise 3-8:

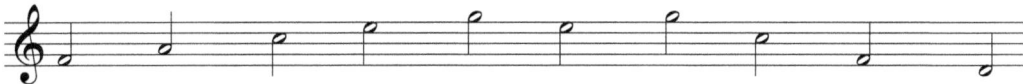

Exercise 3-9:

Exercise 3-10:

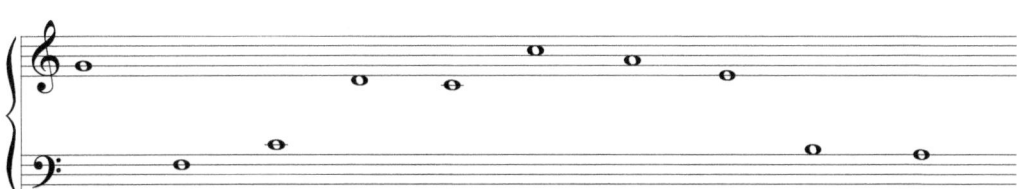

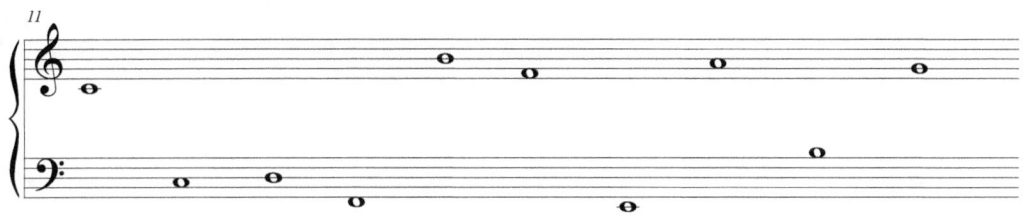

Summary

Clefs have been introduced and letter names of notes have been identified on the treble staff, bass staff, and the grand staff. A bit of practice will help you begin to develop musicianship skills.

Next

We return to the time dimension in the next Chapter with a study of meter, measures, and time signatures.

Quiz 3

1. The treble clef symbol, 𝄞 , is a scripted form of the letter ___ .

2. The bass clef symbol, 𝄢 , is a scripted form of the letter ___ .

3. The letter name of the following note is ___ .

4. The letter name of the following note is ___ .

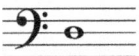

5. The letter name of the following note is ___ .

6. The letter name of the following note is ___ .

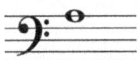

7. The letter name of the following note is ___ .

8. What is the letter name of the following note?

9. Notes on the bass staff portion of the grand staff are normally played with the _____ (right/left) hand.

10. Notes on the treble staff portion of the grand staff are normally played with the _____ (right/left) hand.

CHAPTER 4: METER

Objectives:

1. Recognize definitions for basic concepts of musical meter (meter, accent, beat, measure, bar line, rhythm, time signature).
2. Describe or identify the functions of a double bar line and a repeat bar, and report their symbols.
3. Report the correct interpretations for the top and bottom numbers in a time signature.
4. Draw or identify the correct symbols for cut time and common time, and be able to match them with their equivalent numeric time signatures.
5. Provide (or identify) a general description for each of the ten tempo markings presented in this chapter (You do NOT have to memorize the range of pulses per minute for each.)
6. Demonstrate beginning skill in reciting rhythms for given passages.

Meter in Music

Meter is the use of regular pulses by which time in music is marked and measured. It is similar in this role to poetic meter. Like poetic meter, musical **meter** is created by regular patterns of expected accents in a passage of music. An *accent* is a special emphasis given to a note. There are actually different kinds of accents, but we need discuss only the "dynamic accent" in this chapter: a ***dynamic accent*** creates the emphasis by making that note louder than notes with normal emphasis. Dynamic accent is used to create different meters. Before discussing different kinds of meters, we need to understand what is meant by "beat". The ***beat*** of a certain piece of music is that regular pulse to which the listener could naturally tap his or her foot while listening to the music or playing it. The person writing the music decides what time value is to be treated as a "beat". The ***tempo*** is how fast the beats are being performed, and often is indicated in "beats per minute" (bpm). 60 bpm would be a tempo in which each pulse is one second long; 120 bpm would be a march tempo.

If we use the symbol > to represent an accented beat and the symbol - to represent an unaccented beat, the pattern for triple meter would be: > - - . We can see that such a pattern contains three beats and that the accent is normally located on the first beat.

Here is the pattern for simple duple time: > - .

Notice that there are only two beats for the duple pattern.

Here is the pattern for quadruple time: > - > - .

Yes, in quadruple time, the first accent is heavier than the second one. The quadruple time can be felt as a duple inside of a duple!

Measures and Bar Lines

One time through the regular metric pattern of strong and weak beats constitutes one *measure*, and the composer marks the end of each measure with a *bar line*. The accents that belong to the beat patterns are not actually notated. Instead, the symbols for the time values of notes are used and are divided by bar lines. For example, here is a notation for three measures in quadruple time.

Example 1:

Notice that even when there are no note symbols, the beats are still "felt" (can still be tapped with the foot while the fingers are playing the notes). Try this: tap the note durations with a finger, or sing the notes on neutral syllable "tah", while tapping your foot to the beats.

In the next example, we show the same thing but add numbers for the beats.

Example 2:

Notice that if you are counting the beats, they start over again at the beginning of each measure. Although the accents are not written, use the metric accent pattern for quadruple time, which means a strong emphasis on beat 1 and a moderate accent on beat 3. (Since there is no note for beat 3 in the third measure, you cannot actually perform the accent, but it is still felt.) So, you should also practice saying the beats and tapping the notes. Do not vary the time between beats; keep them absolutely constant, like the ticking of a clock. You can play any note on a musical instrument for this practice. Make sure that you do not release the sound for the whole note until you say "off" after the last beat. Notice that each measure ends in a bar line. Note also that the last bar line is a double line. This *double bar line* (𝄁) is used to mark the end of a piece.

Another kind of bar line at the end of a passage tells the player to repeat the entire previous passage exactly one time only. It is the repeat bar and, on a five-line staff, looks like this: 𝄇.

Time Signatures

The particular meter used for a passage of music is indicated at the beginning of the score by a *time signature*. The time signature consists of two numbers, one written over the other (see the examples below). The lower number indicates the chosen unit of measurement as a note value. A 2 indicates a half note; a 4, a quarter note; an 8, an eighth note; etc. The upper number indicates the number of such units in one measure. (This is similar to a fraction in mathematics, where the top number is the quantity of the fractional unit defined by the bottom number.) For example, here is the time signature for triple time using the quarter note as the unit of measurement: $\frac{3}{4}$, indicating there are three quarter notes in each measure. (For proper alignment on the staff, each number takes up half the height of the five lines.) Here is triple time in which the 8th note is the basic unit: $\frac{3}{8}$. Here is the time signature for quadruple time using quarter notes: $\frac{4}{4}$, indicating there are four quarter notes in each measure. This meter is so common, that it is conventionally called "common time" and can be indicated with a capital "C" in place of the numbers, like this: 𝄴. Shown next is the signature for duple meter using the half note as the unit: $\frac{2}{2}$. This one is sometimes called "cut time" or "alla breve" and can be notated this way: 𝄵.

All of the above meters are examples of "simple meter". Later in the book you will study another classification of meter, but for now, all *simple meter* means is that each beat is subdivided into two equal note values. For example, in $\frac{4}{4}$ meter, each quarter note takes one beat and any such quarter note beat could be subdivided into two eighth notes. Also, in simple meter, the upper number of the time signature always indicates the number of beats in the measure and the lower number, the kind of note that takes one beat. This will not be true of other kinds of meter!

Tempo

Although various tempos can be provided by giving the beats per minute, this degree of precision is not usually practical in a score to be performed live. Therefore, descriptive words are usually written into the score. Different performers, or conductors, will vary in how they interpret the description. Following are some of the most common tempo markings, from slowest to fastest, and how they are normally interpreted. (Approximate pulses per minute rate is given in parentheses, but these are up to arbitrary interpretation.)

largo – *broad; extremely slow (40-52)*
larghetto – *slightly faster than largo (53-58)*
lento – *very slow (59-65)*
adagio – *slow (at ease) (66-75)*
andante – *walking (76-105)*
moderato – *moderate (106-118)*
allegretto – *fast, but not too fast (119-131)*
allegro – *fast (cheerful) (132-169)*
presto – *very fast (170-200)*
prestissimo – *as fast as possible (200-210)*

Then there are words that mean the performers should gradually speed up, **accelerando** (or just **accel.**), or gradually slow down, **ritardando** (**rit.**). There is even one that means the performer should deliberately vary the tempo in an unsteady manner (for expressive purposes), **rubato**. Of course, a composer may choose to use the equivalent of these terms in his/her own language instead of Italian. For some tempo markings, one practically needs an Italian dictionary handy. For *allegro assai*, the *assai* means "much" or "very". So, an allegro *assai* would be on the fast end of *allegro* or the slower end of *presto*. Some can be very expressive. For *largo e mesto*, *e mesto* means "and mournful".

Rhythm

Rhythm is the sense of motion in music that is created by relative durations of notes and the placement of accents. Some rhythms conform very strictly to the expectations of the meter, and some do not. The interplay between familiar and strange in music is a powerful element in creating musical expression. Here is the same passage used in the first two examples, this time with a time signature. The rhythm conforms very closely with expected accents in the meter.

Example 3:

However, if you change it just slightly, you can get a rhythm that plays a bit with this expectation.

Example 4:

We could even add a written accent on one of the notes to tell the performer to play an accent where it is not normally expected:

Example 5:

Some pieces begin with a note or a few notes that precede the first full measure. This is called an *anacrusis*, also often referred to as an "upbeat" or "pick-up". Here is an example:

Example 6:

At the end of the piece or section, the note values used for the anacrusis are often omitted from the last measure.

Rhythmic Practice

Recite the following exercises, on any comfortable pitch, by using the syllable "tah" for accented notes and "dah" for unaccented notes. Tap the beat with your foot. Keep that foot going like the ticking of a clock! Start by doing the exercise slowly, and then try a faster tempo. The beats are numbered for you in the first few examples.

Exercise 1:

Exercise 2:

Exercise 3:

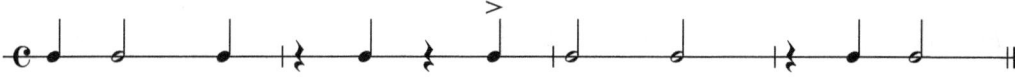

Exercise 4:

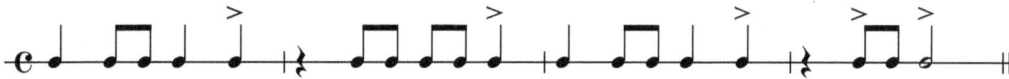

Exercise 5:

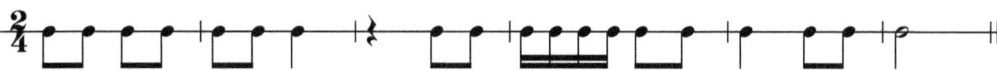

Exercise 6:

SUMMARY

In this Chapter, we have discussed meter, including the use of measures, bar lines, and time signatures. The concept of rhythm has also been introduced, with some beginning exercises.

NEXT

In the next Chapter, you will begin the study of musical intervals, the musical distance between pitches. Understanding musical intervals is very important and will lead (in later chapters of the book) into further studies of musical scales, melody, and harmony.

Quiz 4

1 – 7: For each description on the left, supply the letter on the right that is the name of the concept or item described.

1. Indicates the end of each measure.

2. A regular pulse of non-varying duration that goes all through a passage of music.

3. One time through a repeating pattern of beat accents goes into each one of these.

4. This tells you how many of what time value of note goes into each measure.

5. The sense of motion in music that is created by relative durations of notes and the placement of accents.

6. A special emphasis given to a note or expected at certain points in time in the music.

7. The regular pattern of accents in a certain passage of music.

A. beat

B. accent

C. meter

D. measure

E. bar line

F. rhythm

G. time signature

---

8. The repeat bar directs the performer to play the passage again how many times (in addition to the first time it is played)?

    a. One more time

    b. Two more times

    c. Three more times

9. In a time signature, the top number indicates:

    a. the number of notes, or counts, that make up one measure.

    b. the type of note value to count (quarter note, half note, etc.).

10. Which is the correct symbol for a repeat bar?

    a.　　b.　　c.

11. The following designation tells you that there are ___ beats in each measure and that a _____ note takes one beat.

    𝟯/𝟮

    a. two; third
    b. three; half
    c. three; quarter
    d. two; whole

12. The following designation tells you that there are ___ beats in each measure and that a _____ note takes one beat.

    ₵

    a. two; quarter
    b. four; quarter
    c. four; half
    d. two; half

13. Which tempo marking means "slow and at ease"?
    a. adagio
    b. andante
    c. largo
    d. lento

14. Which tempo marking means "walking"?
    a. adagio
    b. allegretto
    c. andante
    d. moderato

15. Which tempo marking means "very fast"?
    a. allegretto
    b. allegro
    c. prestissimo
    d. presto

CHAPTER 5: INTERVALS: PART 1

Objectives:

1. Define "musical interval".
2. Report how to count intervals on a musical staff, and determine the numeric size of an interval between two given notes on a staff.
3. Report how to count intervals on the white keys of a music keyboard, and determine the numeric size of an interval between two given notes on white keys of a keyboard.
4. Identify the following specific intervals on white keys of a keyboard or on a musical staff: major second, minor second, octave.

An *interval* is the distance in pitch between two tones. The farther apart two tones are in pitch, the wider the interval. Just as two different pairs of cities can be the same linear distance apart, two different pairs of tones can be the same interval apart. For example, the interval between F and the G just above it is the same interval as that between D and the next E above it. An interval has a number that we get by one of two different methods:

(1) On a musical staff, start with one note, count it as "1" and then count each next line and space to the next note to find its interval.

Figure 5-1: Counting ascending interval sizes on a staff.

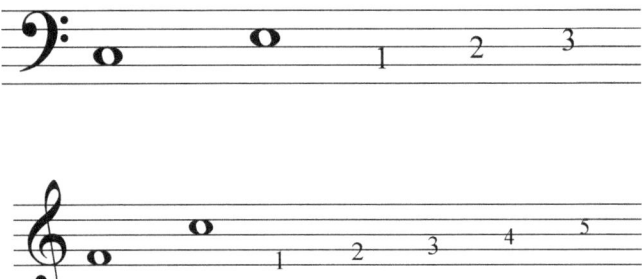

Intervals can be counted either up or down; the interval (that is, the "distance") is the same.

Figure 5-2: Counting descending interval sizes on a staff.

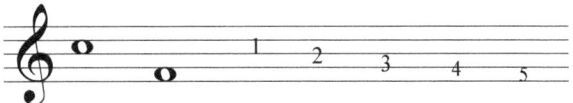

(2) On the keyboard, starting at any white key, count it as "1", then move up to the next note and count each white key. For example, if you start at C and the next note for your interval is E, count the C as "1", the D as "2", and the E as "3". Therefore, the interval between a C and the next higher E is a 3rd.

Figure 5-3: Counting interval sizes on a keyboard.

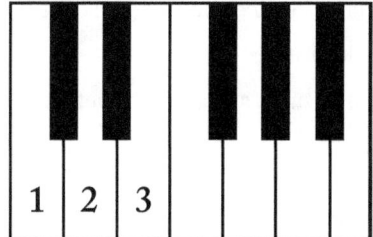

Okay, so we now know how to count to find the numeric size of an interval.

Seconds

If two notes are right next to each other, the interval is a 2nd. Any two white keys that are right next to each other form the interval of a second. Likewise, any two notes on the staff that are right next to each other – one on a line and the other on the space just above or below the line, or one on a space and the other on the line just above or below that space – form the interval of a 2nd.

Figure 5-4: Here are some 2nds on the grand staff:

Figure 5-5: Here are these same 2nds on the keyboard:

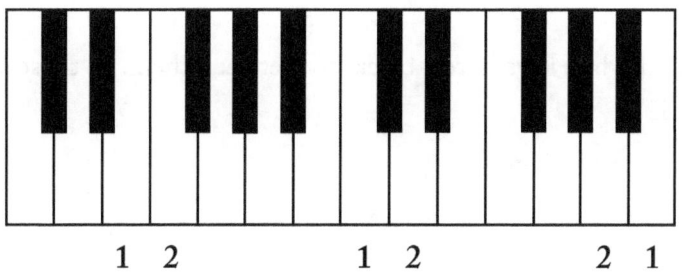

Going up or down by intervals of a second is like going up or down stairs, one step at a time. Therefore, another name for the interval of a second is a *step*. If you step up from A, you get to B; if you step down from G, you get to F.

To return to our staircase analogy, you know that some steps are higher than others; they are not all the same size. In music, there are two sizes of a step: the half step and the whole step. On the keyboard, notice that some 2^{nds}, adjacent white keys, have a black key between them and some do not.

Adjacent white keys that do **not** have a black key between them are *half* *steps*, or *minor* *2^{nds}* (m2).

Figure 5-6: Here are some minor 2^{nds} on the keyboard:

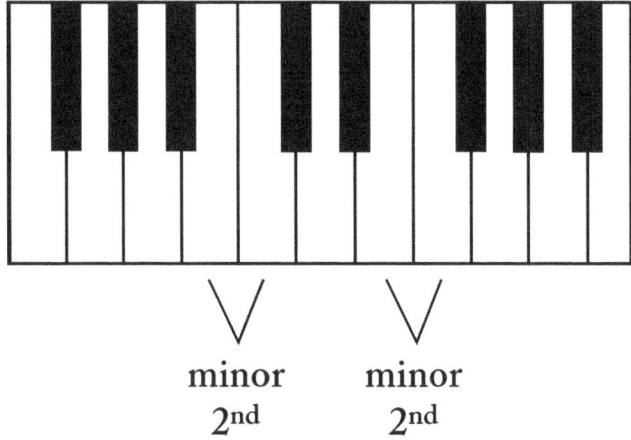

The minor seconds on the white keys are all of those between B and C and between E and F.

Figure 5-7: Here are some minor 2^{nds} on the grand staff:

All other adjacent white keys have a black key between them, so these are *whole* *steps*, or *major* *2^{nds}* (M2).

Figure 5-8: Here are some major 2nds on the keyboard:

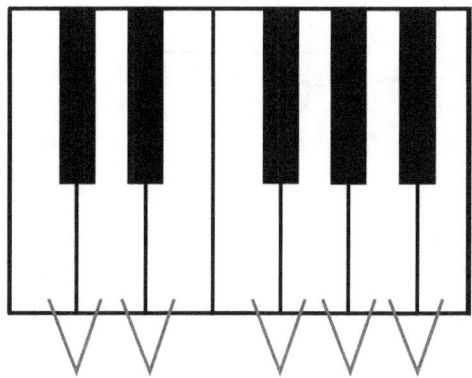

The steps between the following pairs are all major seconds, wherever they appear: C-D, D-E, F-G, G-A, and A-B.

Figure 5-9: Here are a few major 2nds on the grand staff:

All of these have been shown on the staff as ascending intervals, but whether they are major or minor, they may also appear in descending direction or one above the other to be played at the same time. If we tried to stack note heads vertically on a staff to form the interval of a second, it would be unreadable:

So, one of the note heads is shifted horizontally like this:

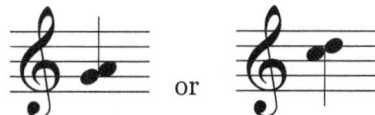

Here are what some whole notes look like as simultaneous 2ⁿᵈˢ:

Notice that the note head of the upper note always goes to the right of the note head for the lower note and they touch one another or both touch the stem.

Seconds are emphasized in many compositions.

Example 1. The French tune Frere Jacques begins with ascending major 2ⁿᵈˢ:

Example 2. The tune for "Three Blind Mice" begins with descending major 2ⁿᵈˢ:

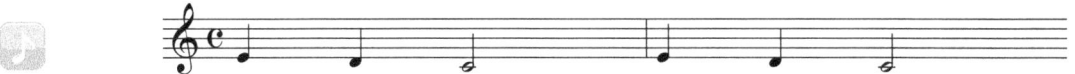

Example 3. You can hear minor 2ⁿᵈˢ – first ascending, then descending (then repeated a bit later) – in the opening of "All the Way", a tune written by James van Heusen and made popular by Frank Sinatra:

(The words that go along with this passage are: "When somebody loves you, it's no good unless he loves …")

Octaves

Let's return to the letter names of notes. You know that the notes are lettered A through G and then they start over again with A. The interval between a given note and the next note higher of lower with the same name is called the *octave*. "Oct" means "eight". Look at the following octave between C and the next C on the keyboard.

Figure 5-10: An octave on a keyboard.

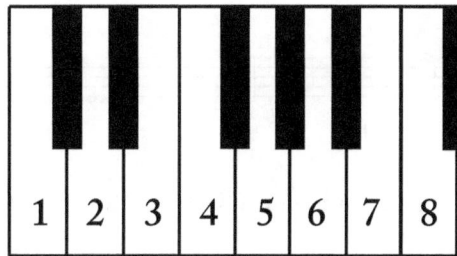

Thus, this could also be called an interval of an **8**th. Following is the octave on a staff, showing how the numerical size of the interval is determined.

Figure 5-11: An octave on the bass staff.

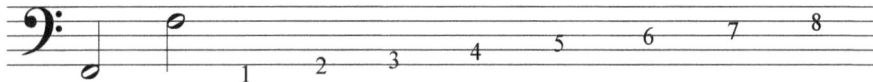

Notice that you have to count every successive line and space, starting with "1" for the first note.

You learned that a sound of a particular pitch is generated by a source that is vibrating at a unique rate (frequency). A musical interval is characterized, in modern tuning, by there being a unique mathematical ratio between the frequencies of two pitches that form the same interval. It so happens that the pitches of two notes that are an octave apart have a 2:1 ratio between their pitches, no matter in what range the interval appears. Hence, the ratio between C and the next lower C is 2:1; the ratio between A and the next lower A is 2:1; and so on. This characteristic gives the octave such a special and strong similarity property that notes at this interval have been given the same letter name. They are the "same note" only in the sense that they have this special property and have the same letter name. They are obviously not truly equal because one note has a much higher pitch than does the other (twice as high, in fact).

Something extra: You may wonder about the ratio for the interval formed by a second. All modern musical pitched instruments are tuned so that the ratio for a minor second is about the twelfth root of 2 to 1; about 1.06:1.

Example 4. "Over the Rainbow" (tune written by Harold Arlen), from The Wizard of Oz, begins with an octave:

Example 5. "Bali Hai", from South Pacific (Richard Rogers), starts with an octave (also emphasizes the minor 2nd):

(The rhythm is somewhat simplified to use only note values you have learned.)

When a note is repeated, it is called a "unison". Also, two people playing different instruments may play the same pitch, and it is also called the "unison". The **unison** is the interval whose frequencies have the ratio of 1:1.

Practice

You must begin to learn to hear intervals in your head. A practicing musician hears, in his/her head, the interval of the next note before playing it. Being able to anticipate the next note is an essential musicianship skill. Following are two suggestions for acquiring skill hearing intervals.

Set 1

1. Play or sing a note of a particular pitch (any pitch).
2. Decide on one of the intervals you have learned: M2, m2, octave. Decide if you will go up or down.
3. Sing the note that is the given interval from the first note.

Set 2

For this one, you will need the help of a partner. Your partner must play, on a keyboard instrument, an interval that you have learned. (Don't look at the keyboard!) Mix the following variants: ascending intervals, descending intervals, simultaneous (harmonic) intervals. Your job is to name the interval.

Summary

An interval is the distance in pitch between two notes (expressible as a mathematical ratio of their frequencies). You studied two sizes of 2nds: major 2nds (two half steps) and minor seconds (one half step). An octave is the interval between a note of a certain letter name and the next higher or lower note with that same letter name; if you count the keys between the notes (starting with the first key as "1"), you find that it is the interval of an 8th. A unison exists between two notes of equal pitch.

Next

Further intervals will be covered in later chapters. For now, you know enough to learn about accidentals, key signatures, and scales. Accidentals (sharps, flats, and naturals) are the topic of the next chapter.

Quiz 5

1. The distance in pitch between two notes is called a/an _____ .
   a. interval
   b. gap
   c. space

2. To count the size of an interval, count the first note as ___ .
   a. 0
   b. 1
   c. 2

3. A _____ second on the keyboard has a black key between the two notes.
   a. major
   b. minor

4. The following interval is a/an _____ .

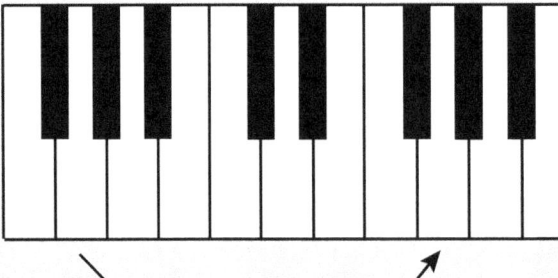

   a. minor 2nd
   b. major 2nd
   c. octave

5. The following interval is a/an _____ .

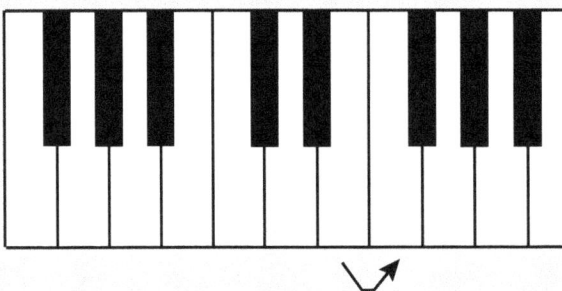

   a. minor 2nd
   b. major 2nd
   c. octave

6. The following interval is a/an _____ .

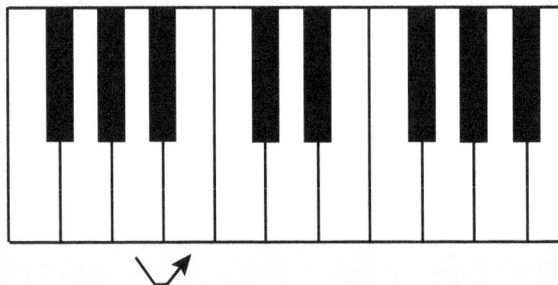

   a. minor 2nd
   b. major 2nd
   c. octave

7. The following interval is a/an _____ .

   a. minor 2nd
   b. major 2nd
   c. octave

8. The following interval is a/an _____ .

   a. minor 2nd
   b. major 2nd
   c. octave

9. The following interval is a/an _____ .

   a. minor 2nd
   b. major 2nd
   c. octave

10. The following interval is a/an _____ .

    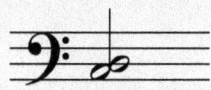

    a. minor 2nd
    b. major 2nd
    c. octave

CHAPTER 6: ACCIDENTALS

Objectives:

1. Report the note that results from altering a given note up or down a half step or canceling its sharp or flat.
2. Given the score for a short melodic passage, determine what accidental, if any, applies to a note that is written on the same line or space as a previous note.
3. Identify the intervallic distance, in half steps, between two notes at least one of which has an accidental.
4. Demonstrate a beginning skill to sing brief stepwise melodic passages, given the tone for the first note.

No, this has nothing to do with "accidents", though they do happen in music and, as in science, can lead to interesting discoveries. The Harvard Dictionary of Music (by Willi Apel, Harvard University Press) indicates that *accidentals* are "signs used in musical notation to indicate chromatic alterations or to cancel them". Okay, but what is meant by "chromatic alterations"? First, a practical example will help. If you are playing a passage on all white keys of a keyboard musical instrument and then decide to play one or more black keys instead, these changes would be examples of chromatic alterations for which you would need to use accidentals.

Sharps

The first accidental we will study is the "sharp". Here is its symbol: ♯ . If, instead of playing the white key F, we play the black key just to the right of the F, we get a tone that is a half step higher than F and we call it F♯. Thus, the *sharp* is an accidental that raises the pitch of a note one half step. The key just to the right of G is G♯, and so on. Following is a picture of the keyboard showing the sharped names of the black keys.

Figure 6-1: Sharps on black keys.

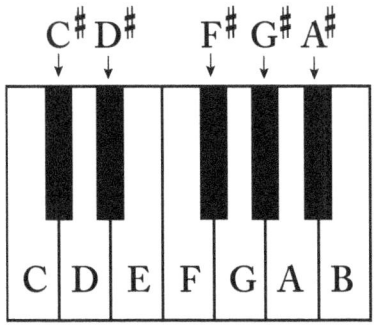

There also are half steps from F♯ to G and from G♯ to A, and each of these is the same size of half step as is the one, for example, from E to F. Also, it now makes sense to understand that the whole step from F to G is made up of two half steps: F to F♯ and F♯ to G. Yes, the interval from F♯ to G♯ is also a whole step.

When you refer to the note in text, you write the sharp sign <u>after</u> the letter name: for example, F#. When the note is written on a musical staff, the sharp sign goes just <u>before</u> the note head. Following is the way that an F# is written on a staff:

When a sharp sign appears before a note, it applies to that note throughout the entire rest of the measure (but <u>not</u> into the next measure). For example, the sharp appears only on the first F in the following example, but the next F is also sharped:

If the note F♯ then appears in the next measure, the sharp is rewritten. There is an exception to this that we will cover when we discuss key signatures in a later chapter.

Flats

The flat is another kind of accidental (a symbol that is used to indicate that a note has been altered in pitch). No, we're not talking about flat tires. However, that may be a way to remember what the flat does. When a tire goes flat, it loses some air; when a note goes flat, it loses some pitch. In fact, the flat lowers the pitch by a half step. Therefore, the way to indicate that you are referring to a note that is one half step **lower** than a note with a certain letter name is to use that letter and add a *flat* (♭) to it. Therefore, the black key just to the left of the B can be indicated as B♭. What would you call the one just to the left of A? Yes! A♭. But haven't we already given this key the name G♯? Yes, any black key can be given one of two names: one with a sharp or one with a flat. Two notes are called ***enharmonic*** if they refer to exactly the same pitch but are spelled differently. Of course, we would normally use only one of these notations for any given note in a score. Following is a picture showing both ways of naming the black keys.

Figure 6-2: Sharps and flats on black keys.

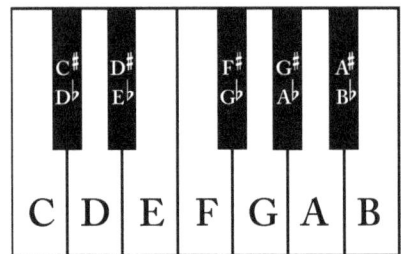

Naturals

Remember that when you write a sharp or flat on a note, that note still carries that sharp or flat to the end of the measure. What if you want it to go back to not having the sharp or flat (back to the white key)? Then you use the accidental called the *natural*, ♮ , which cancels the previous sharp or flat. This is necessary in a large number of passages, including, for example this short excerpt from Irving Berlin's "Easter Parade".

What if you alter a note in one measure, and then it goes back without the sharp (or flat) in the next measure? Since the alteration applies only through the current measure, you would not need to put a natural on the note in the next measure. This could happen to the above example if it were written in duple time, as in the following.

The A in the second measure is A-natural without having to write the natural in this case.

You may wonder whether or not a note that has been sharped or flatted is also sharped or flatted an octave away. The answer is no. The written accidental applies only to the specific pitch on which it is written. In the above example where an A is sharped, any other A on a different pitch level (say an octave above or below) in that same measure would be A-natural unless a sharp is also placed on it.

Double Sharps and Flats

Since a sharp or flat is an alteration of an original note, suppose that the original note is already a sharp and you want to alter it up a half step. Yes, you can do this. Here is the symbol for a *double sharp*: 𝆪 . So, if we wanted to sharp a G♯, it would become G 𝆪 and would look like the following in a score:

Yes, the G 𝆪 has the same pitch as the A, but if you get there by altering a G♯ up a half step, the resulting note would be written as G 𝆪.

The *double flat*, ♭♭, is a half step lower than a flatted note. Here is what an E ♭♭ looks like in a score:

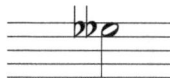

Although E ♭♭ has the same pitch as D, it is written as E ♭♭ if it results from lowering E ♭ by a half step. Thus, from the definition of "enharmonic", E ♭♭ is enharmonic with D ♮.

Practice

Practicing notes that have been altered with sharps or flats is a good ear training exercise in hearing 2nds. For each of the following exercises, play the first pitch on an instrument and then try to sing the given passage on a neutral syllable; then play it on a musical instrument to see how well you did. It will likely take several tries before you can sing the intervals accurately, but the reward is improved ability to hear intervals and anticipate pitches.

Exercise 1: The E♭ goes back to E♮ in measure 3, and the F♯ goes back to F♮ in measure 4.

Exercise 2: In this exercise, notice that you go back to B♮ in the 4th measure. Notice the number of successive half-step motions from the 4th beat of measure 2 through the 2nd beat of measure 4. This is called a "chromatic passage".

Exploring Musical Structure

(If this passage is too low for your voice, just try it an octave higher :)

Summary

This chapter has introduced several accidentals: sharps, flats, naturals, double sharps, and double flats. These provide ways of chromatically altering notes to provide a more rich tonal sound.

Next

In the next chapter, we will introduce scales, which are step-wise successions of notes common to a given piece. A scale provides the tone materials for the melodies and harmonies in a passage of music.

Quiz 6

1. If the note D is altered up one half step, the result will be written as:
   a. D
   b. D♯
   c. D𝄪
   d. E♭
   e. E♮

2. If the note F♯ is altered up one half step, the result will be written as:
   a. F
   b. F♯
   c. G
   d. F𝄪
   e. G♭

3. If the note G♭ is altered down one half step, the result will be written as:
   a. F
   b. G
   c. F♯
   d. G♭
   e. G♭♭

4. If the accidental for the note C♯ is to be canceled (moving the pitch back down a half step), the result will be written as:
   a. C♮
   b. C♭
   c. C♯♭
   d. B
   e. D♭♭

5. If the note B is altered down one half step, the result will be written as:
   a. B♮
   b. B♭♭
   c. B♭
   d. A
   e. A♯

6. In the following passage, the note on beat 3 of measure 1 is:
   a. G-sharp
   b. G
   c. G-flat

7. In the following passage, the note on beat 1 of measure 2 is:
   a. G-sharp
   b. G
   c. G-flat

8. In the following passage, the note on beat 3 of measure 1 is:

   a. G-sharp

   b. G

   c. G-flat

   [musical passage]

9. In the following passage, the note on beat 1 of measure 2 is:

   a. G-sharp

   b. G

   c. G-flat

   [musical passage]

10. How many half steps are there between F and the first G above it?

    a. 1

    b. 2

    c. 3

CHAPTER 7: THE MAJOR SCALE

Objectives:

1. Define "scale".
2. Report the positions of the half steps in a major scale (by scale degrees).
3. Report which major scale has only one sharp / one flat / no sharps or flats.
4. Name the syllables for each major scale degree in the movable solfege system.
5. Supply or identify the functional names of the scale degrees for a major scale.
6. Name the pairs of scales that are enharmonic (same pitch for each scale degree but with different spellings for the notes).
7. Given a major scale identified with its tonic note, report the complete spelling (letter name + accidental, if any) for a specified scale degree.

A *scale* is an ordered set of notes (by letter name) that provide the main tonal materials for the melodies and harmonies of a musical passage. The kinds of scales used varies with changes in styles of compositions in different periods of history and also in different cultures. We begin our study of scales with the one most common in traditional Western music, the major scale. Its pattern is reflected in the layout of the music keyboard.

C Major Scale

Take another look at one octave of the keyboard, starting and ending on the note "C".

Figure 7-1: One octave on keyboard.

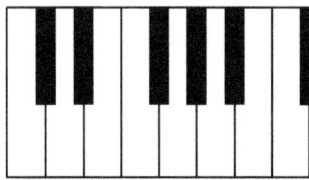

If the left C is middle C, we can write the notes in succession on the treble staff as shown here:

Figure 7-2: C major scale on treble staff.

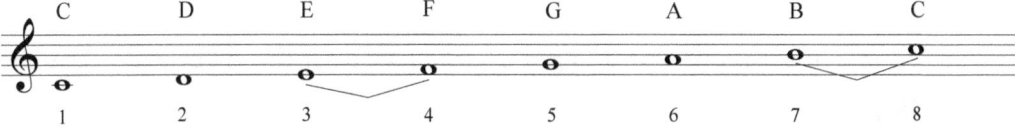

The letter names are given above the notes, **scale degrees** are numbered below the notes, and the two half steps – between E and F and between B and C – are marked. The other steps are all whole steps. The major scale is characterized by the particular pattern of whole- and half-steps. If all are whole steps except for half steps between scale degrees 3 and 4 and between scale degrees 7 and 8, as shown in the example for C Major above, then you have a major scale.

G Major Scale

So, could you build a major scale starting on the note G (instead of C)? Yes! Just follow the whole- and half-step pattern for the major scale:

1-whole-2-whole-3-half-4-whole-5-whole-6-whole-7-half-8

Let's look at how this would work out on the keyboard pattern, starting on G (any G).

Figure 7-3: G major scale on keyboard.

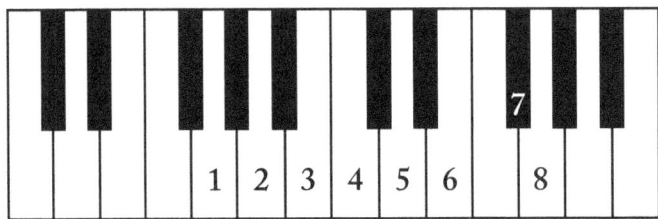

Notice that there is a half step between 3 and 4 (B and C), but for there to be a whole step from 6 up to 7, you have to raise the F up to F♯. Then it is a half step from F♯ to G to complete the octave.

Following is what a G Major scale looks like on a staff (let's use the bass staff this time; either will work fine to show the scale). We show just the scale degrees and mark the half steps this time:

Figure 7-4: G major scale on bass staff.

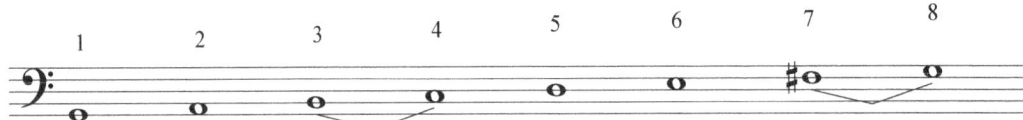

F Major Scale

If we start on F, it turns out that we need a flat to construct the major scale. Use the major scale pattern again:

1-whole-2-whole-3-half-4-whole-5-whole-6-whole-7-half-8

Figure 7-5: F major scale on keyboard.

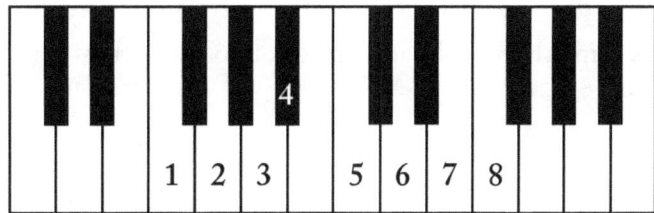

This time, instead of using B, we need B♭ to provide the half step from 3 to 4. Here is what an F Major scale looks like on a staff:

Figure 7-6: F major scale on treble staff.

Could we build a major scale by starting on a black key? Sure!

B♭ Major Scale

First, we show it on the keyboard:

Figure 7-8: B♭ major scale on keyboard.

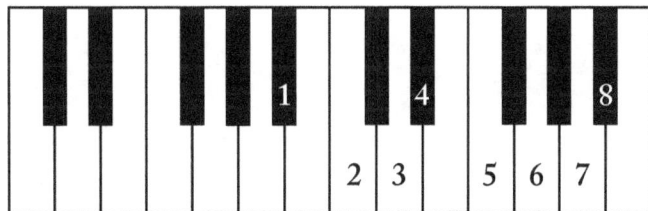

A whole step up from B♭ takes you up to C. For the half step up from 3 to 4, you must use the black key, E♭; then another whole step to 5 takes you back to the white keys. If you follow the interval pattern, you'll always end up at the octave. Here is the B♭ Major scale on a staff:

Figure 7-9: B♭ major scale on bass staff.

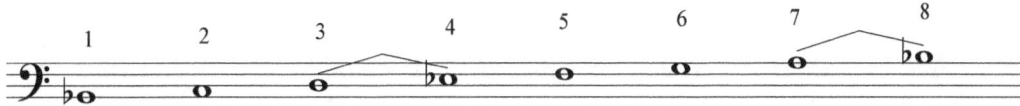

More Major Scales in Sharps

Okay, you've got the idea. Following the same procedure, here are the rest of the major scales that require using sharps. We leave it to you to locate these on a keyboard.

D Major

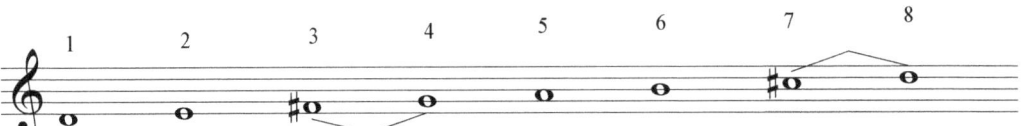

A Major

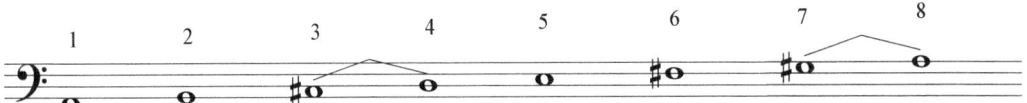

E Major

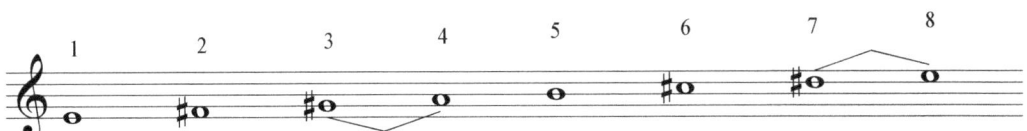

B Major

F♯ Major

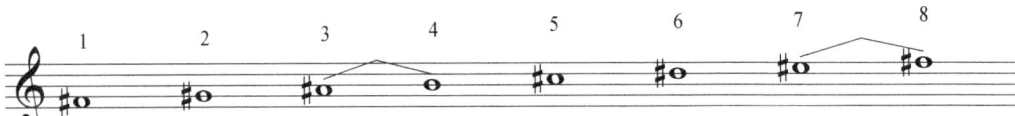

E♯? Yes, even though it is the same pitch as F♮, it would be written as an alteration of E in order to clearly show step-wise motion on the staff. You ran into this situation earlier with double sharps and double flats. In writing these kinds of scales, you must end exactly an octave higher (scale degree 8) on a note spelled exactly the same as scale degree 1, and each letter of the music alphabet must be written in succession.

C♯ Major

More Major Scales in Flats

We developed the scales for F (one flat) and B♭ (two flats). Here are the rest of them in flats:

E♭ Major

A♭ Major

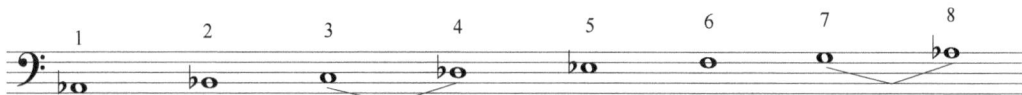

D♭ Major

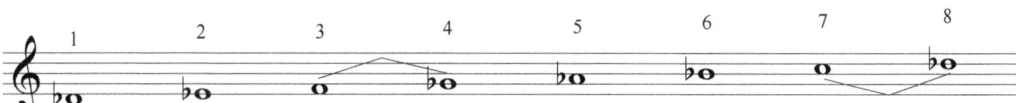

This scale contains the same pitches as does the C♯ Major scale above. However, it contains only five flats whereas the C♯ Major scale requires seven sharps, so D♭ is usually preferred.

G♭ Major

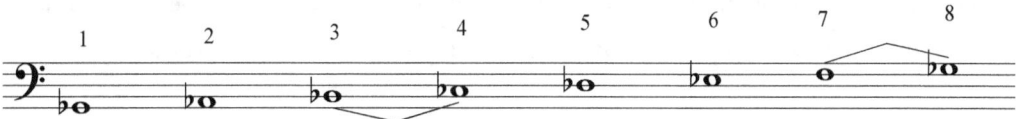

Notice that G♭ Major starts on the same key (and pitch) as does F♯ Major. One scale has six flats; the other, six sharps. The scale can be written either way, depending upon the context of the passage in which it exists.

C♭ Major

Notice that not only C♭ is enharmonic with B; and F♭, with E. This scale has the same pitches as the scale for B Major. Since B Major has only five sharps while C♭ Major contains seven flats, B Major is usually preferred.

Names of Scale Degrees

Besides numbering scale degrees, each degree also has a name that is used in describing special functions of these notes. We will discuss the functions later, but for now, here are these functional names for a major scale:

Table 7-1: Names of scale degrees.

Degree	Name
1	tonic
2	supertonic
3	mediant
4	subdominant
5	dominant
6	submediant
7	leading tone

The 8th scale degree is not shown because it is also the first scale degree for a scale built up from that level and carries the same tonal function, so it is called "tonic" (same as scale degree 1).

Practice

Because of the importance of becoming comfortable with the notes used in a piece, musicians regularly practice scales. Instrumentalists play them on their instruments and singers sing them. If you play an instrument, you will learn all of the scales on your instrument. If you sing, you will sing scales starting on many different pitches. You will just have to be careful that you do not try going too low or too high in pitch, whether you are singing or playing an instrument.

Exercise: Set 1

First practice singing or playing a scale that starts low in the pitch range of your voice or instrument. If you are singing the scale, you may want to play it on a keyboard instrument first, so you know how it sounds. Sing the major scale, one octave up, and then descend, as shown here. (We will start on C Major for this example.)

Then try it on a higher beginning pitch; then higher, until you get to a level that begins to become difficult in the high range.

Exercise: Set 2

Now start with a pitch that is a bit high for you, but still comfortable, and sing the passage upside-down, as shown below. (We will start on G Major for this one.)

Even if you play an orchestral or band instrument, it is good practice to also sing some scales. You can sing the scale using a neutral syllable or using the scale degree numbers. Depending on your instrument, you may start higher or lower than these examples show, and you may use a different clef. If you don't play an orchestral or band instrument, just sing these exercises in a pitch range that is comfortable for you.

Solfege

Besides singing scales using a neutral syllable or the scale degrees, there is another method whereby a conventional set of syllables are used to help musicians learn to sing notes accurately. These systems can be very complicated, and they vary from language to language and culture to culture, even for the same scale. You may already know the one in English used for the major scale: do-re-mi-fa-sol-la-ti-do (descending: do-ti-la-sol-fa-mi-re-do). If you know these and prefer to use them, go ahead. Start with the syllable "do" as the first and eighth scales degree no matter on what pitch level you begin. (This is called the "movable do" system and is much preferred for students just learning what the major scale sounds like.)

Summary

In this chapter, you have studied and practiced the major scale. This is the scale in which there are half steps between scale degrees 3 and 4 and between degrees 7 and 8, the rest of the steps in the scale being whole steps. You have been shown that you can start on any pitch level to generate a major scale, resulting in the use of sharps or flats to create the strict interval pattern in steps and half steps.

Next

In many pieces, the composer wants certain notes always or nearly always sharped or flatted throughout an entire piece or large section. There is a way to indicate this preference without having to write all those sharps or flats every time they occur. This is shown in the next topic, which will cover key signatures.

Quiz 7

1. As you go **up** the major scale there are half steps just **after** which scale degrees?

2. Which major scale contains only one **sharped** note?

3. Which major scale contains only one **flatted** note?

4. G♭ major is exactly the same major scale and on the same pitches as what other major scale?

5. In movable solfege, name the syllable that is used for the 3rd scale degree.

6. For the F Major scale, what is the letter name of the note on the **4th** scale degree? (Specify sharp or flat if it applies.)

7. For the E♭ Major scale, what is the letter name of the note on the **4th** scale degree? (Specify sharp or flat if it applies.)

8. For the G Major scale, what is the letter name of the note on the **5th** scale degree? (Specify sharp or flat if it applies.)

9. For the A♭ Major scale, what is the letter name of the note on the **3rd** scale degree? (Specify sharp or flat if it applies.)

10. For the A Major scale, what is the letter name of the note on the **6th** scale degree? (Specify sharp or flat if it applies.)

11. What is the functional name for the 5th scale degree of a major scale?

12. What is the functional name for the 1st scale degree of a major scale?

CHAPTER 8: KEY SIGNATURES

Objectives:

1. Describe the relationship between the "circle of fifths" and the adding of sharps or flats in a key signature.
2. Report the order in which sharps / flats are added to form a key signature.
3. Given a graphic for a major key signature, supply the complete spelling for the tonic of that key (the name of the major key).
4. Define what is meant by "enharmonic keys".

The "Key" of a Composition

Music is written in many different styles. These vary considerably with different cultures, different times in history, and with individual composers. In Western affluent societies since about the 16th century, many styles have been what is now called Tonal music. A Tonal musical style is one in which the musical piece resolves, by the end of the piece, to emphasize a particular note, usually in the context of a particular scale. This note toward which the piece resolves is the perceived tonal center of the composition as a whole. Part of the expressive interest in a composition is created by the many ways a composer chooses to move away from this tonal center, move back to it, and imply its presence and importance through the piece. The **key** of a piece is this sense of the presence of a tonal centering on a specified note. Usually, it is further specified by whether the piece emphasizes a major scale built on this tone, or a minor scale. Thus, if a passage has G as its tonal center and emphasizes gravitation and resolution to the G major scale materials, we say the passage is in the key of G major.

Introduction to Key Signatures

So, in this Tonal style, an entire passage or an entire composition is based upon a particular scale. This does not mean it stays in that scale through the entire piece; expressive interest is frequently generated by chromatically altering notes. We will return to this idea a little later. If the composer wishes to base a composition on G Major, she/he would not want to write a sharp before every F that appears, since F♯ will likely occur much more frequently than will F♮. Recall the scale for G Major:

Figure 8-1: G Major scale.

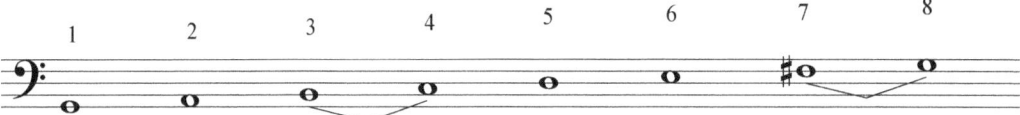

All of the notes are natural except the F, which is sharp. For a composition written in G Major, at the beginning of the piece, there will be a sharp on an F just after the clef (and before the time signature. Here is what this would look like on the grand staff (a time signature is included just to show the proper positioning):

Figure 8-2: Placing a key signature.

These sharps, so placed, make up the "key signature" for the piece. Notice that in the treble staff, the F♯ goes on the top line, not the bottom space, even though it is also an F. In the bass staff, this sharp always goes on the 4th line. These placements are just by convention. Any sharp in the key signature indicates that that same note is sharped in all octaves. Therefore, when a note is written on the bottom space in the treble clef, it will be an F♯; when a note appears in the space just below the bottom line in the bass clef, it will also be F♯. So, all notes on a line or space for "F" will be F♯ unless the composer writes a natural or double sharp sign before the note head. In such case, this is a chromatic alteration and the rules for accidentals apply (only through the current measure and only on that pitch level). Every major key except C requires at least one sharp or flat in its key signature. However, before we list all of the key signatures for major keys, it will help to introduce you to one more interval.

The Perfect Fifth

Let's stay with the scale of G for now. Look at, and count, the first five notes of the G Major scale:

Figure 8-3: First five notes of G major.

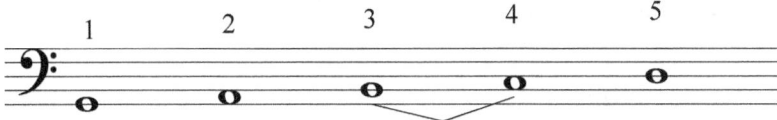

Obviously this is an interval of a 5th. Let's count the whole steps: 1-2, 2-3, and 4-5. That's three whole steps. There is only one half step: 3-4. Any 5th that contains three whole steps and one half step is a **perfect fifth** (P5). Look at the 5th from C up to G. It also contains three whole steps and one half step. Even if you start at B and go up to F♯, you still have three whole steps and one half step; it doesn't matter where the half step is located as long as there is only one of them. Another way to determine the size of an interval is to count the number of half steps, counting all of the black and white keys between. You will find that there are always seven half steps in a perfect 5th. There will be more about the P5 interval in a later chapter. For now let's go back to key signatures and see why this interval is important.

Key Signatures in Sharps

When we showed the major scales, you may have noticed that we first showed the scale with one sharp, then two sharps, then three, etc.

Figure 8-4: Major key signatures in sharps.

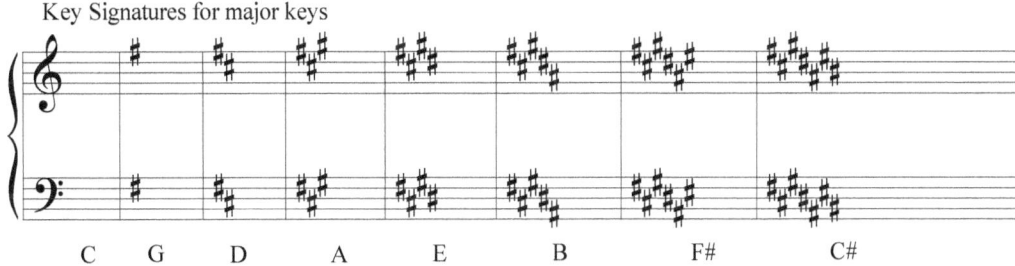

Notice something about the tonic note for each successive key. Each one is up a P5th from the last! Up a P5th from C is G; up a P5th from G is D; etc. Also, each sharp added is up a 5th or down a 4th from the previous one.

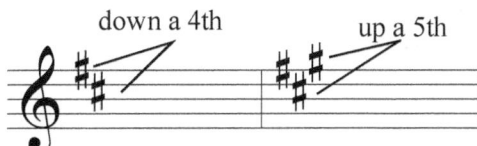

The key will not be identified in the score – just the key signature. Here is an easy way to locate the major key from a key signature in sharps: Go to the last sharp on the right and then go up to the next line or space just above it. For example, for the signature in three sharps, the last sharp on the right in the signature is G♯; the next note up is A. Therefore the major key with three sharps is A Major.

Key Signatures in Flats

We also showed scales that use flats. Therefore, pieces that emphasize these scales also have key signatures, and they use flats instead of sharps.

Figure 8-5: Major key signatures in flats.

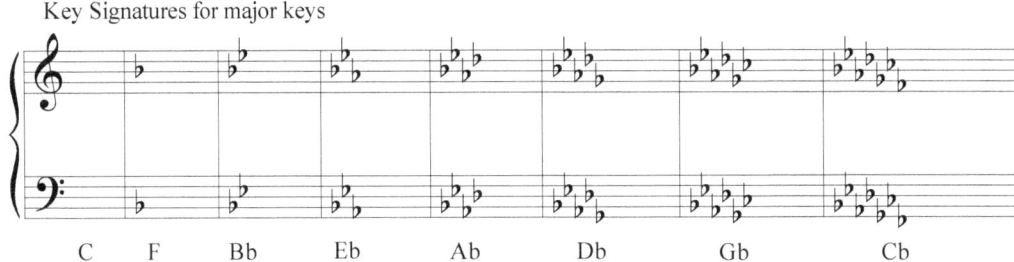

For key signatures in flats, go down a P5th to the next one. For example, down a P5th from C is F; down a P5th from F is B♭; down a P5th from B♭ is E♭; etc. Also notice that each flat added is down a 5th or up a 4th from the previous one.

Here is an easy way to locate the major key from a key signature in flats: Go to the next-to-last flat. For example, for the signature in three flats, the last flat on the right in the signature is A♭; the flat right before it is E♭. Therefore the major key with three flats is E♭ Major. Since the key signature for F Major contains only one flat, there is no "next-to-last flat", so just memorize this one. Also, just memorize the key with no sharps or flats: C Major.

Circle of Fifths

Because of this relationship between the key signatures, one can put these keys into a circle, called the "circle of fifths".

Figure 8-6: Circle of Fifths: major keys.

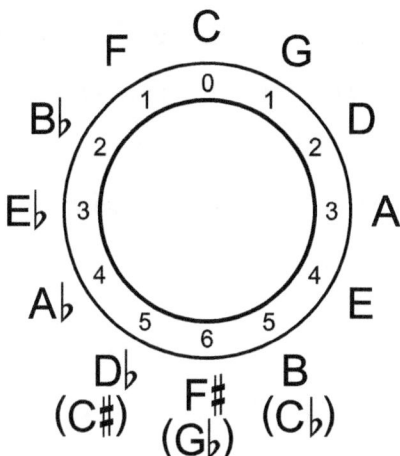

As you go clockwise around the circle, you add a sharp or take away a flat; as you go counterclockwise, add a flat or take away a sharp.

Order in which sharps are added: F♯, C♯, G♯, D♯, A♯, E♯, B♯
Order in which flats are added: B♭, E♭, A♭, D♭, G♭, C♭, F♭

Enharmonic Keys

Look again at the major scale for the key of F♯ Major:

Figure 8-7a: Scale for F♯ Major.

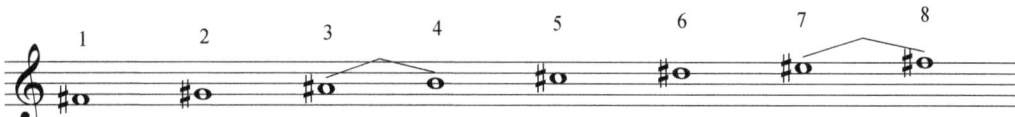

Now examine the scale for G♭ Major (in the same clef this time):

Figure 8-7b: Scale for G♭ Major.

Each corresponding scale degree is on the same pitch even though they are musically spelled differently (in flats in one case; in sharps in the other). You could easily confirm this by playing the scales on a keyboard instrument. Such keys are called ***enharmonic keys***. Which notation a composer chooses to use will depend upon a number of factors which may include which instruments will play the piece and the overall harmonic scheme (which will be discussed in a later unit).

Summary

This chapter described what is meant by the "key" of a piece and then went on to introduce key signatures. The interval of the perfect fifth was defined in order to present the circle of fifths, a graphic way to help understand relationships among keys and their key signatures. All of the major key signatures were described, including a discussion of enharmonic keys.

NEXT

The next chapter will present the following additional note values: dotted notes and tied notes. This will give you access to a greater variety of rhythms and musical examples. You will also be introduced to articulations, which alter notes in certain ways.

Quiz 8

1. As you go clockwise around the "circle of fifths" you add one _____ or take away one _____ .

2. Each flat added to a key signature (after the first one) is up a _____ or down a _____ from

    the previous flat.

3. Following is the major key signature for ____ (letter name plus sharp or flat if it applies).

4. Following is the major key signature for ____ (letter name plus sharp or flat if it applies).

5. Following is the major key signature for ____ (letter name plus sharp or flat if it applies).

6. Following is the major key signature for ____ (letter name plus sharp or flat if it applies).

7. Following is the major key signature for ____ (letter name plus sharp or flat if it applies).

8. Following is the major key signature for ____ (letter name plus sharp or flat if it applies).

9. Following is the major key signature for ____ (letter name plus sharp or flat if it applies).

10. Following is the major key signature for ____ (letter name plus sharp or flat if it applies).

CHAPTER 9: ALTERING TIME VALUES; ARTICULATIONS

Objectives:

1. Describe the exact effects produced by ties and by dotted notes; interpret these where they appear in notation.
2. Demonstrate elementary skill in playing or singing short rhythmic passages containing dotted notes and/or ties.
3. Describe the performance effects to be performed for various articulations, and identify graphic symbols for those which have them. Articulations discussed in this chapter include: accent, slur, staccato, trill, fermata, pizzicato, arco, bowings, tremolo, pedal.

Not all rhythms can be written by using just the note symbols presented in Chapter 2 (quarter notes, eighth notes, etc.). We will next show more ways of indicating note durations by making alterations that use the note values previously learned plus special symbols to create additional durations.

Ties

Suppose you have a note that you want to hold over into the next measure. For example, if, in common meter (four quarter notes per measure) you want to play a quarter note and then two half note durations, you would not have enough time in one measure of common time to do this.

One quarter and two halves would be the equivalent duration to **five** quarter notes, but a measure in 4-4 time can contain only **four** quarter notes. Here is how this would be indicated in a short passage in a score:

The curve under the two quarter notes on the same pitch is a *tie*, which indicates that the note is to be held through the duration of the note to which the previous note has been tied. In the case above, it is to be held for a duration of two quarter notes (= one half note). Now you can see that each measure has exactly four quarter notes, as required by the time signature.

Example 9-1. Here is an example from a popular (if old) tune, "I've Got You Under My Skin", by Cole Porter:

(Recall from the chapter on key signatures that the A, E, and B are all flatted wherever they appear because they are in the key signature.) The third note has the duration of a whole note, but has to be expressed as two half notes tied together so that there are only four quarter notes per measure. The last note in this sample has the duration of three half notes.

You can also tie notes together within a measure.

Example 9-2. The opening of Scott Joplin's "The Entertainer":

Each of the tied 16^{ths} provides the duration of an eighth, but it extends over the beat, so it is much easier to see where the beats go if you tie the notes.

Look at how much more difficult it would be if this rhythm were written without the tie:

This is supposed to be 2/4 time, but where do you see the second quarter?

Let's return to the "Easter Parade" example we first showed you in Chapter 6, but let's keep the sound going and use a tie:

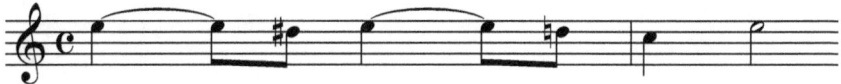

However, there is a more conventional way to indicate the note that has the duration of 1 and ½ quarter notes (or 1 and ½ of any note).

Dotted Notes

Any time you want to indicate that a note should last 1½ of its value (its value plus half again), you just put a dot after the note head. The dot adds half of its duration to whatever note it follows. So, here is the "Easter Parade" example using dotted quarter notes instead of the ties:

Example 9-3. "The Easter Parade", by Irvine Berlin:

The third beat is still very easy to read, so it is not difficult to perform even though the weaker 2nd and 4th beats are a bit disguised.

If you are in 3/4 time, although you can indicate a full measure of rest with a whole rest, a note that lasts for a full measure must be the dotted half note (the half note takes two beats, and the dot the third beat). Notice the dotted note values in the following.

Example 9-4. "My Country 'Tis of Thee":

The last note has the value of 1½ half notes (= 3 quarter notes, a full measure). Look at the note values in the rhythm of the 2nd and 4th measures. The dotted quarter takes up the length of a quarter plus an eighth; then the eighth note, then the quarter note. So, you have a quarter + an eighth + another eighth + a quarter. The result is the three quarter notes of duration that must be in each measure in this meter.

Any note value can be dotted. Following is an example that includes a dotted eighth note. A dotted eighth note has the duration of an eighth and a sixteenth. The dotted eighth note followed by a sixteenth note (= a quarter note in duration) is a very common rhythm.

Example 9-5. Here is an example from "The Stars and Stripes Forever" by John Philip Sousa:

Practice

Here are some rhythmic practice exercises that include dotted note values and tied notes. Play these on your instrument or sing them on a neutral syllable. Tap the beat with your foot.

Exercise 9-1:
We'll start out with the rhythm of the Sousa example:

Exercise 9-2:

Exercise 9-3:

Articulations

There are several notations, called **articulations**, that tell the performer to produce a certain effect by the way a tone or sequence of tones is produced. Although these are handled differently on various instruments, a few are quite general in the effects specified and are in common use. Here are a few of the common articulations:

Accent – You have already learned about this symbol, which directs the performer to apply a special dynamic emphasis to a note.

Legato – an Italian term that means "smoothly". This is indicated in a score by placing a curved line, called a ***slur***, over or under the notes to be smoothly connected.

Example 9-6. Example showing slurs:

(Note: a slur looks like a tie, but whereas the tie connects two notes of the same pitch, the slur is placed over or under notes of different pitches.) If the passage to be played smoothly is very long, this might be indicated simply by writing the word "legato" at the beginning of the passage.

Staccato – another Italian term, this time meaning "detach", directs the performer to play the note/notes shorter than written, adding a rest for the remainder of the note's duration. (Usually the rest takes up half or more of the notated duration for the tone.) A staccato is indicated by placing a dot directly above or below the note head of the affected note.

Example 9-7. Staccatos in "Twinkle, Twinkle, Little Star" (Mozart):

Trill – an indication that the performer must rapidly alternate the note written with the one just a step (in the key) above it. This is done throughout the written duration of the note to which it is applied. It is indicated with *tr*, sometimes with a small, wavy line following it.

Example 9-8. Trills in "Minuet" (Opus 14, No. 1) by Paderewski:

Fermata – a symbol that directs the player to hold the note for a duration longer than written, creating a musical pause of the tempo on the given note. The exact duration is up to the performer or conductor. Here is the symbol: 𝄐.

Example 9-9. An example that contains staccatos, slurs, and fermata:

Okay, what are those little numbers above some of the notes? They are sometimes included for a keyboard player to indicate recommended fingering to facilitate playing.

Some articulations are specific to the type of instrument being played. The ancient Chinese instrument called the Chin, a small plucked, stringed instrument, had over a hundred ways of "touching the Chin", each one with its specific notation. Modern instruments also have some specific notations. Following are but a few of the most common ones:

Pizzicato/Arco (bowed stringed instruments) – Pizzicato means to pluck the string. When you want to go back to bowing it, indicate arco. There are no special symbols for this one, just use the Italian words above the first note to which it applies.

Down bow/up bow (bowed stringed instruments) – symbols to tell the player to drag the bow downward or upward on the strings.

Down bow: ⊓ ; up bow: V

Tremolo – for bowed, stringed instruments, this is an effect produced by rapid successions of up and down bows. (The effect can be imitated on some other instruments, but this is not as commonly used.) It is indicated by short slash marks through the stem of the note or just above or below the note head:

Pedal – Here is one specifically for instruments with sustain pedals (such as the modern piano):

Example 9-10. The following is a passage showing the use of a pedal in Beethoven's Piano Sonata Opus 53 (taken from the Henle 1953 edition, last movement, measures 251-252). Use the symbol *Ped* just under the staff where the pedal is to be pressed; then use * at the place where it is to be released, as shown in the example.

(One should be a bit cautious about pedal markings; they often are added by editors, and may or may not represent the composer's wishes. They do often make the passages easier to play.)

There are many more articulations than those shown above; these are but a beginning sample.

> **SUMMARY**
>
> This chapter has dealt with extending note values through the use of dotted rhythms and ties. Some practice has given you the opportunity to integrate these into your ear training. Then you were introduced to several articulations that are used to further specify how a note is to be played.

> **NEXT**
>
> In the next chapter, you will learn more intervals in preparation for then studying more kinds of scales in a later chapter.

Quiz 9

1. A/An _____ is a symbol between two notes of the same pitch that indicates that the player should hold the sound through both note values (not re-attacking the second note).
   a. accent
   b. fermata
   c. slur
   d. tie

2. A/An _____ is a symbol drawn over or under two or more notes to indicate that they should be played in a smooth, connected manner.
   a. accent
   b. fermata
   c. slur
   d. tie

3. The following symbol is a _____ .

   a. quarter note
   b. half note
   c. dotted half note
   d. whole note

4. The following note would have the duration of a quarter note

   a. plus an eighth note
   b. minus an eighth note
   c. plus a sixteenth note
   d. minus a sixteenth note

5. The presence of a slur tells you to play the notes
   a. in a sharp, detached manner
   b. in a smoothly connected manner
   c. by moving the bow up and down very quickly
   d. by holding the pedal down

6. The following symbol tells the player to rapidly alternate the note written with the one just a step above it.

   a. V

   b. (tremolo notation)

   c. (staccato note)

   d. *tr*

7. The following is the symbol for a down bow.

   a. Ped.

   b. ⊓

   c. V

   d. >

8. The word "arco" in a score means:
   a. Change from plucking a string to bowing it.
   b. Change from bowing a string to plucking it.
   c. Play the following passage in a smoothly connected manner.
   d. Hold the current note for longer than notated.

9. Which notation means "play in a detached manner"?

   a.

   b.

   c.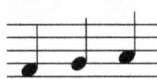

   d.

10. The following shows a/an _____ .

   a. tie
   b. pedal
   c. up bow
   d. slur

CHAPTER 10: INTERVALS, PART 2

Objectives:

1. Given two notes on a staff (with clef), report the specific size of the interval between them, including whether it is perfect, major, minor, augmented, or diminished.
2. Describe how major and minor 9ths and 10ths are formed.
3. Name the exact size of the inverse of a given interval.
4. Demonstrate the ability to name the exact size of an interval by ear.

Review Interval Size

Chapter 5 introduced interval size and how to determine it. Here, we review this concept and then cover it more thoroughly, showing all interval sizes through the octave and providing practice in quickly recognizing these on keyboard and staff. The numeric size of an interval (whether it is a 2nd, 3rd, 4th, etc.) is determined by one of two ways: On the white keys of a keyboard: Start with the first key as "1", then count up or down from there for each successive key.

For example, the interval between a C and the next higher E is a 3rd.

Figure 10-1: Interval of 3rd on keyboard.

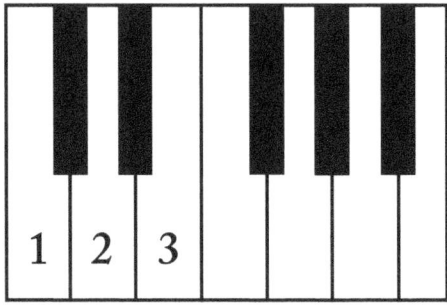

(You could also count from the E down to the C and get a third; it works in either direction.)

Figure 10-2: A third on a staff:

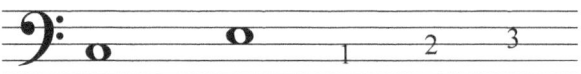

The following reviews the numeric sizes of intervals through the octave (8th).

Figure 10-3: Intervals (numeric sizes) on a staff.

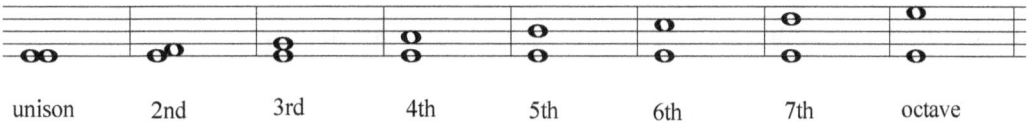

You also learned that there are different sizes of 2nds: major and minor. These have the same numeric classification, but are different sizes in terms of the pitch differences: the minor second having a half step between; the major second, a whole step (or two half steps).

Perfect Intervals

You already know that the interval of the 8th that contains 5 whole steps and 2 half steps (or 12 half steps, or 6 whole steps), as between F and the next higher F, is the perfect 8th (or perfect octave). There are three other intervals within the octave that are classified as "perfect".

Perfect fifth

You were introduced to the perfect fifth when the topic of keys was being explained. The perfect fifth is a fifth that contains 3 whole steps and 1 half step (or 7 half steps). In appearance, the notes of a P5th are both on lines, with a line between, or both on spaces, with a space between them. However, B up to F contains only 6 half steps and is <u>not</u> a P5th. Look at the last P5th in Figure 10-4 below and notice the B-<u>**flat**</u>.

Figure 10-4: Some P5ths on staff.

If you count the steps in each, you will find 3½ whole steps (or 7 half steps). The following shows counting the half steps on a keyboard pattern from D up to A:

Figure 10-5: A P5th on keyboard, showing half steps.

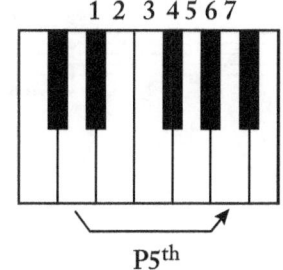

As you have done with the other intervals, you should learn how to identify the perfect fifth when you hear it.

Example 1. Ascending P5th:

After the opening unison, "Twinkle, Twinkle, Little Star" moves up a P5th.

Example 2. Descending P5th:

The opening interval in "The Way You Look Tonight", by Jerome Kern:

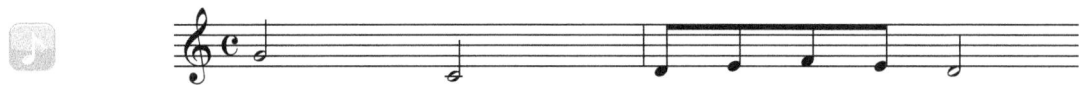

Perfect fourth

The perfect fourth is the fourth that contains 2 whole steps and 1 half step (or 5 half steps). The P4th appears just a bit smaller than the P5th and has one note on a line and the other on a space.

Figure 10-6: Some P4ths on staff.

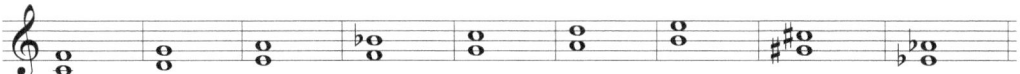

Example 3. Hear the ascending P4 in "Here Comes the Bride":

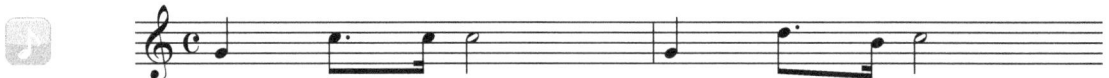

Example 4. The following example from "Eine Kleine Nachtmusik" (A Little Night Music) by Mozart opens with perfect fourths, descending and ascending.

Example 5. You might recognize the theme from the opening of L'Arlesienne Suite No. 1, by Georges Bizet, which also begins with a descending and an ascending P4th:

Perfect unison

The unison is created between two notes at the same pitch and notated on the same line or space. "Twinkle, Twinkle Little Star" starts with the unison.

Something extra: You may be wondering why these particular intervals are called "perfect". What's so "perfect" about them? The "perfection" is (or was) a mathematical one: the ratio between the vibration rates that produce the pitches. For a perfect unison, that ratio is 1:1. For the octave, the ratio of frequencies is 2:1. So, the A just below middle C has a frequency of 220 cycles of vibrations per second. Because the ratio of frequencies for an octave is 2:1, the note that is a perfect octave above that A (the first A above middle C) has a frequency twice that of the lower note of the octave. So, the A above middle C has a frequency of 440. The next A above that has a frequency of 880 (2:1 ratio again). These intervals were named "perfect" way back in the Classic Greek period, attributed to Pythagoras or one of his followers (such musical ratios were documented much earlier than that). At that time, the perfect fifth was assigned the ratio of 3:2, and the perfect fourth, a ratio of 4:3. Today, the unison and the octave still have their "perfect" ratios (1:1 and 2:1). However, although we still have a 5th and a 4th that we call "perfect", in today's tuning, the ratios between the notes are close to but not exactly the older Pythagorean ratios. The Pythagorean 3:2 ratio is equivalent to 1.5:1. Today's "perfect" 5th has a ratio of about 1.498:1, so it is very close to the older P5th. The 4:3 ratio of the Pythagorean P4th is equivalent to about 1.3333:1. Today's P4th is about 1.3348:1 – again, very close to the older P4th. The reason for this change is so that musicians could play pieces that change keys in the middle of a piece without having to retune the instruments. This could not be done with the older tuning. If you want to find more information about modern tunings, look up "equal temperament tuning" on your Internet search engine.

Major and Minor Intervals

You have been introduced to the minor and major 2nd already, so we will now deal with the other minor and major intervals within the span of an octave.

Thirds

The **minor third** is that third that contains 1½ steps.

Figure 10-7: Some minor 3rds on staff.

Example 6. Beethoven's Piano Concerto No. 3 begins with an ascending minor 3rd:

Example 7. The "Hawaiian Wedding Song" also begins with an ascending minor 3rd:

Example 8. Our national anthem, "The Star-Spangled Banner", begins with a descending minor 3rd:

The **major third** contains 2 whole steps.

Figure 10-8: Some Major 3rds on staff.

The second and third intervals of the national anthem are major 3rds.

Example 9. Hear the major 3rd between C and E in the opening of "Frère Jacques" (Even though there is a D in between, you have no trouble hearing the ascending major 3rd followed by the descending major 3rd):

We have covered some unisons, 2nds, 3rds, 4ths, and 5ths. Now for a couple of 6ths.

Sixths

The **minor sixth** contains 3 whole steps and 2 half steps (= 8 half steps).

Figure 10-9: Some minor 6ths on staff.

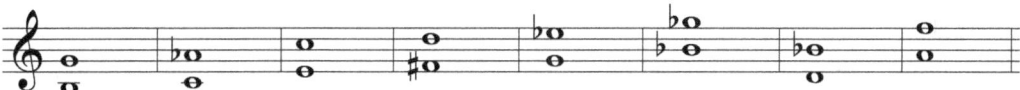

Since the P5th is such an important interval, notice that the m6th is ½ step wider than the P5th (and written as a 6th).

Example 10. The theme from Love Story ("Where do I begin"), by Francis Lai, opens with descending and ascending minor sixths:

Example 11. "Sunrise, Sunset" from Fiddler on the Roof begins with an ascent to a minor 6th (1st and 3rd notes):

The **major sixth** is one whole step wider than the P5th, and has 4½ steps.

Figure 10-10: Some Major 6ths on staff.

Example 12. "The Days of Wine and Roses", by Henry Mancini, opens with an ascending M6th:

Example 13. For a descending M6th, here is the opening to "Over There", by George M. Cohan:

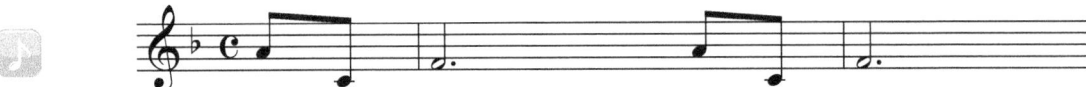

Sevenths

The **minor seventh** is just one whole step smaller than the P8th (the octave), and contains 10 half steps.

Figure 10-11: Some minor 7^{ths} on staff.

Example 14. Hear this ascending m7th at the beginning of "Somewhere" from Leonard Bernstein's West Side Story:

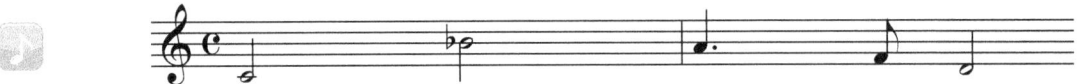

The **major seventh** is only a half step smaller than the octave and contains 11 half steps.

Figure 10-12: Some Major 7^{ths} on staff.

Example 15. You can hear a M7th (after the octave) in the opening of "Bali Hai", from South Pacific, by Richard Rogers:

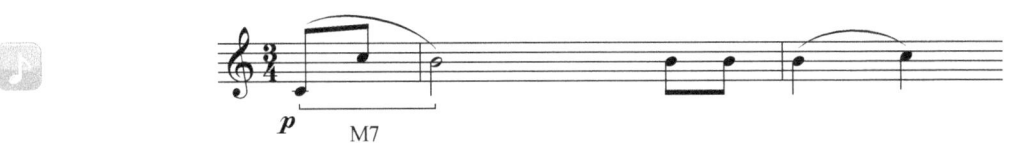

Example 16. Near the end of "Have Yourself a Merry Little Christmas" (by Hugh Martin and Ralph Blane; featured in the movie Meet Me in St. Louis) is a descending M7th:

Augmented and Diminished Intervals

Many intervals can be raised a half step to make them augmented, or lowed a half step to make them diminished. All of these intervals are enharmonic to other intervals. For example, a diminished 3rd is the same size in half steps (2) as is the major second. However, when written in a score as a diminished 3rd, it has a different structural function than does a major second. We will deal more with such functions in later chapters. For now, understand that many intervals create a kind of tonal tension that is resolved into a more stable tonal sound. For example, the diminished third (as between F♯ and A♭) usually will soon move to a unison (G). Such motion would not be implied if they were written as a M2nd (e.g., F♯-G♯). Such explanation is offered at this point to clarify that there is a good reason for enharmonic spellings in a score – it has to do with tonal motion and its relationship to tension and resolution in music.

<u>The diminished fifth and augmented fourth</u>
In terms of the size of an interval as the number of half steps, we have covered all sizes except one: the interval for which the pitches are six half steps apart. One of these is the diminished fifth (○5th). It is a half step <u>smaller</u> than a P5th. B to F♯ is a P5th; so if we lower the F♯ a half-step to F, we get the following diminished 5th (○5th):

If we write the notes with the B on top of the F, we get an augmented 4th (+4th):

The +4 is a half step <u>larger</u> than the P4. This is a unique interval in that the dim 5th is the same size, in half steps, as is the aug 4th. (The word "augmented" is sometimes symbolized as "+" and sometimes as "aug"; likewise, "diminished" may be shown as "dim" or "○".)

Figure 10-13: Some dim 5^{ths} and aug 4^{ths} on staff.

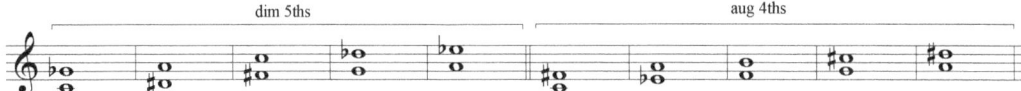

Example 17. While it is quite unusual for pieces to start with augmented or diminished intervals, the song "Maria", from Bernstein's West Side Story opens with an augmented 4th:

More augmented intervals

Any perfect or major interval can be augmented by increasing its size by a half step without changing its numeric size (written on the same lines and spaces on the staff). For example, if you change the P4th from G up to C by adding a sharp to the C, you get an augmented 4th:

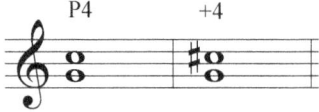

As another example, a major sixth enlarged by a half step, and still spelled as a 6th, is an augmented sixth (you can augment by moving the upper note up a half step or lowering the lower note down a half step):

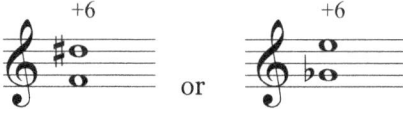

Figure 10-14: A few more augmented intervals.

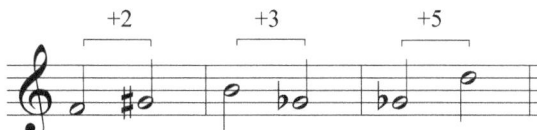

More diminished intervals

Any minor or perfect interval (except the unison, which has no pitch difference between the tones) can be diminished.

Figure 10-15: From P4th to dim 4th.

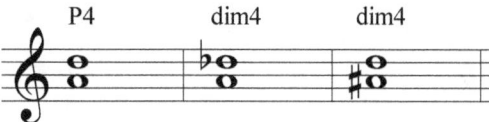

Notice that you can diminish an interval by moving the <u>upper</u> note <u>down</u> a half step or the <u>lower</u> note <u>up</u> a half step (just the opposite of augmenting). Although these might **sound** like major 3^{rds}, they are spelled, and they function as diminished 4^{ths}.

Figure 10-16: More diminished intervals.

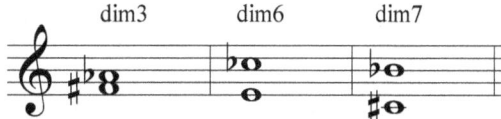

Okay, here is a little challenge. Can you classify the following interval? (Cover up the text below the example until you are ready to see if you are correct.)

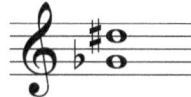

Well, from G up to D♯ would be an augmented 5th. Since this is even another half step larger, and yet still spelled as a 5th, it is the double-augmented 5th. (A rare interval, but that is how it would be classified.)

Pitch Class

We revealed the unique similarity property of the octave (due to the 2:1 ratio of the frequencies of the pitches) that resulted in giving notes an octave apart the same letter name. Notes of the same letter name, including any accidental, if present, are in the same "pitch class". In fact, ***pitch class*** refers to not only octave duplications but also all enharmonic equivalents of the pitch or its octave duplications. In fact, in the 12-tone, equal temperament tuning system, there are only twelve pitch classes (correlating to the 12 keys of a music keyboard that are less than an octave apart). For example all of the following belong to the "pitch class C":

Figure 10-17: Pitch class C.

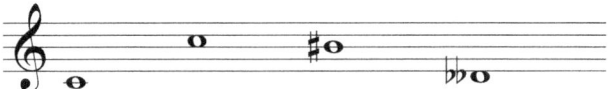

Remember that even if two notes are enharmonic and have the same pitch, they still have different tonal functions in a composition.

Inverted and Compound Intervals

Another result of the special similarity property of the octave leads to interval inverting. In the topic on the augmented 4th and diminished 5th, we showed that if you start with the diminished 5th and then moved the lower note up an octave, you got the augmented 4th as a result. This process of generating a related interval by moving a note up or down an octave past the other note is called **interval inverting**. First, look just at the numeric size changes. If you invert a 2nd, you get a 7th (and vice versa: inverting a 7th yields a 2nd), an inverted 3rd is a 6th (an inverted 6th is a 3rd) and an inverted 4th is a 5th (and invert a 5th to get a 4th).

Figure 10-18: Inverting intervals: numeric size changes.

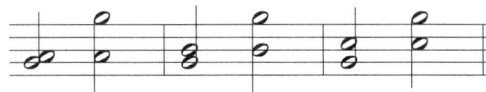

Notice that the numeric sizes always add up to 9.

Now, let's look at specific intervals. The inversion of a minor interval is always a major interval, and vice versa; inverting a perfect interval yields another perfect interval; and inverting a diminished interval yields an augmented interval (and vice versa). Here are some of the most common intervals and their inversions:

Figure 10-19: Common intervals and their inversions.

You can also invert an interval by moving the upper pitch down an octave, as in the following:

Of course, the intervals must be within an octave of one another, and one note must be moved on the other side of the other note.

If you move one of the notes an octave away from the other, you form a compound interval. For example, the interval of an octave plus a 2nd is a 9th, and the interval of an octave plus a third is a 10th, as shown here:

Figure 10-20: Compound intervals: 9^{ths} and 10^{ths}.

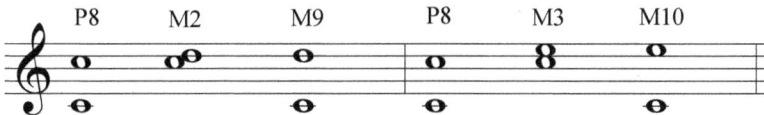

Summary of Intervals

There has been a lot of information in this chapter, and the student needs to begin hearing the intervals in order to anticipate their sound when performing. Knowing what the next note should sound like will help to hear when you make a mistake, and when you are playing exactly the correct pitch. Knowing how the intervals sound is an important step in this ear training. Following is a table summarizing all of the intervals covered in this and the previous chapter on intervals.

Table 10-1: Summary of intervals and their inverses.

Interval	No. half steps	Example	Inverse
P1	0		-
m2	1		M7
M2	2		m7
aug2	3		dim7
dim3	2		aug6
m3	3		M6
M3	4		m6
aug3	5		dim6

Interval	No. half steps	Example	Inverse
dim4	4		aug5
P4	5		P5
aug4	6		dim5
dim5	6		aug4
P5	7		P4
aug5	8		dim4
dim6	7		aug3
m6	8		M3
M6	9		m3
aug6	10		dim3
dim7	9		aug2
m7	10		M2
M7	11		m2
P8	12		-

Next

In the next two chapters, we return to the study of scales: first minor scales and then additional scales. Your studies in intervals will assist in the subsequent study of different scales.

Quiz 10

1 – 15. Name the specific interval, including whether it is perfect (P), major (M), minor (m), augmented (aug), or diminished (dim).

1.
2.
3.
4.
5.
6.
7.
8.
9.
10.
11.
12.

13.

14.

15.

16. The inverse of a major interval is always a/an _____ interval.
    a. diminished
    b. minor
    c. major
    d. perfect
    e. augmented

17. The inverse of a diminished interval is always a/an _____ interval.
    a. diminished
    b. minor
    c. major
    d. perfect
    e. augmented

18. The inverse of a perfect 5th is a/an:

19. A major 9th is an octave plus a/an:

20. A minor 10th is an octave plus a/an:

CHAPTER 11: MINOR SCALES AND KEYS

Objectives:

1. Report the intervals between scale degrees for each of the forms of the minor scale, and name each form.
2. Identify important characteristics for each of the forms of minor scales.
3. Identify a minor key by the number of sharps or flats.
4. Name the specific notes for a given form of a minor scale for a given tonic.
5. Define or identify parallel keys and relative keys.
6. Given a starting pitch, sing a minor scale in a specified form (natural or melodic; ascending or descending).

Review Major Scale

Let's take another look at the major scale. Here is one version of it:

Figure 11-1: The C Major scale.

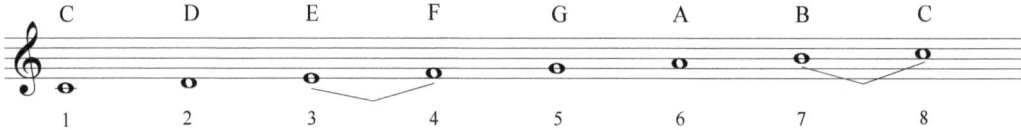

Notice that as we go up the scale, we number the scale degrees, starting with 1. Each successive step of the scale is either a whole step or a half step. We can notice in the pattern of the major scale several important facts:

1. The half steps are between scale degrees 3&4 and 7&8.
2. The 5th scale degree (dominant) is a perfect fifth up from tonic (scale degree 1).
3. The 3rd scale degree (mediant) is a major 3rd above tonic.

Given that the 5th scale degree is a P5th, naming the scale "major" is derived from the 3rd scale degree being a major third above tonic. Further evidence of the importance of this scale degree will be apparent when we study harmony (chords) in later chapters. No matter what note the scale starts on, the relationships of the intervals remain the same: half steps between 3&4 and 7&8, scale degree 5 is a P5 and scale degree 3 is a M3 above tonic.

Figure 11-2: The B♭ Major scale.

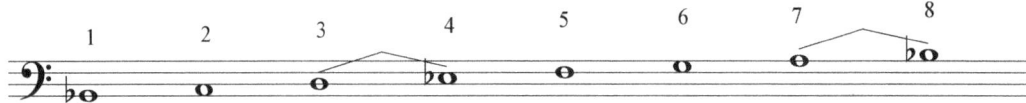

Starting a scale on a different pitch is called transposing the scale. You can think of the scale immediately above as a "transposition" of the major scale from C to B♭.

Forms of the Minor Scales

Natural minor

If we start on the note A and write or play, on a keyboard, a scale upward on all white notes, we get a minor scale:

Figure 11-3: The A natural minor scale.

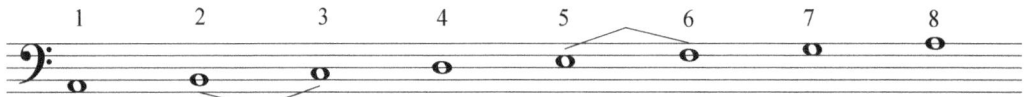

This scale has the following attributes:

1. Half steps are between 2&3 and 5&6.
2. The 5th scale degree is a P5th above tonic.
3. The 3rd scale degree is a minor 3rd above tonic.

This scale is called "minor" because of the minor 3rd on the 3rd scale degree. Compositions written for minor scales and keys make frequent use of chromatic alterations of scale degrees 6 and 7, so there are different forms of minor scales in use. The one shown above is called the natural minor scale.

Melodic minor

For a composition written in minor, frequently a melodic passage will sharp the 6th and 7th scale degrees when ascending from 5 to 8. These alterations result in a form of the minor scale called the melodic minor scale. In the next figure is the ascending melodic minor form built on A.

Figure 11-4: The A melodic minor scale, ascending.

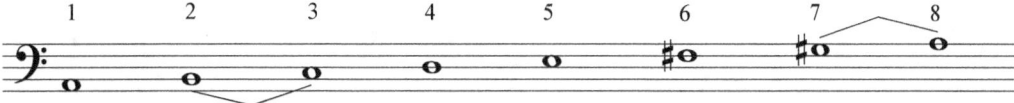

Notice that this removes the half step that was between 5&6 and relocates it between 7&8. When practicing this scale on an instrument, you should use the raised 6th and 7th degrees on the way up but put them back on the way down. Here is a melodic practice example for the melodic scale of A minor:

Figure 11-5: The A melodic minor scale, ascending and descending.

It's melodic minor on the way up and natural minor on the way down. Sometimes a passage in a composition will stay in the melodic minor mode even when descending from 8 if it will be going right back up again, as in the following example.

Example 1. Staying in melodic minor:

If it goes on down after going up to 8, it is much more likely to use the natural minor on the descent.

Example 2. Switching back to natural minor notes in descending passage.

Harmonic minor
In the harmonies of a passage that uses a minor scale, the 6th scale degree is not usually raised (from its natural form) but the 7th scale degree is normally raised, resulting in the harmonic form of the minor scale:

Figure 11-6: The harmonic minor scale.

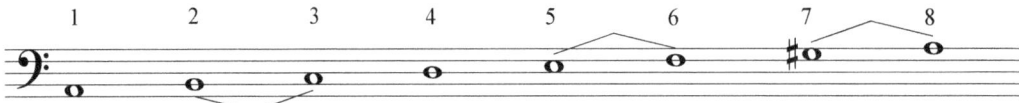

This form of the minor scale contains three half steps. Notice that the interval between scale degrees 6 and 7 is the augmented 2nd.

<u>Scales in C minor</u>

The three forms of a minor scale can be constructed on any note. As one example, let's construct minor scales starting on the note C. We just follow the pattern of step sizes for the minor, starting with those for the natural minor form.

Figure 11-7: C natural minor:

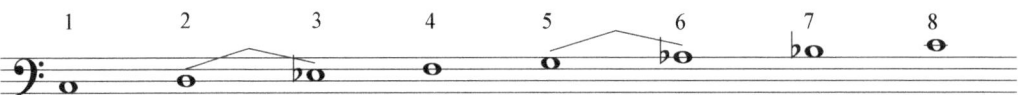

Figure 11-8: C melodic minor:

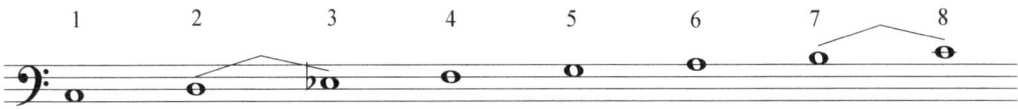

Figure 11-9: C harmonic minor:

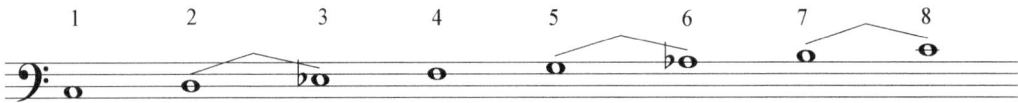

In the ascending melodic and in the harmonic forms of the minor scale, scale degree 7 is just a half step from tonic (at scale degree 8). In this position, it still has the same scale degree name as does the 7th scale degree in a major scale: "leading tone". However, when it is a whole step down from scale degree 8, as it is in the natural minor and descending form of the melodic minor, the 7th scale degree is named the "subtonic". (It no longer "leads" as strongly into 8 as it does when it is only a half step away. "Sub"-tonic merely means "below" tonic.) The other scale degrees have the same names as they do in a major scale: tonic, supertonic, mediant, subdominant, dominant, submediant – for the first six scale degrees. Remember that 8 always has the same name as 1: tonic.

Minor Keys

When a piece is in a minor key, the piece will gravitate toward, and usually resolve to, the tonic note. Whether a piece is in major or minor, a tonal composition will gravitate toward the tonic note. The sharps or flats used in the key signature for a piece based on a minor scale will be those used in the natural minor form of the scale. Since A natural minor contains no sharps or flats, the key signature for A minor also contains no sharps or flats. Notice that the C natural minor scale contains three flats (E♭, A♭, and B♭); so, the key signature for C minor is the one that has three flats in it. Yes, these are the same three flats that are in the key signature for E♭ Major!

Notice also that the key signature for A minor is the same as that for C Major (no sharps or flats). Keys that have the same key signature are called **relative keys**. The relative minor for C Major is A minor, and the relative major for A minor is C Major. Likewise, C minor and E♭ Major are relative keys. In fact, the location of the tonic note for any minor key is a minor third below the tonic for its relative major (or, the major key is a minor third above its relative minor key). So, when we list key signatures below, each key signature will be the signature for two keys: the major key and then its relative minor key.

There is also a close, special relationship between a major and a minor key that has the same tonic note. These are called **parallel keys**. So, C Major and C minor are "parallel". These do NOT have the same key signature.

<u>Minor key signatures</u> (with their relative major)

Figure 11-10: Key signatures in sharps and flats.

Circle of fifths

Since the key center (tonic) for the minor keys is a fixed interval from major keys with the same signature, the tonics of the minor keys are also a P5th apart as you add one sharp or flat. Therefore, we can now show one circle of fifths with both major and minor keys represented.

Figure 11-11: Circle of Fifths (all keys)

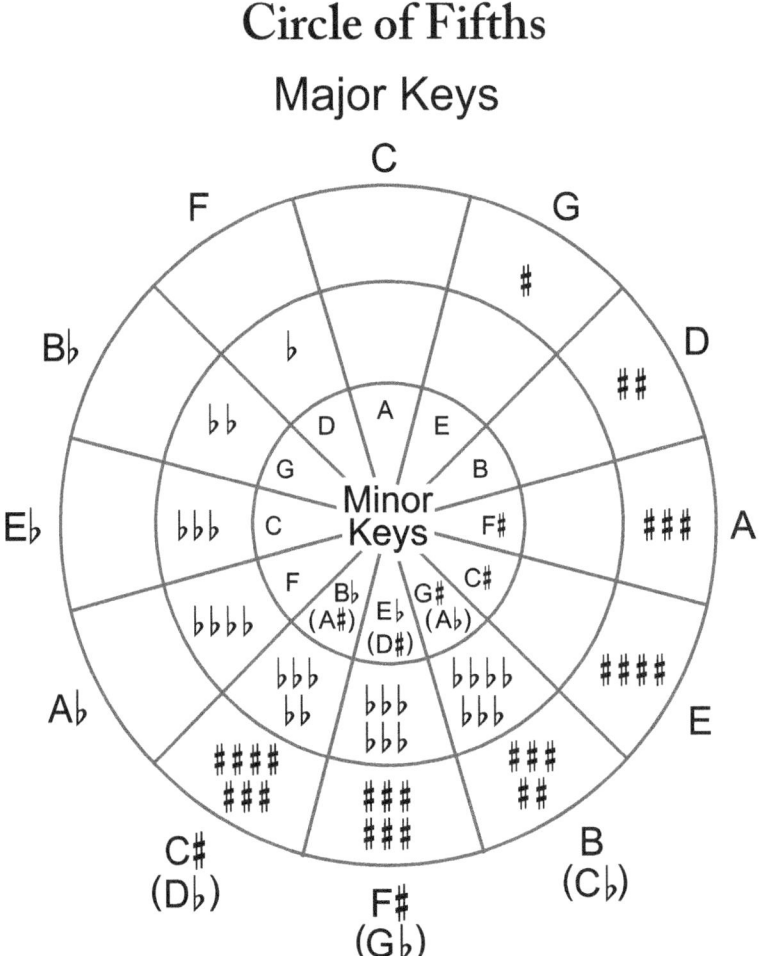

Practice Minor Scales

As we did for major scales, you need to practice minor scales on your instrument or with your voice. Practice descending and ascending, natural minor and melodic minor forms, and choose the range so that the lowest and highest notes are relatively comfortable to perform.

Practice Set 1. Natural minor, ascending first.

Start on a note relatively low in your comfortable range. Play or sing the natural minor scale for one octave ascending and then descending to the starting pitch. If you are singing the passage, you may wish to play it first on a keyboard instrument so you know how it should sound. Remember which notes are already flatted in the key signature.

Remember that even though the E♭ in the key signature is located on the top space, all E's are to be flatted, including the one on the bottom line (3rd note). Then do it again on a higher beginning pitch. Play or sing this scale in this form in as many keys as you can manage at this point in your performance skills. Keys with more sharps or flats are generally more difficult.

Practice Set 2. Natural minor, descending first.

Now try starting on a pretty high pitch and go downward first.

Remember: Even if you play an orchestral or band instrument, it is good practice to also sing some scales.

Practice Set 3. Melodic minor, ascending first.

Watch measure 3: Remember that when you change measures, the notes go back to the flats that are in the key signature, so play or sing the B♭ and A♭ on the way down. Now try this in different keys.

Practice Set 4. Melodic minor, descending first.

As with the other sets, try this pattern in different keys.

Unless your instrument teacher directs otherwise, it is not advised for you to do scales in the harmonic minor form because this collection of notes is used in harmony, not usually the melody.

SUMMARY

This chapter has introduced you to the three forms of the minor scale and to minor keys and key signatures. Practice examples have been provided to extend ear training to the minor scales.

NEXT

In the next chapter, you will study some more scales other than the major and minor scales of traditional tonal music.

Quiz 11

1. In minor scales, there is always a half step between which two scale degrees, regardless of the form of the scale?
    a. 2&3
    b. 5&6
    c. 6&7
    d. 7&8

2. Which form of the minor scale contains an augmented 2nd?
    a. harmonic
    b. melodic
    c. natural

3. Which form of the minor scale uses different pitches depending upon whether you are ascending or descending through the scale?
    a. harmonic
    b. melodic
    c. natural

4. The notes for all scale degrees contain the same sharps or flats as found in the key signature for which form of the minor scale?
    a. harmonic
    b. melodic
    c. natural

5. Which minor key has three sharps in its signature?

6. Which minor key has four flats in its key signature?

7. For the G natural minor scale, which note is on the 6th scale degree?

8. For the G harmonic minor scale, which note is on the 6th scale degree?

9. For the G ascending melodic minor scale, which note is on the 6th scale degree?

10. _____ keys have the same tonic note.
    a. Parallel
    b. Relative

CHAPTER 12: COMPOUND METER, TUPLETS, AND ORNAMENTS

Objectives:

1. Report or identify the correct beat subdivision for compound meter.
2. Given a compound time signature, report the note value for each beat.
3. Given a group of beamed or bracketed notes written as a tuplet, identify which kind of tuplet is being represented (triplet, quintuplet, or septuplet).
4. Given the notation for a specific tuplet, identify what note value would have the same duration.
5. Describe how the following ornaments are performed: grace note, trill, tremolo, mordent, inverted mordent, and turn.
6. Identify the symbol for each of the ornaments presented in this chapter.

Review Simple Meter

Recall that in **simple meter** each beat is subdivided into two equal note values. If the subdivision of the beat is an eighth note or shorter, the beaming of the beat subdivisions usually reflects this, as in the following:

In the above example, there are two beats to each measure, the quarter note takes one beat, and this quarter note is subdivided into two eighth notes within each beat.
In simple meter, the top number in the time signature gives you the number of beats in each measure, and the bottom number indicates the kind of note that takes one beat.

Compound Meter

In *compound meter*, sometimes called *compound time*, each beat is subdivided into <u>three</u> equal note values. This presents a small challenge with rhythmic notation. Suppose that we want the **sub**division to be eighth notes. If this is the case, then three 8th notes would make one beat. So, what time value would be taken in the duration of three 8th notes? One dotter quarter note. Well, there is no natural number that we can use to indicate a dotted quarter note, unless we are going to invent a 6th note, which the theorists of the past decided not to do. Therefore, in compound time, the time signature indicates the number of total **sub**divisions of the beat that make up each measure.

Suppose we want to indicate duple time, but wish each beat to be divided into three parts instead of two. Let's also suppose that we wish to use the 8th note as the value of this subdivision. Thus, you need two groups of three 8th notes. The time signature must indicate the number of 8th notes in each measure (which is six: 3 x 2). Following are examples of duple, triple, and quadruple compound meter showing, for each, the proper time signature and the way the eighth notes are beamed to indicate the proper subdivision of each beat:

Figure 12-1: Three compound meters.

Compound duple meter:

Compound triple meter:

Compound quadruple meter:

Notice that in each case, the top number is divisible by 3 (the number of notes subdividing each beat). So, it turns out that if you see a time signature in which the top number is divisible by 3, not including 3 itself, then you have compound meter and the beat is equal to the dotted note value indicated by three of the notes of the value shown by the bottom number. In the last example above (12/8 time), the time signature tells you that there are 12 8th notes in each measure, that a dotted quarter note (= three 8th notes) takes one beat, and that therefore there are four beats (12 ÷ 3) in each measure.

Naturally, other note values can be used for the beat subdivision.

Figure 12-2: Two more examples of compound meters.

(Each of the 3 beats is a dotted eighth.)

(Each of the two beats is a dotted half.)

Since one cannot beam quarter notes, the subdivision is not as apparent in the measures. The time signature and the rhythmic context of the piece will tell you that this is a compound meter in which each beat is a dotted half note subdivided into three quarter notes. (However, you could also fit six quarter notes into each measure in such a way that each group of two quarter notes is one beat, in which case each beat would be represented by a half note, and there would be three of them. The time signature would be 3/2, a simple meter.)

Tuplets

Sometimes, a composer or arranger will wish to indicate that one particular note value is to be subdivided into some number of parts different from what is normal for the current meter. This requires special notation which consists of a beam or bracket with a number to indicate the number of subdivisions. Following is an example. Below the notes are indicated the count for the steady beat:

Figure 12-3: Triplet 8^{ths} (= one quarter).

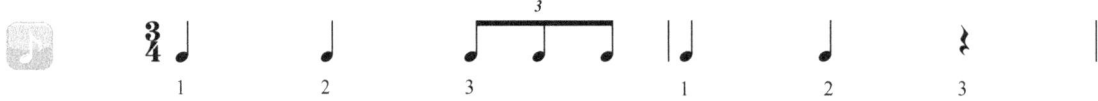

The 3 above the beamed 8th notes tells the performer to play three evenly-spaced notes in the time of one quarter note instead of the normal two. These are called **triplets**. Here is an example in which one would wish three equally-spaced notes in the duration of one half note. Since the half note is normally divided into subdivisions using quarter notes, you use three quarter notes and bracket them with the number 3, as shown here:

Figure 12-4: Triplet quarters (= one half).

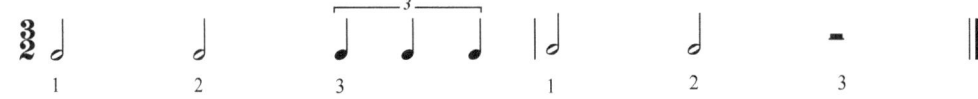

When you practice such passages, make sure you keep the beat going at a steady pace. It sounds just like the previous example. The only difference is that the beat is a half note instead of a quarter note.

You could divide the beat into 5 equally-spaced notes, as here:

Figure 12-5: Quintuplet 16^{ths} (= one quarter).

The 5 indicates that one should play five equally spaced 16th notes in the time span normally taken by four 16^{ths} (one quarter note). A five-note tuplet is called a *quintuplet*.

Example 1. Here is an example of a quintuplet (a tuplet of five notes, as above). This is from the beginning of Minuet in G by Ignace Paderewski:

Even a note value that is less than one beat can be subdivided irregularly.

Example 2. In the following excerpt from Piano Sonata No. 8, Beethoven notates six 64th notes (a sextuplet) and then seven 64th notes (a *septuplet*) each in the time span of one 16th note (normally, there are four 64th notes in one 16th).

(Remember that every time you add another flag or beam, you cut the previous note value in half. Therefore, notes with three flags or beams are half a 16th note, or 32nd notes; notes with four beams are 64th notes. Beethoven even used 128th notes: five beams!)

Musical Ornaments

Now let us examine a few examples of **ornamentation** in music: grace note, trill, tremolo, mordent, and turn. There are many more than these, but these are among the most common musical ornaments. In early music, these were not notated but were part of the performer's way of improvising. Later on, composers started notating ornaments that they considered essential. Such ornaments are rapid successions of notes that rhythmically and melodically embellish a single note. They are indicated by notes of physically diminished size or by special symbols. Because these are just ornamentation for a given note, they share the time value of the note so ornamented.

The *grace note(s)* is "a note(s) printed in small type to indicate that its time value is not counted in the rhythm of the bar and must be subtracted from that of an adjacent note." (from Harvard Dictionary of Music) Following is an example that uses grace notes.

Example 3. From Moments Musicale, Op. 94, No. 3, by Franz Schubert:

Since the grace note takes up part of the note value to which it is attached, these grace notes are played on the beat (not before it).

A *trill* is "a musical ornament consisting of the rapid alternation of a given note with the diatonic second above it". (Harvard Dictionary of Music) It is indicated in a score by a symbol placed above the note to which it applies. The most common symbol for the trill is: *tr*. When applied to long, tied note values, one often will see the following notation: *tr*~~~~~. The wavy line ends where the trill should stop.

Example 4. From the Rondo in D by Mozart

With a bowed, stringed instrument, a *tremolo* is produced by moving the bow very rapidly up and down, creating a kind of shimmering or agitated sound. It is notated with short, slanted slash marks going all the way through the note stem. Other instruments produce the tremolo effect by rapidly repeating a single note or rapidly playing back and forth between two notes (often the octave).

Example 5. The tremolo strings and xylophone provide a very dramatic background for the opening of Shostakovich's Fourth Symphony. Here is a simplified reduction of this passage:

Notice that the xylophone can also do a tremolo, produced on that instrument by playing the same bar rapidly with the two mallets. The effect with the entire orchestra is very dramatic.

The ***mordent*** (✳) is produced by rapidly alternating the written note with the diatonic note immediately below it, usually only once, but sometimes twice (depending upon the style of the music and the performer's preference). There is also an ***inverted mordent*** (✳) for which the alternation is with the note immediately above the written note. From the definition on the Wikipedia site, (http://en.wikipedia.org/wiki/Mordent):

Could be performed, at moderate tempo as:

Example 6. From Bach's Goldberg Variation No. 7:

The ***turn*** (∽) is played by a quick succession of: the note above the notated note, the notated note, the note below, and the notated note again.

103

Example 7. Here is a turn in the beginning of the second movement of Mozart's Piano Sonata No. 10:

Whether the embellishment begins at the beginning or near the end of the note value depends upon whether the symbol is placed exactly above the note head or to the right of it. The way it is notated above, the B ♭ would be part of the turn. However, Mozart wanted the B ♮ played, so he wrote out the turn as grace notes, as indicated here:

Summary

In this chapter, we have studied compound time, tuplets, and some of the most common ornaments. All of these affect the time values of notes, and ornaments also affect melodic patterns. We will now begin referring to examples that include these structures.

Next

The next chapter continues the study of scales by examining some scales commonly used in Western music that contain more or fewer than seven pitch classes.

Quiz 12

1. In compound meter, each beat is subdivided into ___ notes of equal duration.
   a. two
   b. three
   c. four
   d. five

2. There are ___ beats per measure in 12/8 compound time.
   a. two
   b. three
   c. four
   d. twelve

3. In 9/8 compound time, a _____ note takes one beat.
   a. eighth
   b. ninth
   c. quarter
   d. dotted quarter

4. The following tuplet is called a _____ .

   a. triplet
   b. quadruplet
   c. quintuplet
   d. septuplet

5. The following tuplet would take a time equal to the duration of one _____ note.

   a. eighth
   b. quarter
   c. half
   d. whole

6. The following tuplet would take a time equal to the duration of one _____ note.

   a. whole
   b. half
   c. quarter
   d. eighth

7. Notes printed in small type to indicate that their time value is not counted in the rhythm of the bar are called _____ .

   a. grace notes
   b. trills
   c. tremolo
   d. mordents
   e. turns

8. A _____ is played by a quick succession of the note <u>above</u> the notated note, the notated note, the note <u>below</u>, and the notated note again.

   a. grace note
   b. trill
   c. tremolo
   d. mordent
   e. turn

9. Following is the symbol for a _____ .

   a. grace note
   b. trill
   c. tremolo
   d. mordent
   e. turn

10. Following is the symbol for a _____ .

    tr

    a. grace note
    b. trill
    c. tremolo
    d. mordent
    e. turn

CHAPTER 13: NON-DIATONIC SCALES

Objectives:

1. List the names of the four non-diatonic scales discussed in this chapter.
2. Report the number of pitch classes for a given non-diatonic scale and report the structure of intervals in the scale.
3. Given a score showing a short passage that emphasizes a non-diatonic scale, identify the scale.
4. Identify a non-diatonic scale by listening to it being played.

In this chapter, we will study a few more scales that are commonly used as materials in today's tonal style of music, as practiced in Western, affluent societies. In a later unit, we will get into scales used in Jazz and in the musical styles in non-Western societies.

So far, each of the scales we have studied have consisted of seven different pitch classes, with the 8th scale degree being of the same pitch class as the 1st. Following are scales that have more or fewer than seven pitch classes.

Although the use of these scales can be found throughout musical history, they have been used very frequently as a normal part of musical materials since the early part of the 20th century, particularly in the Impressionistic period and in modern Jazz and avant garde. During the Impressionistic movement in musical art, composers sought to give some emphasis to tonally colorful moments in musical passages, moments during which the tension-resolution direction of music were temporarily suspended. Numerous examples of such treatment can be found in works of Claude Debussy, Maurice Ravel, Bela Bartok, Igor Stravinsky, and Charles Griffes. The scales studied in this chapter help to create these moments of musical color and suspension of tonal direction.

The Chromatic Scale

First, we need to classify some of the scales that we have been studying as "diatonic" scales. A *diatonic scale* is one that contains five whole steps and two half steps, has seven different pitch classes, and can (in one transposition) be played on all white keys of the keyboard. The major scale can be played on all white keys by starting on C; the natural minor scale can be played on all white keys by starting on A.

We have already seen two scales that are non-diatonic: the harmonic minor and the ascending melodic minor scales. The alterations made to the natural minor in order to create these other forms are called *chromatic alterations.*

The ***chromatic scale*** consists entirely of successive half steps and is therefore played on all of the white and black keys, in succession. Thus, each note is a half step from the notes on each side of it, and there are twelve different pitch classes in this scale. Since the interval pattern is the same no matter which note you start on, it makes little sense to distinguish different transpositions of the modern 12-note chromatic scale. Just start on any note and play half steps. While it is slightly more conventional to write sharps ascending and flats descending, composers often use either regardless of direction of the melody. Here is a version of the chromatic scale using sharps on the way up and flats on the way down:

Figure 13-1: The chromatic scale.

Example 1. A piece of a chromatic scale can be heard in the opening of "Prelude to the Afternoon of a Faun" by Claude Debussy.

Example 2. The following passage shows just the last two beats at the end of the introduction to Beethoven's Pathetique Sonata (Piano Sonata No. 8, Opus 13). This one contains a very long chromatic scale spanning over two octaves!

Whole-Tone Scales

Okay, we have seen a scale that consists of all half steps. There is also one that consists of all whole steps: the whole-tone scale. With the ***whole tone scale***, there are two possible scales: one contains the three black notes that are grouped on the keyboard and the rest are white notes; the other whole-tone scale contains the two black keys that are grouped together and the rest are white keys. There are six different pitch classes represented in a whole tone scale. Start on any note and you can get only one or the other of these two scales. Again, we will show an octave for each and show both ascending and descending.

Figure 13-2: Whole-tone scales.

Here is one of the two possible whole-tone scales:

Here is the other:

Again, the reason there are only two whole-tone scales is that no matter what note you start on, you will get the pitch classes of one or the other of these.

Notice in the above examples that in notation, some of these "whole steps" get written as diminished 3rds, but this does not interfere with the whole-tone sound of such passages.

Example 3. Often, a passage can be predominantly whole-tone with just a few notes outside of that scale, as in the following melody from the first movement of La Mer by Debussy:

Only the F and E♭ are outside of the whole-tone scale to which the rest of the notes belong, and you can hear the whole-tone sound.

Octatonic Scales

There are also scales that alternate whole- and half-steps in succession. If you do this, when you get to the octave, you will find that the scale has eight different pitch classes in it. "Octa" means "eight"; "tonic" means "tones". Hence an **octatonic scale** has eight different tones, or eight different pitch classes. There are three different octatonic scales, each containing a particular set of pitch classes. No matter what note you start on, or whether you begin with a whole- or half-step, you will get the pitch class set of one of these three scales. (Whether it is written in sharps or flats depends upon context.)

Figure 13-3: Octatonic scales.

Example 4. Here is an example of an octatonic scale from a jazz tune, "Please Send Me Someone To Love" by Percy Mayfield, and arranged by Ray Brown:

When the 32nd notes begin, all of the remaining notes in this example except the B-flat are in the C Major-minor octatonic scale (the first one in the above list).

Pentatonic Scales

There are five black keys in each octave on the keyboard. If you play these, you will hear a *pentatonic scale*. "Penta" means "five", and a pentatonic scale contains five different pitch classes. A pentatonic scale has a pattern of intervals that repeats only once every octave, so it can be transposed to start on any note. One common form of pentatonic scale in Western music **looks like** a major scale with degrees 4 and 7 missing. As you move from one note to the next, you find only successive whole steps or minor 3^{rds}. Here is a form of a pentatonic scale starting on C:

Figure 13-4: A pentatonic scale.

Here is a different form of pentatonic scale. The first minor 3rd is in a different location and this transposition is on all black keys:

Figure 13-5: Another pentatonic scale.

Example 5. First look at the main melody at the beginning of "Morgenstimmung" from the Peer Gynt Suite by Edvard Grieg:

Example 6. For a more involved example, there is a pentatonic collection near the beginning (ms. 5-6) of "The Fountain of the Aqua Paola" from Roman Sketches by Charles T. Griffes:

All of the notes in the above example (both hands) are in the following pentatonic scale:

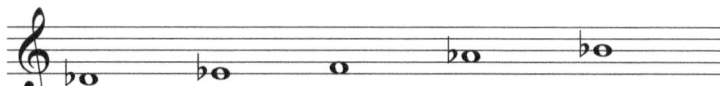

Practice

Have someone play some non-diatonic scales and identify each by listening to it.

SUMMARY

All of the scales studied in this chapter contain more or fewer than seven pitch classes and thus are all non-diatonic. Although the pentatonic and octatonic scales have non-Western origins, they find frequent expression in Western musical compositions. Here are the scales covered:

Chromatic: 12 pitch classes, successive semitones.
Whole tone: 6 pitch classes, successive whole-tones.
Octatonic: 8 pitch classes, successive alternations of whole- and half-steps.
Pentatonic: 5 pitch classes, containing successions of whole steps and minor thirds.

NEXT

Next, we will begin our study of harmony in music, beginning with triads (chords of three notes). We will study the structure of chords, their role in musical consonances, and ways in which they are notated.

Quiz 13

1. Which scale contains only successive **major** 2nds?
    a. chromatic
    b. octatonic
    c. pentatonic
    d. whole-tone

2. Which scale successively alternates minor 2nds and major 2nds?
    a. chromatic
    b. octatonic
    c. pentatonic
    d. whole-tone

3. Which scale contains only successive **minor** 2nds?
    a. chromatic
    b. octatonic
    c. pentatonic
    d. whole-tone

4. Which scale contains exactly five pitch classes?

    a. chromatic

    b. octatonic

    c. pentatonic

    d. whole-tone

5. Which scale contains exactly eight pitch classes?

    a. chromatic

    b. octatonic

    c. pentatonic

    d. whole-tone

6. Which scale is used in the following passage? 🎵

    a. chromatic

    b. octatonic

    c. pentatonic

    d. whole-tone

7. Which scale is used in the following passage? 🎵

    a. chromatic

    b. octatonic

    c. pentatonic

    d. whole-tone

8. Which scale is used in the following passage? 🎵

    a. chromatic

    b. octatonic

    c. pentatonic

    d. whole-tone

9. Which scale is used in the following passage?

   a. chromatic
   b. octatonic
   c. pentatonic
   d. whole-tone

10. Which scale is used in the following passage? (Consider the entire passage – not just pieces of it.)

    a. chromatic
    b. octatonic
    c. pentatonic
    d. whole-tone

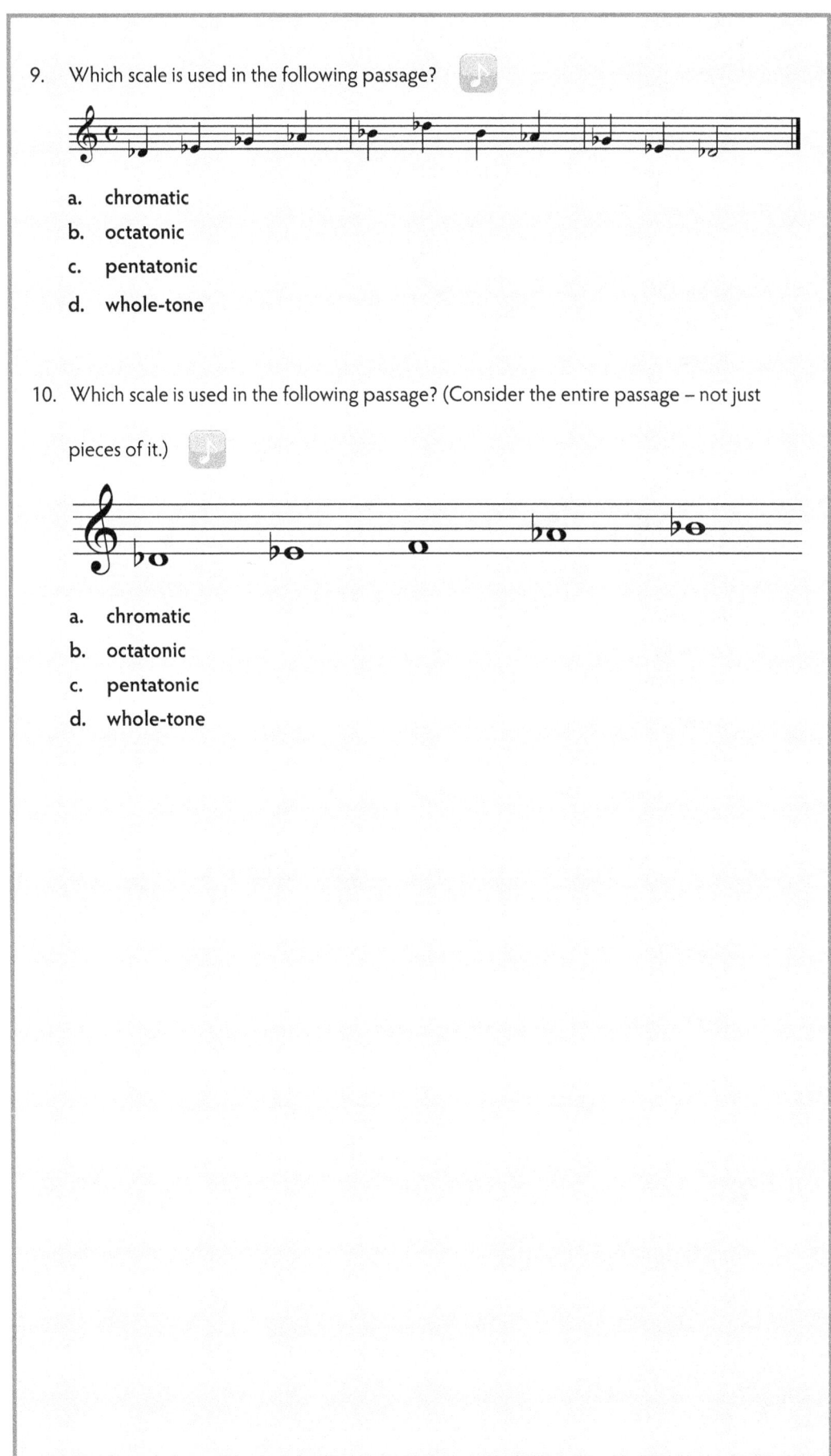

CHAPTER 14: CHORDS, PART 1

Objectives:

1. Define "chord" and "tertian harmony".
2. Construct each of the four forms of a triad on a given chord root.
3. Name the correct quality for a triad by listening to it.
4. Given a chord notated in close position on a single staff, name the chord, including its quality, and state its position (root, 1st inversion, 2nd inversion).
5. Identify or write the chord represented by given chord symbols that would be written above a melody line.
6. For triads written in open position on a grand staff, use the given step-by-step procedure to identify the triads, including their positions (root, first inversion, or second inversion).

A *chord* is produced by the simultaneous sounding of three or more tones. In this chapter, we will study triads. A triad is a chord of three tones consisting of a root, a note that is an interval of a third above the root, and another note that is an interval of a fifth above the root (or another third above the second note). Such chords are produced by stacking notes in intervals of thirds. Chords so formed are said to form **tertian harmony**.

Four Qualities of Triads

There are four possible structures of the triad, each with its own, aurally identifiable musical quality determined by the relationship of the intervals in the chord. The three tones are identified as the root, the third, and the fifth of the triad. The root is always the note on the bottom of the stack of thirds; the 3rd is so named because it is an interval of a 3rd above then root; and the 5th is an interval of a 5th above the root. These are shown below.

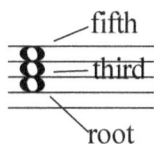

There are two thirds: the one between the root and the third, and that between the third and the fifth of the triad. Each of these thirds must be either a major third or a minor third. This allows exactly four options:

(1) Both 3rds are major,
(2) both 3rds are minor,
(3) the bottom 3rd is major and the top minor, or
(4) the bottom third is minor and the top major.

Let's examine each of these.

(1) Both 3^{rds} are major:

The bottom 3rd is major and the 5th is augmented. This is called the ***augmented triad*** (because the fifth is augmented).

(2) Both 3^{rds} are minor:

The bottom 3rd is minor and the 5th is diminished. This is called the ***diminished triad*** (because the fifth is diminished).

(3) The bottom 3rd is major and the top 3rd is minor:

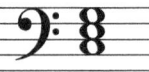

The bottom 3rd is major and the 5th is perfect. This is the ***major triad***.

(4) The bottom 3rd is minor and the top 3rd is major:

The bottom 3rd is minor and the 5th is perfect. This is the ***minor triad***.
Play or listen to all four forms of the triad: augmented, diminished, major, and minor. Pay attention to the darker qualities of the minor and diminished structures; the open, hollow sound of the augmented triad; and the more brilliant quality of the major triad.

Example 1. Let's look at these built on D this time. The four triads:

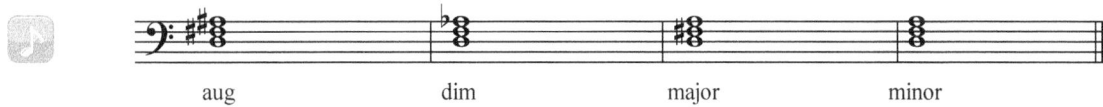

Consonance and Dissonance

Consonance and dissonance in music are on opposite ends of a bipolar concept in which *consonance* is sensed as stable and as a condition of resolution; *dissonance* is sensed as unstable and needing to move toward resolution to more consonant sounds. These are related to musical intervals in the Tonal style. Thirds are sensed as more consonant and seconds as more dissonant. The perfect octave and the perfect fifth are sensed as the most stable intervals, while augmented and diminished intervals are sensed as very unstable. It is for this reason that the major triad and minor triad are heard as consonant chords, whereas – because of the fifths – the augmented and diminished triads are dissonant, needing resolution in music of the Tonal period (roughly since the 15th century, in Western harmonic styles).

Inversions of Triads

In Tonal harmony, which note is in the bass determines the stability of the prevailing harmony. For tertian chords (recall these are chords built in thirds), the most stable condition is for the root of the chord to be in the bass (and the other two notes above it). When this is the case, the chord is said to be in **root position**. If any other note of the chord is in the bass, the chord is in one of its inversions. In the ***first inversion***, the 3rd of the chord is in the bass (root and 5th above it). You can get the first inversion by moving the root of the chord up an octave, as shown here for the G Major triad:

If the B is then move up an octave, you get the ***second inversion***, in which the 5th of the chord is in the bass (root and 3rd above it):

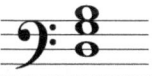

The position of the chord depends only upon which note of the chord is lowest. Therefore, root, first inversion, and second inversion of the G major triad could also be notated in the following ways:

Figure 14-1: Positions of triad on grand staff.

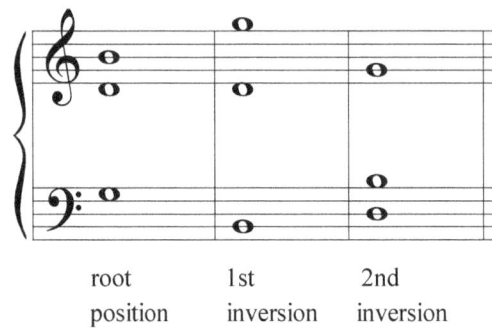

While all of these sounds are consonant relative to some other chords, of the three positions of the triad, the root position is the most stable, and the 2nd inversion is the least. It would not sound "complete", for example, to end a piece on a triad in second inversion. (Though we will explain this in more detail later, this has to do with the fact that a note at an interval of a 4th above the bass has a strong tendency to move by step to another note.)

Let's try to hear the difference in the following pair of examples.

Example 2a. From Sonata No. 5, K.283, end of second movement, the way Mozart wrote it:

The final C in the bass gives the ending a solid feeling.

Example 2b. Now let's change the ending:

The G in the bass at the end just doesn't sound as stable as does the root of the chord.

You may have noticed a new notational practice in Example 2: Writing stems in opposite directions on a staff can be used to separate notes being played in different rhythms in the same hand or on the same five-line staff.

Identifying triads

No matter how the notes of a tertian chord are distributed throughout the range shown, to identify what kind of chord has been written, you will need to reconstruct the chord as stacked thirds. Identify the letter names and then arrange the notes in stacked thirds.

Here is an example.
Given the following chord, identify the root note and name the type of chord.

Steps:
(1) Letter names: **F♯, D, A**.
(2) Rearrange in thirds: **D-F♯-A**.
(3) Rewrite

(4) Name the root note: **D**
(5) Examine the 3rd and 5th of the triad: **Major 3rd**, **Perfect 5th**.
(6) Name the triad: **D Major triad**.
(7) State the position from the originally notated chord: Since F♯ was in the bass and that note is the 3rd of the chord, it is in **first inversion**.

Here is another one – try it yourself:

Cover up the following lines until you are ready to see the answer.

- - - - - - - - - - - -

Ready for the answer?

E diminished triad in second inversion.

(1) Letter names: B♭, G, E.
(2) In thirds: E, G, B♭.
(3) Rewrite (if you need to)
(4) Root of chord: E
(5) m3, dim5
(6) E diminished
(7) 5th of the chord (B♭) is in the bass, so 2nd inversion.

Chord Symbols

In collections of popular songs and jazz pieces, it is common for there to be only the melody line written out in conventional musical symbols and then the harmony – the supporting chords that should be played along with it – shown above the melody notes in an abbreviated, symbolic notation. For triads, this is quite simple. Here are the symbols used:

- Major triad: just the letter name of the root. For a C Major triad: C.
- minor triad: letter name of root + "m". For an A minor triad: **Am**.
- diminished triad: letter name of root + "dim". For F♯ diminished: F♯ **dim**.
- Augmented triad: letter name of root + "+". For a C augmented triad: C+.

The above are the conventions we will use in this course. There are several variations from the above.

Sometimes the augmented chord is specified as a major triad with an augmented 5th, like this: **C+5**. Sometimes the "+" is replaced with "aug". At times, you will see a small circle representing the diminished interval. So, an E diminished triad could be shown as **Edim** or as **Em♭5** (an E minor chord with a diminished instead of a perfect 5th).

We point these out just so you will know how to interpret them if you see them in other sources.

SUMMARY

- A chord is produced by the simultaneous sounding of three or more tones.
- Chords formed of stacked thirds are called tertian chords.
- The three notes of a triad, when arranged vertically in 3rds, are (bottom to top): root, 3rd, and 5th.
- The four qualities of triads, based on specific interval structure, are: major,
- minor, diminished, and augmented.
- Triads with a perfect 5th in them are more consonant than are those containing the diminished or augmented 5th.
- The three positions of a triad are based only upon which note of the triad – root, 3rd, or 5th – is in the bass. These are: root position, first inversion, and second inversion.
- The most stable position of a triad is root position; the least stable: 2nd inversion.
- You have gone through a step-by-step procedure for identifying triads in notation.
- Abbreviated symbols for the four qualities of triads have been shown.

NEXT

You will continue into the next chapter the study of tertian chords by stacking more than three notes in thirds. You will also be introduced to non-tertian chords (those whose notes are formed by stacking them in intervals other than 3rds).

Quiz 14

1. In a B♭ Major triad, the **third** of the chord is what note?

2. In an A♭ Major triad, the **fifth** of the chord is what note?

3. In a G♯ diminished triad, the **fifth** of the chord is what note?

4. In a C minor triad, the **third** of the chord is what note?

5. In an E♭ augmented triad, the **fifth** of the chord is what note?

6. Name the chord and its position.

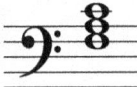

7. Name the chord and its position.

8. Name the chord and its position.

9. Name the chord and its position.

10. Name the chord and its position.

11. When written above a melody, what chord is represented by: **Fm**?

12. When written above a melody, what chord is represented by: **Edim**?

CHAPTER 15: CHORDS, PART 2

Objectives:

1. Supply or identify the interval structure for each of the seven most common qualities for seventh chords (interval of each note above the root when in root position).
2. Identify the type of a tertian chord (7th, 9th, 11th, or 13th) when shown on a single staff (the 7th chord might be inverted; others will be in root position).
3. Identify the position (root, 1st inv., 2nd inv., or 3rd inv.) of a 7th chord shown on a single staff.
4. Identify the name of the specific quality of seventh chord written on a single staff.
5. Given a non-tertian chord notated on a staff, identify the type of chord based on its interval structure.

Continuing our examination of tertian harmony, we will extend our study to chords of more than three notes. We will also introduce non-tertian chords, those constructed of stacking notes at intervals other than thirds.

Non-Triadic Tertian Chords

We can create additional tertian chords by simply stacking more notes at intervals of a third. In each case, you name the chord (except for the triad) by the interval formed above the root by the top note.

Figure 15-1: 7th, 9th, 11th, and 13th chords.

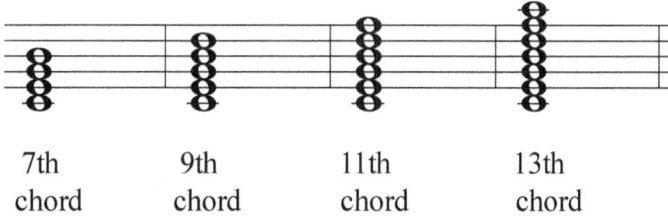

7th chord   9th chord   11th chord   13th chord

There is no 15th chord because the next note an interval of a third above the 13th is back to the original root of the chord. In classical musical styles, chords above the 7th are quite rare, but they are commonly used as harmonic structures in jazz music and some popular music. Often, not all of the notes are needed to provide the sound and function of the chord. It is common to see a 7th or 9th chord with the fifth omitted; it is also common to see the 11th or 13th chord with both the 5th and the 9th omitted.

Figure 15-2: Chords with omitted members.

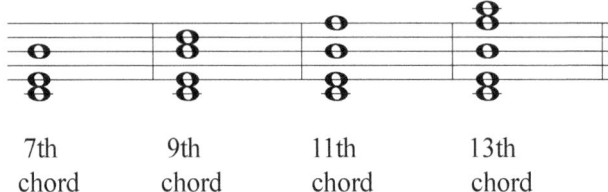

It does not work as well for some other notes to be missing. For example, look at the structure of a 9th chord with a missing 7th:

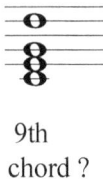

9th
chord ?

This looks like, and in most cases would sound like, a triad with a note that does not belong in the chord. However, the study of such "non-harmonic tones" will be covered in a later chapter.

Inversions of the Seventh Chord

Just as a different note can be in the bass in a triad, you can have inversions of a 7th chord. As with the triad, the first inversion has the 3rd of the chord in the bass; the second inversion, the 5th. Therefore, the position that has the 7th of the chord in the bass is called the ***third inversion***. Following shows the four positions of the 7th chord, first in closed position (notes as close together as possible), then in a more open distribution. As with any chord, the position is determined only by which note of the chord is in the bass.

Figure 15-3: Inversions of a 7th chord.

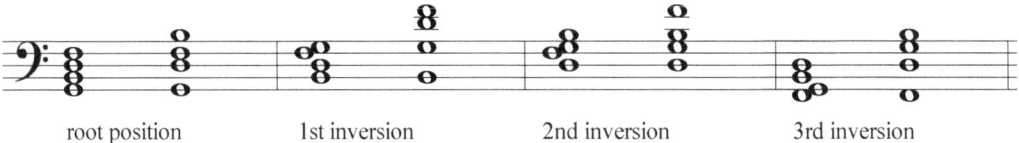

In chord abbreviations used in song books, the inversion of the chord is not usually indicated. Where it is important to the composer or arranger for a particular note to be in the bass, it will be indicated as shown here for an example in which the second inversion of the G7 is required: G7/D. This indicates that the performer should play a G7th chord with the D in the bass.

Qualities of Seventh Chords

The seventh chord can be seen as constructed from a triad plus a note that is an interval of a 7th above the root. The qualities of seventh chords are classified by the type of the triad and the size of the 7th. Following is a table showing these classifications for seventh chords.

Table 15-1: Classifications of 7th chords (by quality).

Classification	Meaning	Example	*Symbol
Major-minor	Major triad + minor 7th		G7
Major-Major	Major triad + Major 7th		GM7
minor-minor	minor triad + minor 7th		Gm7
minor-Major	minor triad + Major 7th		Gm(M7)
diminished-diminished	diminished triad + diminished 7th		Gdim7 or G°7
diminished-minor	diminished triad + minor 7th		Gm7(°5) or Gm7(♭5)
Augmented-Major	Augmented triad + Major 7th		GM7(+5) or GM7(♯5)

*Chord symbols are shown for root on G. Sometimes "M" is shown as "Maj"; and sometimes "m" as "min".

Another way to think of the structure of these seventh chords is as each of the four triads plus either a major or minor third added to the stack of thirds. (The only one of the resulting eight possibilities that does not result in a 7th chord is trying to add a major 3rd on top of an augmented triad. Look at a keyboard and see that this would place the fourth note of the chord on the tonic pitch, so that possibility is not included as a seventh chord.)

Figure 15-4: Three major 3rds = augmented triad, not a 7th chord.

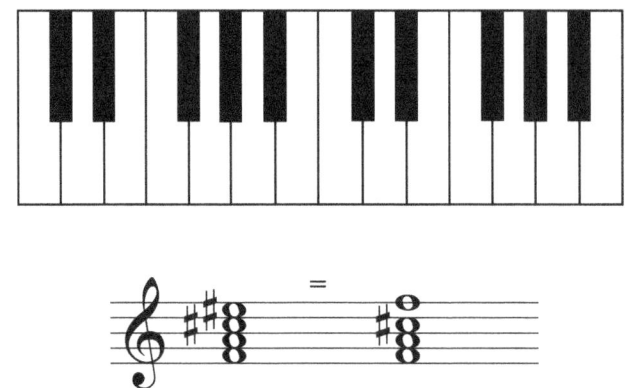

Examples

Following are a few examples containing seventh chords.

Example 1. Near the beginning of Beethoven's Moonlight Sonata (Opus 27, No. 2, in C♯ minor) is a Major-minor 7th in 1st inversion (measure 6):

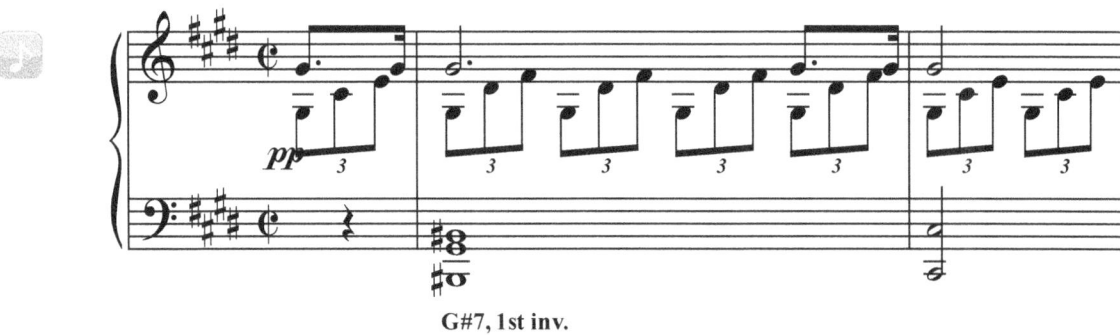

G♯7, 1st inv.

Example 2. Later on in that same piece in measures 34-35, Beethoven presents two different diminished 7th chords in the right hand (over a note in the bass that is not a member of either chord!):

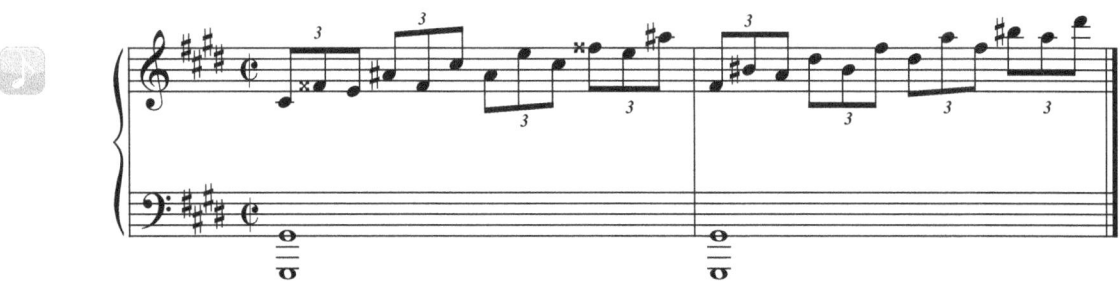

Example 3a. Let's examine a harmonization of the first eight measures of the tune "My Funny Valentine", by Richard Rogers. First, we will use all triads (not the way Rogers wrote it):

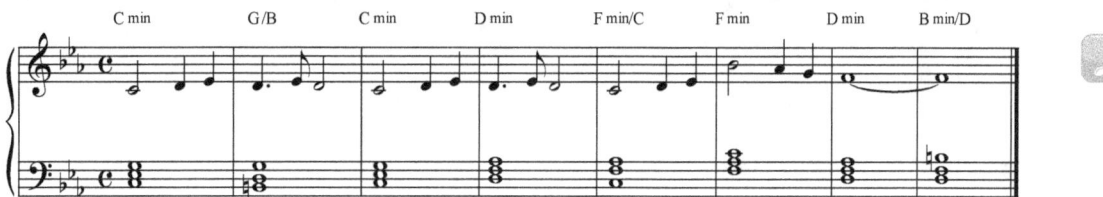

Example 3b. Listen now to the denser, more interesting sound when it is harmonized with 7th chords (plus 11th and 13th in two chords):

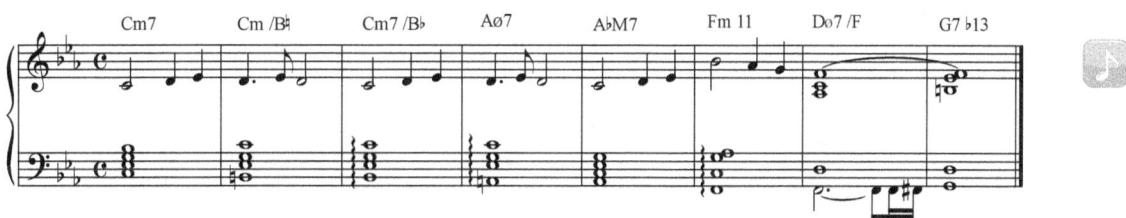

Chord qualities in this passage:

Meas. 1: minor 7th (root pos.);

    2: minor-Major 7th (3rd inv.);

    3: minor 7th (3rd inv.);

    4: diminished-minor 7th (root pos.);

    5: Major-Major 7th (root pos.);

    6: minor triad + the 11th (root pos.);

    7: diminished-minor 7th (1st inv.);

    8: Major-minor (dominant) 7th + the 13th.

Non-Tertian Chords

Some chords are also formed by stacking notes in intervals other than the third.

Quartal harmony

A harmonic system in which chords are formed by stacking notes at intervals of fourths is called **quartal harmony**. Several jazz arrangements make use of these structures. If you stack chords in fifths, since their inversion is 4ths, they may look and sound like quartal harmony. Only examining the specific musical context can tell you which was intended.

Example 4. Listen to the open sound of the succession of quartal chords in the following passage:

Secundal harmony (clusters)

A harmonic system in which chords are formed by stacking notes at intervals of seconds is called *secundal harmony*. The chords so formed are often referred to as clusters. Clusters can be found in all styles of music, especially since the early 20th Century.

Example 5. The following excerpt from the "Polka" in The Golden Age by Dimitri Shostakovich contains a cluster of minor 2nds:

SUMMARY

Tertian chords (those built in stacked thirds) can be constructed in 7th, 9th, 11th, and 13th chords. Not all notes of such chords need be present. Seventh chords often occur in inversions, with the following possible positions: root, 1st inversion, 2nd inversion, and third inversion. The position of the chord depends only upon which note of the chord is in the bass, not the distribution of chord notes above the bass.

Seven different qualities of 7th chords were presented, categorized by the type of triad, and the size of the seventh:

Major-minor; Major-Major; minor-minor; minor-Major; diminished-diminished; diminished-minor; Augmented-Major

Non-tertian chord structures were explained: chords built in fourths (producing quartal harmony) and chords built in seconds (producing secundal harmony, or "clusters").

Next

In the next chapter, we will begin our study of functional harmony, starting with building chords on each scale degree in a key and then discussing phrases and how they end in what is called "cadences".

Quiz 15

1. The following is a/an ___ chord.

   a. 7th
   b. 9th
   c. 11th
   d. 13th

2. The following is a/an ___ chord.

   a. 7th
   b. 9th
   c. 11th
   d. 13th

3. The following is a/an ___ chord.

   a. 7th
   b. 9th
   c. 11th
   d. 13th

4. The following is a/an ___ chord.

    a. 7th
    b. 9th
    c. 11th
    d. 13th

5. The following is a/an ___ chord.

    a. 7th
    b. 9th
    c. 11th
    d. 13th

6. The following chord is in _____ .

    a. root position
    b. 1st inversion
    c. 2nd inversion
    d. 3rd inversion

7. The following chord is in _____ .

    a. root position
    b. 1st inversion
    c. 2nd inversion
    d. 3rd inversion

8. The following chord is in _____ .

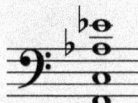

   a. root position
   b. 1st inversion
   c. 2nd inversion
   d. 3rd inversion

9. The following is a/an _____ - _____ seventh chord.

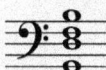

10. The following is a/an _____ - _____ seventh chord.

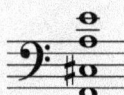

11. The following is a/an _____ - _____ seventh chord.

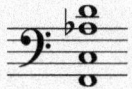

12. The following is a/an _____ - _____ seventh chord.

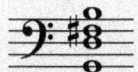

13. The following is a/an _____ - _____ seventh chord.

14. The following chord is an example of _____ harmony.

    a. quartal
    b. secundal
    c. tertian

15. The following chord is an example of _____ harmony.

    a. quartal
    b. secundal
    c. tertian

16. The following chord is an example of _____ harmony.

    a. quartal
    b. secundal
    c. tertian

CHAPTER 16: FUNCTIONAL HARMONY, PART 1

Objectives:

1. Given a triad written on a grand staff, and the key, report the functional designation for the chord (Roman numeral + inversion numbers if inverted).
2. Define or identify the following: phrase, antecedent phrase, consequent phrase, period, cadence.
3. Identify a terminal or a progressive melodic cadence and distinguish the difference between them.
4. Given a functional chord sequence (via Roman numerals) at a harmonic cadence, report or identify the type of cadence (authentic, plagal, half, or deceptive).

In Western Tonal style, musical passages progress toward conclusion, with all elements of the music structured logically and expressively to move the piece from beginning through its unfolding to the end. There are some works in which such progression is of minor importance. However, we will focus in our study of harmony on the very large body of musical art in which the elements of the music are structured so that the work takes advantage of learned senses of tension and relaxation, of development and resolution, of movement away from and toward musical goals. Most of Western Classical music, popular songs, folk music, country music, rock, sacred music, jazz, and music for the theater and movies, possess this property of motion in a perceivable direction. *Functional harmony* is the study of how chords relate to one another in the prevailing key, and how their succession leads the music away from or toward the natural harmonic goals. In these sections on functional harmony, we will examine, and hear, how chord progressions in Tonal music help generate this sense of tonal direction. First, we need to take an inventory of chords available in the context of the key of a piece.

Triads in Major Keys

A diatonic scale gives us a collection of notes available to us in a given key. One can build a triad on each scale degree in any particular key to show the triads normally available in that key. Following, for example, are the triads constructed on each scale degree in the key of C Major. Only notes in the C Major scale can be used for the notes in each triad. For each, the name of the scale degree (and the chord built on it) and the quality of the triad is shown.

Figure 16-1: Triads on each scale degree in C Major.

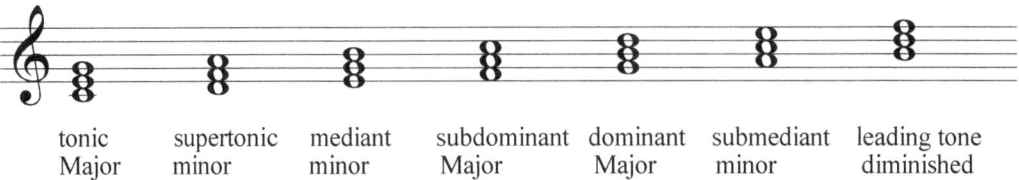

Whereas scale degrees by themselves can be indicated by plain (Arabic) numerals, for the purposes of theoretical discussion, the chords built on these degrees are referred to by Roman numerals. Now look at the chords available in D Major – plus the Roman numerals this time.

Figure 16-2: Triads on each scale degree in D Major.

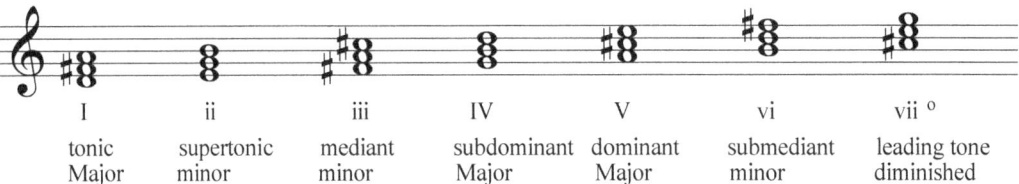

Notice that uppercase Roman numerals are used to indicate major chords, lowercase for minor chords, and the small circle after the lowercase is used to indicate diminished. The Roman numerals are shown below the chords and are used for study, not performance, purposes. (Chord symbols used above the notes are used in performance and follow different conventions for how they are indicated.)

No matter in what major key these chords are constructed, they will have the same qualities and will carry the same functions. Some of these chord qualities sound harsh (dissonant) and others, more pleasing (consonant). In a major key, all diatonic triads except vii are classified as "consonant". Recall from chapter 14 that the diminished 5th is heard as a very dissonant interval; hence the chord containing that interval sounds more harsh than does a major or minor triad, both of which contain a perfect 5th, a very consonant interval, and a 3rd, a relatively consonant interval.

Triads in Minor Keys

Triads in a minor key are normally constructed upon two different forms of the minor scale. As was done for chords constructed upon a major scale, we will construct a triad upon each scale degree, starting with the root of the triad on the scale degree and then stack thirds to complete the chord. For a minor key, there will be two sets: one for natural minor and one for harmonic minor. Notice that these scales differ by only one note: the 7th scale degree.

Figure 16-3: Triads on each scale degree in C natural minor.

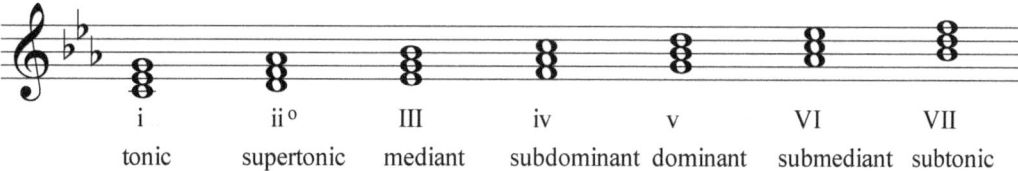

Notice that the chord on the 7th scale degree is named "subtonic", as it is for the natural minor scale.

Figure 16-4: Triads on each scale degree in C harmonic minor.

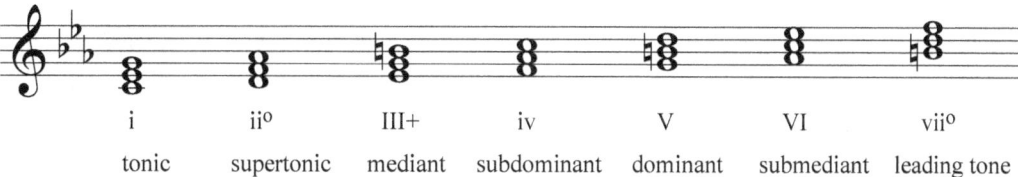

To strictly follow the pitches in the harmonic minor scale, the mediant triad in Figure 16-4 should be augmented. However, the mediant triad from the natural minor form (Figure 16-3), which is a major triad, is also very frequently used. Which form is used depends upon the context, especially whether a melodic line uses the leading tone or the subtonic note in the scale. The 7th scale degree appears in two other triads: those built upon the 5th and the 7th scale degrees. For these, the most common structure of the triads are those shown in the harmonic minor form of the scale: V (major triad) and viio (diminished triad).

Showing Inversions with Roman Numerals

If a triad is in root position, we just indicate the chord with the Roman numeral. If the triad is in first inversion, a "6", in smaller type, is placed beside the Roman numeral. So, a Major tonic triad in first inversion would be indicated like this: I^6. Let's go back and look at what happens to the structure of a triad when it is inverted. Following is an example in F Major, with the tonic triad shown in root position, first inversion, and second inversion. In each case, one can write the size of each interval above the bottom note of the chord:

Figure 16-5: Intervals above bottom note of triad in each position.

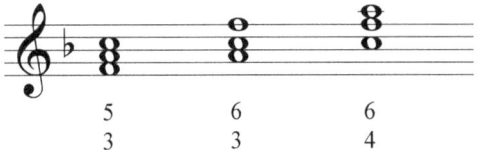

Hence, a $^5_3$ chord is a triad in root position; the 3 indicates a note at an interval of a third above the bass, and the 5 indicates a note at an interval of a 5th above the bass. A $^6_3$ is a triad in first inversion; notice the notes above the bass are at intervals of a 3rd and a 6th. Finally, a $^6_4$ indicates a triad in second inversion, with notes above the bass at intervals of a 4th and a 6th. However, theorists are sometimes efficient people, so it was decided that if one wishes to indicate a triad in root position, these numbers (the 5 and the 3) would not be shown; also, if one wants to indicate a 1st inversion triad, only the 6 is indicated (not the 3). If one wants to show a second inversion triad, both the 6 and the 4 are written beside the Roman numeral. Here are these three chords again with the correct and conventional indications of position:

Figure 16-6: Tonic triad: functional notation for each position.

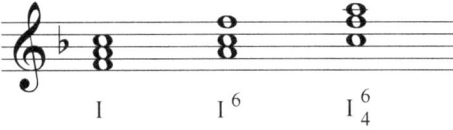

This convention for triad position is used with any Roman numeral for inverted triads.

Before we continue with our discussion of chords within the context of keys, we need to deal with the existence in Tonal style of final and intermediate goals, and how the music is divided into musical gestures that last over the span of several measures.

Phrases

A *phrase* is a division of the musical line into segments, similar to phrases or clauses in prose, with the clear sense that a phrase is one relatively complete musical gesture in the passage. It is a short musical expression, typically two to eight measures in length, that has a clearly discernible beginning and ending. Phrases are in every piece of music. Following are a few examples of musical phrases.

Example 1a. "Oh Susannah!" by Stephen Foster – first four measures:

The point in time at which the musical line seems to end or take a pause, however brief and subtle, marks the end of a musical phrase, similar to commas or semicolons in prose.

The phrase above can be further classified as an *antecedent phrase* because it implies, by its incomplete sound, that another is to follow.

Example 1b. Here is the *consequent phrase* for "Oh Susannah":

Where phrases are obviously grouped as in the antecedent-consequent phrase sequence, the overall structure is sometimes called a *period*.

Cadences

A *cadence* is a melodic or harmonic formula that marks the end of a complete musical gesture. The gesture terminates at the end of a composition, or at the end of a phrase, period, or section of a composition. Cadences are classified in relation to how permanent or temporary is the sense of ending.

Melodic Cadences
Even without a harmonic context, a single-line melody is organized into phrases that end in ways that are relatively permanent or temporary. A *terminal melodic cadence* is one in which the phrase ends on the 1st or 3rd scale degree in the key. Look back up at the second phrase of "Oh Susannah", Example 1b. It ends on scale degree 1 (F Major); therefore, the ending of that phrase is classified as a terminal melodic cadence.

A *progressive melodic cadence* is one which ends on some scale degree **other than** 1 or 3. The first phrase of "Oh Susannah" ends on the 2nd scale degree; thus this is a progressive melodic cadence.

Why is this distinction musically important? A piece in a Tonal style will not sound completely resolved and "settled" until it ends on a terminal note. While the 3rd scale degree is frequently the terminal note, Tonic is always the final goal of a piece in the Tonal style. Certainly, pausing on the second scale degree would not sound "final"; the music "wants" to go on, to "progress", to a more settled, stable resolution.

Harmonic Cadences

Each phrase ends not only melodically but also harmonically. In the Tonal style, there are a limited number of models, or formulas, for how a phrase or section ends harmonically.

An *authentic cadence* is one characterized by the V-I motion. This cadence is further classified as one of two types: perfect or imperfect. A *perfect authentic cadence* meets both of the following criteria:

(1) Both tonic and dominant chords are in root position.
(2) The soprano, or top line, ends on the tonic scale degree.

Example 2. Here are perfect authentic cadences – one in G Major and one in G minor:

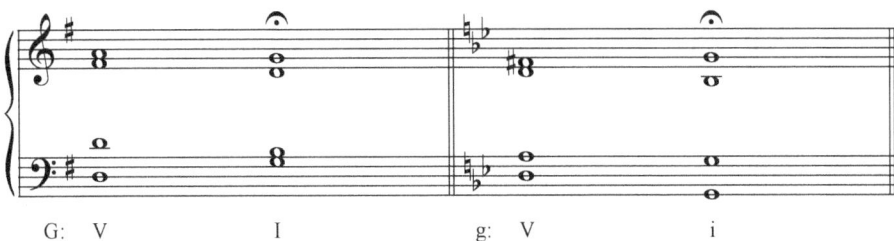

An *imperfect authentic cadence* is one that moves from dominant to tonic but does not meet at least one of the above criteria: either the top note does not end on scale degree 1 or at least one of the two chords is inverted, or both conditions might apply.

Example 3. Following are some imperfect authentic cadences:

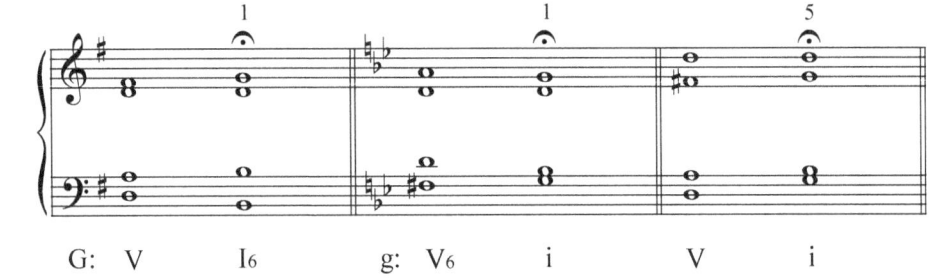

In the first example above, the tonic chord is in 1st inversion; in the second example, the dominant chord is in 1st inversion; and in the last example, the top line ends on scale degree 5 (instead of 1). In each case, these changes make the ending less complete than is the case with the perfect cadence.

A *plagal cadence* ends with the tonic chord, but moves into it from the subdominant, IV, instead of dominant.

Example 4. Following is a plagal cadence, first in D Major, then in D minor:

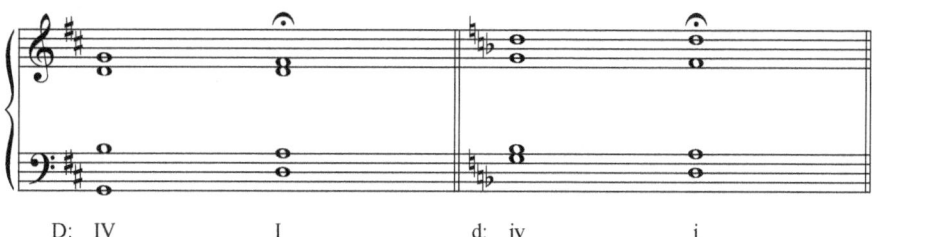

Often, the phrase before the one that ends in an authentic cadence is a phrase that ends in a *half cadence*, which is a cadence that ends on the dominant, V. There are several ways to approach the V chord at the end of such a phrase. Among the most common penultimate (next-to-last) chords in the half cadence are ii, IV, and I.

Example 5. Following are four-part examples of such progressions in both Major and minor. In each case, we play the tonic triad with a short melodic figure in order to establish tonic in the key.

There is one more cadence to examine before we continue with other topics in functional harmony. The **deceptive cadence** is one in which dominant leads, at the end of a phrase or section, to a substitute for tonic. The substitute chord is usually the submediant, VI. This device is normally used to delay movement to the tonic in order to allow for an extension of a musical idea near the end of a piece or major section. The listener "expects" a motion to the tonic, so the deception is that the music goes somewhere else instead.

Example 6. In this example, we show what the authentic cadence would sound like (if it occurred), then show the deceptive cadence:

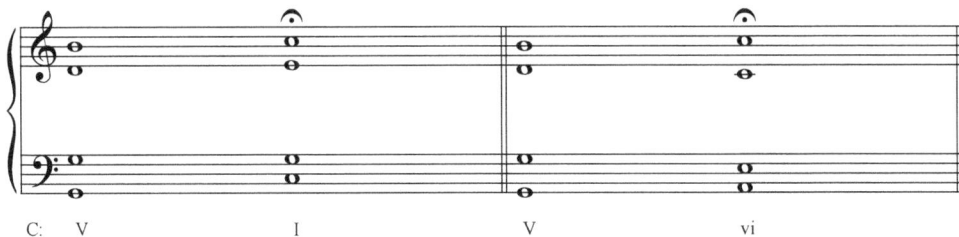

C: V   I   V   vi

> **Summary**
>
> Triads in the context of a key can be built on every scale degree. We showed how Roman numerals are used to indicate chords for the purpose of theoretical explanations and analysis. Arabic numbers can be added beside the Roman numerals to indicate chord positions, based upon intervals above the written bass note. Then we discussed phrases, which break up a passage into units similar to phrases and clauses in prose. Finally, we dealt with a number of formulaic melodic and chord progressions, cadences, which occur at the ends of phrases.

> **Next**
>
> Our next task is to delve further into chord progressions. How does a piece move harmonically into the cadences and toward the end of the piece? How do the individual notes of a chord move into those of the next chord?

Quiz 16

1. In the key of B♭ Major, write the Roman numeral designation for the following chord (include any numbers to indicate inversion, if applicable).

2. In the key of B minor, write the Roman numeral designation for the following chord (include any numbers to indicate inversion, if applicable).

3. In the key of C Major, write the Roman numeral designation for the following chord (include any numbers to indicate inversion, if applicable).

4. In the key of D minor, write the Roman numeral designation for the following chord (include any numbers to indicate inversion, if applicable).

5. In the key of E♭ Major, write the Roman numeral designation for the following chord (include any numbers to indicate inversion, if applicable).

6. An antecedent phrase followed by a consequent phrase is often called a _____ .

7. A melodic phrase ending on scale degree 2 is classified as a ____ melodic cadence.

   a. terminal

   b. progressive

8. The progression V – I is classified as a/an ____ cadence.

   a. authentic

   b. plagal

   c. half

   d. deceptive

9. The progression V – VI is classified as a/an ____ cadence.

   a. authentic

   b. plagal

   c. half

   d. deceptive

10. The progression ii – V is classified as a/an ____ cadence.

    a. authentic

    b. plagal

    c. half

    d. deceptive

CHAPTER 17: FUNCTIONAL HARMONY, PART 2

Objectives:

1. Report or identify the interval structure of a dominant seventh chord (interval of each note above the root when in root position).
2. Report, by Roman numerals, which chords are dominant preparations.
3. Explain the purpose of a dominant chord and of a dominant preparation chord.
4. Identify or write the correct numeric designations for each inversion of a dominant seventh chord.
5. Locate the diminished fifth in a dominant seventh chord.
6. Report, by Roman numeral, a chord that usually functions as a substitute for the dominant.
7. Given a passage on a grand staff that shows a succession of two or three chords, supply the missing Roman numeral designation (with inversion numbers, if inverted).

All Tonal works move away from "home" (tonic) and back to home. Much of the harmonic interest of a piece lies in the variety of chords and chord progressions that are used to produce harmonic digression, momentum and final resolution. Certainly phrase structure and cadences help to produce the sense of resolution, whether temporary or permanent. We continue in this chapter to examine additional structural features that help generate this tonal momentum in musical passages.

The Dominant Seventh Chord

The final goal of a tonal piece is usually a perfect authentic cadence at the end of the piece. Imperfect authentic cadences also give a sense of arrival at intermediate goals. (These cadences, with examples, were presented in the last chapter.) In all such cases, the V – I motion is very important in clearly establishing the key of the piece and producing this sense of arrival at tonic.

In the section on seventh chords, you were shown how to construct these chords, including inversions. Since the V chord is so important as a way to announcing the probable arrival of the tonic triad, we will focus on this chord and learn more about how it helps create this pull to tonic. First, let's show the 7th chord built on the 5th scale degree in C Major, the V^7 chord. We show here all of the intervals to the bass note in root position:

We have referred to this 7th chord structure as the Major-minor 7th because of the Major triad plus the minor 7th. To reflect the harmonic importance of this chord as built on the 5th scale degree, it has the more common name: ***dominant seventh***. A dominant seventh is always a Major-minor 7th, even in a minor key, as shown below for the dominant 7th in C minor:

It acquires the same quality (same intervals) as the one in a major key because of using the harmonic minor scale, resulting in raising the 7th scale degree in the key (which is the B♮ in C major).

The fact that the 5th above the root of the chord is perfect adds to the chord's stability. However, look at the interval between the 3rd of the chord and the 7th:

Yes, this interval is the **diminished 5th**, which is a very dissonant interval. The presence of this diminished interval creates a pull toward resolution to a more stable, consonant chord. When present in a dominant seventh, this diminished 5th interval creates an extra pull to resolve to the tonic.

Example 1. Following shows the V⁷ moving to I in a four-part texture:

Notice how the diminished fifth in the treble staff moves strongly into the interval of the third: the root and 3rd of the tonic triad.

Inverting the Dominant Seventh

As with other seventh chords, the dominant 7th can be in different inversions. Here are inversions of V⁷ in G Major (as was the case with triads, the numbers beside the Roman numerals indicate the intervals above the bass for the upper notes of the chord):

Figure 17-1: Inversions of dominant 7th.

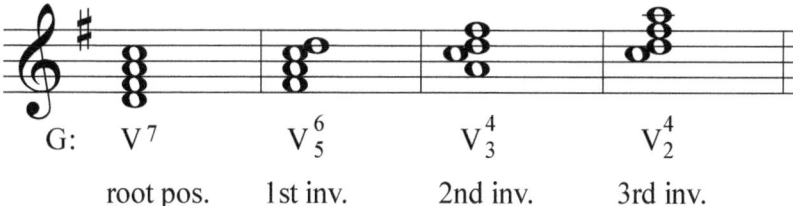

The numbers beside the Roman numeral define the inversion. It does this efficiently by identifying the location in close position of the interval of a 2nd between the relocated root and the 7th of the chord. For example, in the first inversion, there are notes at intervals of a 6th, a 5th, and a 3rd above the bass. However, it is the 6 and 5 that show where to find the 2nd between the inverted root and the 7th of the chord, so it is unnecessary to indicate the 3rd.

Chord Functions and Progressions

Tonic

The final harmonic goal of a piece in the Tonal style is the tonic note and chord. Therefore, the tonic chord ("I" in Major, "i" in minor) is "home base". However, this tonic triad does not occur only at the end of a piece. When it does occur before the end, there is usually something in the structure of the piece – harmonic, melodic, or rhythmic – that is incomplete. Arriving at an imperfect authentic cadence will usually signal that the end is yet to come. Still, the pause on tonic will sound like "touching home plate", so at such a cadence, it carries this sense of resolution to a goal even if temporary.

Example 2. In the following phrase (Bach Chorale #153, "All Men Must Die"), hear how the pause on I is "home", but temporary because the top line is on ^3, not ^1:

Notice also that the I chord is incomplete in that the 5th of the chord (A in this case)

is missing. Still, this sound is clearly identified by the ear as the tonic chord. It is quite common at a cadence in four-part music for the I chord to have a tripled root and no 5th.

Dominant

The strongest and final functional purpose of V chord is to lead to I. The V⁷ chord provides the extra pull to tonic because the diminished 5th (or augmented 4th, in inversion) is a dissonance that receives resolution to consonance in the I chord. In the example above, notice that the V⁷ chord resolves to I, with the diminished 5th between C♯ and G moving to the root (D) and 3rd (F♯) of the tonic triad.

Figure 17-2: V⁷ → I.

Dominant Substitutes

Take another look at a dominant seventh chord and notice that the top three notes form a diminished triad built on the leading tone. Here is the V⁷ in G Major:

If we omit the root of this chord, we get vii°. This chord can also lead to I:

Example 3. vii to I:

We can also build a diminished 7th chord on top of the dominant root to get a V⁹ chord. This has two forms: one in a Major key, and one in minor. Here are V⁹ chords in G Major and G minor:

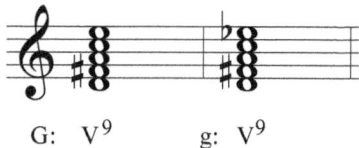

G: V⁹   g: V⁹

Now, if we omit the root of the dominant, we get seventh chords that substitute for and carry the same function as dominant.

Example 4. Following are vii⁷ chord motions into the tonic triad, one in G Major and one in G minor:

vii ⌀7   I   vii ⌀7   i

The first diminished 7th is called a "half-diminished seventh"; it is a diminished triad plus a minor 7th. The second diminished 7th is called just the "diminished seventh" (or full diminished 7th); it is a diminished triad plus a diminished 7th.

Dominant Preparation Chords

From here onward, chord function varies. The important functional consideration is that there are musical expectations in the Tonal style. V is **expected** to go to I (even if it gets momentarily diverted by, for example, the existence of a deceptive cadence to VI). Likewise, ii and IV (or iv in minor) are expected to go to V. Because their most expected motion is to resolve to dominant, they are called ***dominant preparations***.

Example 5. Here are examples of ii and IV going to V, and then V to I. One pair in C Major and one in C minor:

C: ii   V⁷   I   IV   V⁷   I   c: ii⌀⁶   V⁷   i   iv   V⁷   i

Frequently VI also is a preparation for the dominant, but another relatively strong resolution of VI is to ii. VI might also go immediately to IV.

Exploring Musical Structure

Example 6. This example shows VI in its role as dominant preparation:

C: vi   V   I   c: VI   V⁷   i

> **SUMMARY**
>
> Functional roles of chords vary in different contexts. Still, there are "most expected" resolutions. The major role of V is to resolve to I. The ii, IV, and sometimes the vi chords function normally as "dominant preparations". vii and vii7 normally function as substitutions for the dominant chord (missing root).

> **NEXT**
>
> Next, we will continue the study of harmonic functions of diatonic chords in a key and then study chords that function as "dominants" of scale degrees other than tonic.

Quiz 17

1. Which of the following has the interval structure of a dominant 7th chord?

    a.

    b.

    c.

    d.

148

2. The functional purpose of a dominant chord is to resolve to the _____ .
   a. tonic
   b. supertonic
   c. subdominant
   d. submediant

3. The Roman numeral designation for a **second** inversion dominant 7th chord is:
   a. V_2^4
   b. V^7
   c. V_5^6
   d. V_3^4

4. The Roman numeral designation for a **first** inversion dominant 7th chord is:
   a. V_2^4
   b. V^7
   c. V_5^6
   d. V_3^4

5. The highly dissonant interval in a dominant 7th chord is the diminished 5th between the ___ and ___ of the chord.
   a. root; 3rd
   b. root; 5th
   c. 3rd; 5th
   d. 3rd; 7th
   e. 5th; 7th

6. The dominant substitute chords discussed in this chapter are constructed in 3rds beginning on the ___ scale degree.

7. Which of the following is NOT a dominant preparation chord?
   a. ii
   b. iii
   c. IV
   d. vi

8. Supply the correct Roman numeral designation for the chord with "??" below it.

D: IV   ??   I

9. Supply the correct Roman numeral designation for the chord with "??" below it.

a: ??   V⁷

10. Supply the correct Roman numeral designation for the chord with "??" below it.

g: ??   V⁷   i

CHAPTER 18: FUNCTIONAL HARMONY, PART 3

Objectives:

1. Report or identify common resolutions for the III chord and the VI chord.
2. Define "secondary dominant".
3. Given a number of seventh chords written on a staff, and the key, identify which one is a specified secondary dominant.
4. Given a Roman numeral designation for a secondary dominant, report the specific note or scale degree of the root of this chord.
5. Given, on a staff, a chord with a dominant seventh structure, report or identify by Roman numeral the chord to which it would normally resolve.
6. Report the strongest resolution of a tonic six-four chord.

Common Resolutions of VI

The submediant chord is one of those chords that could go to any one of several other chords in the prevailing key. You have already seen that one of its normal resolutions is to the dominant. Closely related to this resolution is a resolution to a dominant substitute, the vii° or vii°⁷ chord.

Example 1. Following is an example of vi going to vii:

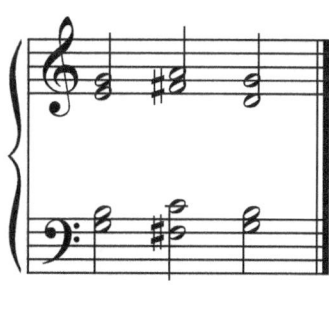

G: vi⁶ vii I

Another quite common resolution of vi is to ii.

Example 2. vi – ii – V – I progression:

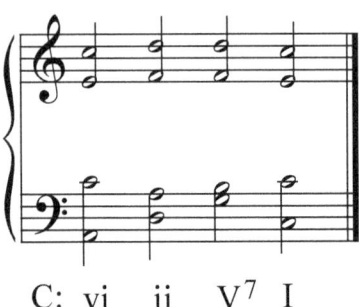

C: vi   ii   V⁷   I

The vi chord has two notes in common with I and two other notes in common with IV. This means that it can move to I or to IV by moving only one note by step to a note of the next chord.

Example 3. Here, vi resolves to I or to IV:

G: vi   I$^6_4$ vi   IV⁶

Common Resolutions of III

The mediant triad also has several common resolutions. One of the strongest of these is resolution to the submediant, VI.

Example 4. In the following passage, the progression from mediant is III – VI – V⁷ – I:

d: III   VI   V⁷   i

The mediant triad might also go to one of the dominant preparation chords, ii or IV.

Example 5. III to ii, and iii to iv:

d: III   ii°   V$^4_3$ i^6 D: iii   IV   V^7 I

Secondary Dominants

There is a particular way to place a special emphasis on a chord built on a scale degree other than tonic. We can make that scale degree sound like a momentary tonic by preceding it with a chord that sounds like the dominant of the chord built on that scale degree. A *secondary dominant* is a chord with the dominant interval structure that functions as the dominant of a consonant triad built on a scale degree other than tonic. You can have a dominant of ii (notated V/ii), a dominant of III (V/III), etc. In terms of chord quality, either a Major triad or a Major-minor seventh chord can take this function. In all but a very few cases, this will require at least one chromatic alteration.

In Major keys, the triads that can take secondary dominants are: ii, iii, IV, V, and vi. Remember the restriction that the target chord must be one whose triad is consonant; hence, the vii° chord cannot have a secondary dominant.

Figure 18-1: The triads in F Major that can have secondary dominants.

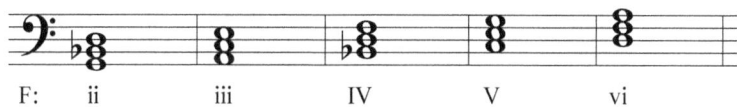

F: ii   iii   IV   V   vi

Figure 18-2: The triads in G minor that can have secondary dominants:

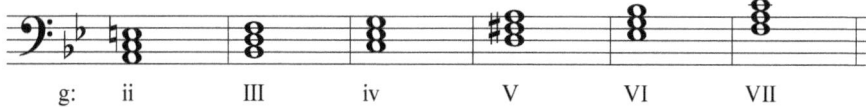

g: ii   III   iv   V   VI   VII

Notice that for the ii chord to take a secondary dominant it must have the 5th of the chord (6th scale degree in G minor) raised a half step in order for it to meet the requirement that it must be a consonant triad. Similarly the VII chord must be the consonant, diatonic triad built on the subtonic scale degree (not on the leading tone, which would make it a diminished triad).

Now for the secondary dominants themselves. The following shows the secondary dominant for each of these consonant triads.

Figure 18-3: Secondary Dominants for F Major:

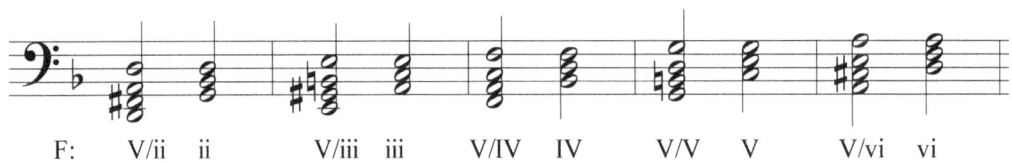

Figure 18-4: Secondary dominants for G minor:

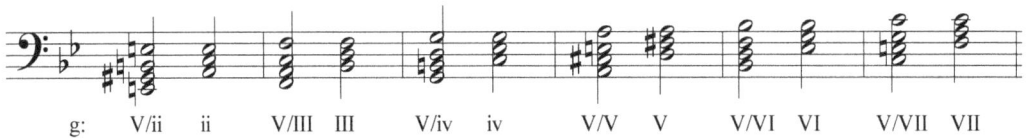

More often than not, these secondary dominants are written as 7th chords. In fact, in a major key, the only way one can tell for sure that a chord built on ^1 is V/IV instead of I is to chromatically alter the chord by adding the flatted 7th (minor 7th needed for the dominant 7th interval structure).

Example 6. Here is an example of a V^7/IV in the context of a normal chord progression in F Major. Notice the E♭ added to I to make it V^7/IV:

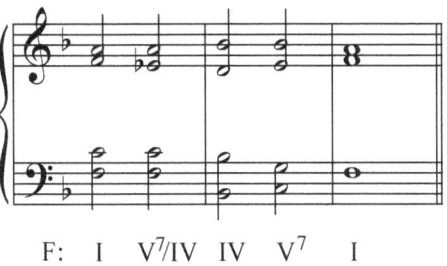

Example 7. Notice how Mozart uses this V^7/IV at the beginning of his Piano Sonata in F, K.332:

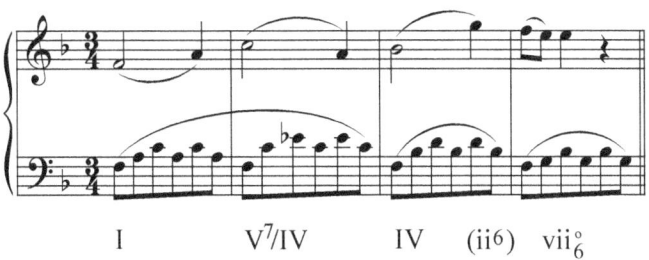

Example 8. How about a V^7 of V?

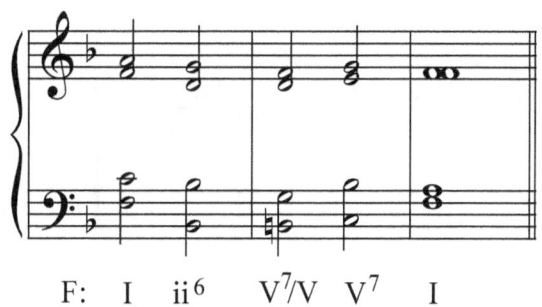

F: I   ii^6 V^7/V   V^7 I

Notice in Example 8 that a secondary dominant 7th can lead to a dominant 7th instead of a triad. In fact, one secondary dominant can lead to another secondary dominant – and then to another. For a chord to be a dominant of another, it must be a P5th above (or P4th below) it. When one secondary dominant leads to another – and perhaps another – you travel a circle of fifths by root progression.

Example 9. In this example, we start on I, move to iii, then alter the iii to a V^7 of VI and continue through a succession of secondary dominants, with each being the dominant of the next chord.

F: I   iii   V^7/vi   V^7/ii   V^7/V   V^7 I

Inversions of Tonic

While the tonic triad may appear at the end of a phrase, there are uses within phrases for I$\,^6$ and I$\,^6_4$.

Example 10. Consider the following progression:

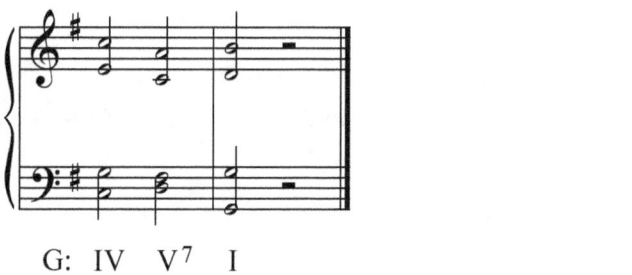

G: IV   V^7 I

155

Example 11. The leaps in the upper voices can be smoothed out with stepwise motion by inserting a I$^6_4$ chord, as shown here:

G: IV   I$^6_4$ V^7 I

Example 12. Notice how the I^6 chord smooths the motion between ii and V^7:

c: ii   i^6 V^7 i

Don't worry about the F in the bass; we will cover notes that are not part of chords in a later chapter.

SUMMARY

Continuing functional harmony, common resolutions of the VI and III chords have been discussed. The vi chord can commonly resolve to ii, IV, V, or vii. The III chord can commonly resolve to ii, IV, or vi.

Secondary dominants function to serve as "dominants" of consonant chords other than tonic. In a Major key, one can have a "V (or V^7) of" any of the following: ii, iii, IV, V, or vi. In a minor key, one can have "V (or V^7) of" ii, III, iv, V, VI, or VII. The target chord itself can be altered to form yet another secondary dominant of the chord a P5th below or P4t^h above that one (if such chord is consonant and built on a diatonic scale degree in the key).

The tonic triad in 1st or 2nd inversion can function in the middle of a phrase to connect two other chords in a progression. While the first inversion can connect any two chords, the strongest resolution for the second inversion of tonic is to the dominant chord.

Next

Future chapters will get into syncopated rhythms, modal music, non-harmonic tones, voice leading, and writing some two-part and four-part musical passages.

Quiz 18

1. The vi chord does NOT normally move directly to:
   a. ii
   b. iii
   c. IV
   d. V

2. The iii chord does NOT normally move directly to:
   a. ii
   b. IV
   c. vi
   d. vii

3. Which of the following chords is the V^7/ii in G Major?

   a.

   b.

   c.

   d.

4. Which of the following chords is the V⁷/V in C minor?

   a.

   b.

   c.

   d.

5. The V/IV has its root note on what scale degree?

6. The V/VI has its root note on what scale degree?

7. The V/VII in a minor key has its root note on what scale degree?

8. The following chord, in G minor, is expected to go to:

   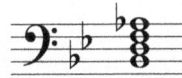

   a. VII
   b. VI
   c. V
   d. iv

9. The following chord, in F Major, is expected to go to:

   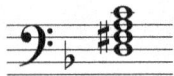

   a. ii
   b. iii
   c. V
   d. vi

10. The strongest resolution for the I $^6_4$ chord is to:
    a. I
    b. IV
    c. V
    d. vi

CHAPTER 19: EXTENDED METRIC AND RHYTHMIC PRACTICES

Objectives:

1. Define the following terms: syncopation, composite meter, mixed meter, and polyrhythm.
2. Describe three ways that syncopation can be produced.
3. Write a composite time signature given sufficient information about the meters to be represented.
4. Given groupings of beamed notes for one measure, write the correct composite time signature.
5. Given a composite time signature, write notes beamed properly to show the correct groupings for that signature.
6. Recognize and identify examples of syncopation, composite meter, mixed meter, and polyrhythm in short passages of written music.

In this chapter, we will study unconventional beat patterns and meters, and attacks and accents that occur off the beat.

Syncopation

A particular meter establishes expectations about where notes begin – that there is a note that begins on each beat – as well as the expected pattern of heavy or light accents on those beats. If one actually followed these expectations, the music would be quite rhythmically and metrically simple (and perhaps uninteresting). Whenever an expected pattern of the attacks or accents is disturbed, the resulting rhythmic effect is known as *syncopation*.

There are a number of ways that syncopation occurs. Here, it happens by a shift of the normal positions of accents:

Sometimes the attack of one or more notes is delayed by a rest:

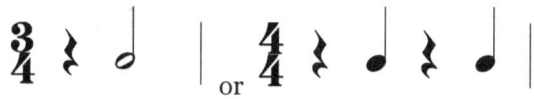

It can happen by the duration of a note being extended through a beat by using a tie:

The rag-time jazz of the early 20th Century is resplendent with examples of syncopation.

Example 1. Check out the syncopation just after the intro of the "Maple Leaf Rag", by Scott Joplin:

Notice that the left hand keeps to the metric pattern while the right "disturbs" this pattern and plays against it. This is a common feature of rag-time style.

Shifting meter effect: Sometimes the syncopation can give the effect of shifting the metric accent.

Example 2. Here is an example of the melody from the beginning of the 3rd movement of Symphony No. 40 by Mozart:

Not only is there an accent on the 3rd beat, but the note duration is extended beyond the downbeat of the next measure. (The accent is not usually written in this score, but is usually performed in order to emphasize this metric shift.) The effect is to create a temporary pattern of two instead of the expected three. It is interesting to look at this line with shifting meter:

Figure 19-1: Shifting meter in Mozart Symphony No. 40.

Of course, this is not the way Mozart wrote it, and it is an oversimplification because of what he put against this in the other instruments, but it helps to see the metric shift that clearly comes out in the performances. We will return to this passage when we cover polyrhythms later in this chapter.

Example 3. At the beginning of the Turkish march section in Beethoven's *Symphony No. 9*, the opening gives the impression of establishing the metric beat. Then when other lines enter, one senses that this was not, if fact, the beginning of the measure. It continues with the actual metric pattern expressed in the bass and a syncopated accent in the upper lines – a very interesting metric surprise:

Meters with Unequal Beat Durations

Beats traditionally have equal durations. However, some music contains beats within each measure that are not of equal duration. Here is a division of 9/8 time that uses **four** beats per measure, but the last one has the duration of 3 eighth notes instead of 2.

This same meter might also have a *composite meter signature*:

The eighth notes form an unvarying pulse within the changing beats.

Example 4. Here is this rhythmic pattern in Dave Brubeck's "Blue Rondo a la Turk":

The first three measures could have used the following composite time signature:

Figure 19-2: Composite time in "Blue Rondo a la Turk".

If the tempo is relatively slow, one may find music with unequal <u>groupings</u> of beats. Following is a 5/4 meter, grouped by accent or melodic pattern into 3 beats + 2 beats per measure:

Figure 19-3: Unequal groupings of beats.

Example 5. Dave Brubeck's "Take Five" provides an example of this meter.

Mixed meter: Sometimes composers write music in which meter changes, but then often the metric pattern repeats. Sometimes a bar line is placed between the two meters, and sometimes, as shown in the following example, it is not.

Example 6. Here is an example of mixed meter in the song "America" from Leonard Bernstein's *West Side Story*:

Polyrhythms and Polymeters

In some works, the metric pattern in one line, or instrument, is different from that in another, simultaneous line. This is called *polyrhythm*. These are sometimes called "cross rhythms". If the lines have different meter signatures, it is called *polymeter*.

Let's go back to the Mozart example and look at what he put against the main line. Refer to Example 7. You will notice that the lower strings keep to the pattern of the notated time signature (except for the viola line in measure 8), while the upper strings have the shifted metric pattern. This creates two different metric ideas going on at the same time: upper strings vs. lower strings.

By the way, you will see a clef that is new to you: the "alto" clef. This is also called the C clef because it is an older form of the letter C. The center of the C clef defines where middle C is located: in this case, on the middle line of the staff. Violas usually are written in this alto staff.

Listen for the following interplay of timings – 3 against 2 – between the two parts:

There are 3 half notes in the top parts to two measures in the bottom. The actual rhythms are expressed this way:

Example 7. String section from 3rd movement ("Menuette"), Symphony No. 40, by Wolfgang Amadeus Mozart:

Example 8. Here is a portion of the String Quartet No. 3 by Bela Bartok:

Although the entire passage is written in 3/8 time, the shifted meters are apparent. The violins are each in 3/4 time, but their entrances are staggered with the 2nd violin imitating the 1st violin part (an octave below), but three 8th notes later. Here is the rhythmic pattern of each violin line shown in 3/4 time:

Figure 19-4: Rhythmic motive in Bartok Quartet.

These are set against the lower strings which are clearly in 3/8 time. The lower strings take a two-measure pattern that is repeated over and over again. (Such repetition is called an *ostinato*.) Try to hear all three rhythms playing against one another: the 3/4 in the 1st violin against the delayed 3/4 in the 2nd violin, against the 3/8 ostinato in the lower strings.

Summary

Several additional rhythmic and metric practices have been introduced in this chapter. This brief treatment just scratches the surface of these interesting ideas in timing.

Syncopation: shifting the accent or the beat;

Mixed meters and composite meter signatures (e.g., 2/4 + 3/8);

Unequal beats (usually also examples of composite meter);

Odd meters (5/4, 7/8, etc.; these are also examples of unequal subdivisions of the measure);

Polyrhythm (different meters played at the same time – **polymeter** if with different time signatures).

You may wish to extend your listening and sample a few of the following examples:

Drums of Passion, by Babatunde Olatunji;

"Afro Blue", on *Afro Blue Impressions* (CD), artist John Coltrane, composer Mongo Santamaria;

"Happiness is a Warm Gun", *White Album*, the Beatles;

"Canon X", or "Study #1", by Conlon Nancarrow;

"Ragtime Dances" (4), by Charles Ives;

any of the rags of Scott Joplin.

Next

Next, you will study modal scales and music written using them. These are still diatonic scales, but the half steps go in different places. Some of the music using these are early European styles, and some were introduced in non-Western countries (e.g., Asian).

Quiz 19

1. The rhythmic effect produced when the expected pattern of accents defined by a meter is disturbed, or shifted:
   a. mixed meter
   b. composite meter
   c. polyrhythm
   d. syncopation

2. Sounding different meters at the same time in different voices or instruments is called:
   a. mixed meter
   b. composite meter
   c. polyrhythm
   d. syncopation

3. Write a composite time signature in which triple meter in 8th notes is followed by a duple meter in quarter notes.

4. Describe three ways that syncopation can be produced.

5. Using the grouping shown by beaming of notes, write a composite time signature for the following measure.

6. Using the grouping shown by beaming of notes, write a composite time signature for the following measure.

7. Write beamed notes to reflect the following time signature:

   $\frac{3}{8} + \frac{2}{4}$

8. Write beamed notes to reflect the following time signature:

   $\frac{1}{4} + \frac{6}{8}$

9. Name the type of metric device employed in the following passage:

   (from "Tango of the Merchant's Daughters", in the ballet The Incredible Flutist, by Walter Piston)

10. Name the rhythmic device used in the following passage:

    (from "Stompin' at the Savoy", by Benny Goodman, Edgar Sampson, Chick Webb, and Andy Razaf)

CHAPTER 20: MODAL AND NON-WESTERN SCALES

Objectives:

1. Recognize or explain features of the scales studied in this chapter.
2. Given notes on a staff for one of the Western modal scales, identify or name the scale.

Some History of Modes

The use of modal scales goes back as far as the Greek Classic period (circa 5th century BCE). The early modal scales back then were very different from today's modal scales. The scale was divided into two tetrachords (collections of four notes). Each tetrachord was bounded by two fixed notes and two movable notes. In the following example, only the D and G of the lower tetrachord and the A and D of the upper tetrachord were fixed. The other two notes in each tetrachord varied in a pattern that defined the particular mode for a given chant.

Figure 20-1: Greek Classic scale pattern.

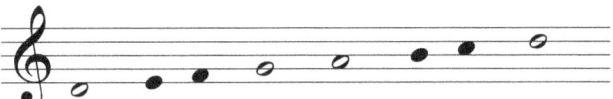

In addition, none of these notes (except the reference octave) would be playable on a modern keyboard instrument because the pitches were tuned to ratios not commonly used today.

Another complication to tracing the history of derivation for today's modal scales concerns the loss of information and inaccuracies in transferring knowledge from early practices to today. Before the printing press was invented by Gutenberg about 1437, manuscript was written by hand and stored in libraries and monasteries. Fires were quite common in these libraries. The great library in Alexandria, Egypt was burned probably four different times, destroying many volumes. Before the age of the printing press, it was difficult to make copies, so when a large library burned, it was not just books that were lost; it was the knowledge they contained.

One of the consequences of this loss of knowledge was that how the modes were formed and named was unclear when theorists later decided to draw on this uncertain knowledge to form theories about modal scales. As a result, today's modes have the same names as did earlier modes, but the structures are different. What follows in the next topic are descriptions of modes that conform with the more modern interpretation and which can be played on modern instruments (with equal-tempered tuning).

Modal Scales

The modern (Western) modal scales are all diatonic. Therefore, they can be played on all white notes of a keyboard instrument. As realized on all white keys, here are the seven possible modes, beginning with the one starting on C (which corresponds to the Major tonal scale). The half-steps are marked (the rest being whole-steps).

Figure 20-2: Western modal scales.

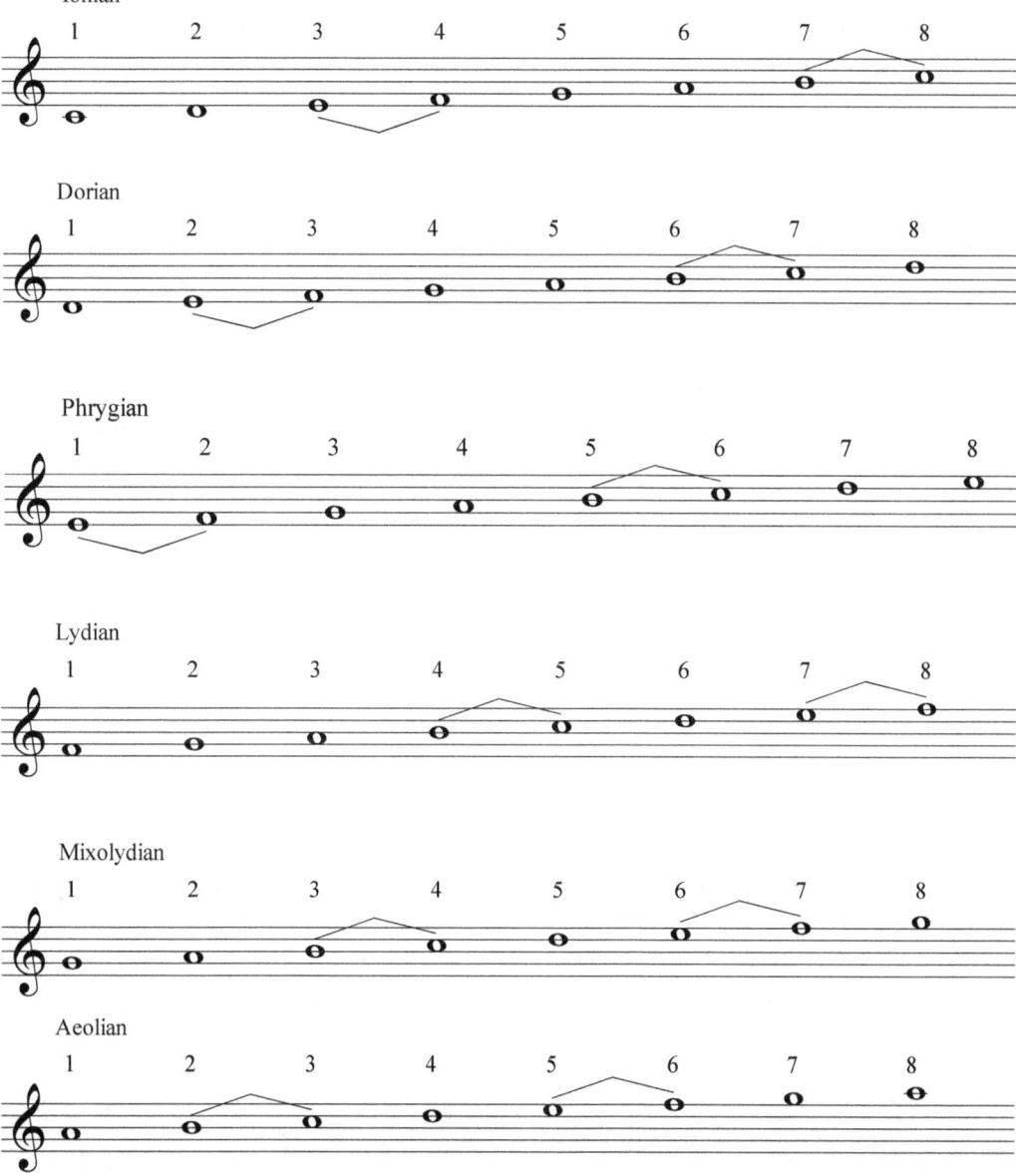

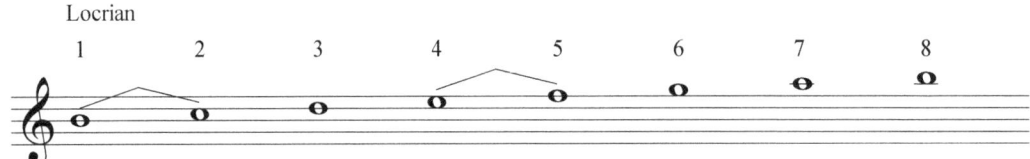

Notice that the Ionian scale is the same collection as the major scale, and the Aeolian is the same collection as the natural minor scale. In addition, the modes can also be classified by the size of the interval between the 1st and 3rd scale degrees. This would classify Ionian, Lydian, and Mixolydian as major scales; and Dorian, Phrygian, Aeolian, and Locrian as minor scales.

In modal music, the 1st scale degree is normally called the "final" because a passage gravitates toward and ends (finds its "final" resting place) on the 1st (or 8th) scale degree. The 5th scale degree is called the "dominant" (as it is in Tonal music) because it has a dominant position in the melodic line. In liturgical chant (which is written in modes), the dominant is that note on which the melodic line spends most of its time.

The Locrian mode was a theoretical possibility but not frequently used as a mode on which to base a musical passage. This is due to the fact that the 5th scale degree is a diminished instead of a perfect 5th and was therefore not considered a good choice for a "dominant". However, in the 20th century, when composers began to challenge tonal centricity, several pieces used this mode.

Modal Examples

Example 1. The song "Scarborough Fair" – one version made popular by Simon and Garfunkel – was probably originally an old Scottish ballad dating back to the 17th century. It is in Dorian mode:

Example 2. "Impressions" by John Coltrane is also in Dorian:

Example 3. Some folk songs are in modal scales. "I Am a Man of Constant Sorrow" (made popular in the movie *Oh Brother, Where Art Thou*) is in Mixolydian in this version:

An interesting feature of this song is that in several renderings, the 3rd scale degree is sometimes major and sometimes minor, and the 7th scale degree might also vary between major and minor or be completely missing in the melody.

The main difference between Aeolian mode and the Tonal minor key is the presence in the minor key of the leading tone to provide the strong half-step pull to tonic. If the subtonic is always there instead of the leading tone, you are in Aeolian mode, not a minor key. An example is the traditional Christmas carol "God Rest Ye Merry Gentlemen". Here is the Aeolian scale it uses (built on D):

Figure 20-3: Aeolian scale for "God Rest Ye Merry Gentlemen".

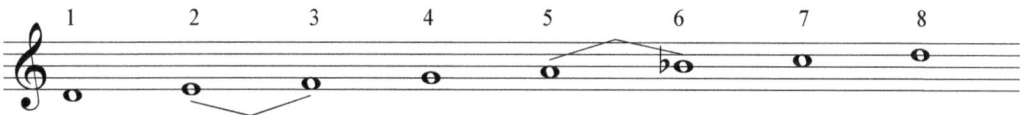

To make the mode clear, here are the first and last phrases:

Example 4. "God Rest Ye Merry Gentlemen" – two phrases.

Notice that the line in the last phrase ascends stepwise to tonic and does not use the melodic minor form, so it is in Aeolian.

Pitch Materials from Non-Western Cultures

When you study the arts of other cultures, the names of things and the ways they are categorized are different. In most non-Western cultures, there are no scales that truly correspond exactly with our "modes". Usually, the categories of pitch materials are expressed by patterns of notes used in pieces and often with particular rhythmic formulas as well. Still, there are similarities, and at least a portion of what they may translate from their language into English as a "mode" or "mood" includes pitch collections similar to Western modal scales. Added to this is the fact that in most cases their traditional songs do not use our equal-tempered tuning system, so the pitches and intervals will not be exactly the same as ours. Given these precautions, let's talk about the similarities. This is important in our culture because we have borrowed so much from other cultures. Many of the Western composers of the last 100 years – especially in the field of modern jazz – have utilized pitch and rhythmic ideas and materials from other cultures, translated to allow performing in our tuning system.

Australia

Transcriptions of songs from early Australian aboriginal practice reveal use of the following two six-tone scales:

Figure 20-4: Australian six-tone scales.

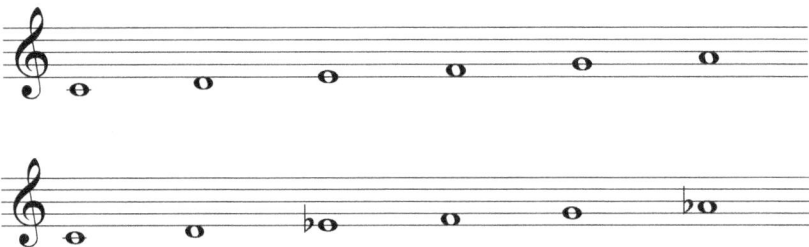

These look and sound like the Ionian and Aeolian modes, respectively, but with the noticeable absence of a leading tone (or subtonic).

In Melanesia (islands just northeast of Australia), pentatonic scales formed the basis of early songs:

Figure 20-5a: A pentatonic scale.

Many of the islanders in Indonesia also used pentatonic scales, although there were many pitch slides (glissandi) and the pitches were not in our tuning system.

Some of early African music used pentatonic scales:

Figure 20-5b: Another pentatonic scale.

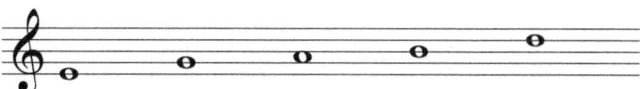

Others, a form of Aeolian without the 7th scale degree.

Islamic Countries

In Islamic (Turkish) tradition, one of the three following forms of scale was often used.

Figure 20-6a: Rast maqam:

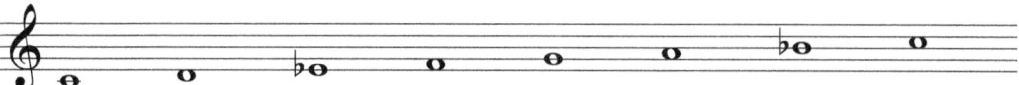

This looks like the Western Dorian mode, but the pitches were not exactly the same.

Figure 20-6b: Hijaz maqam:

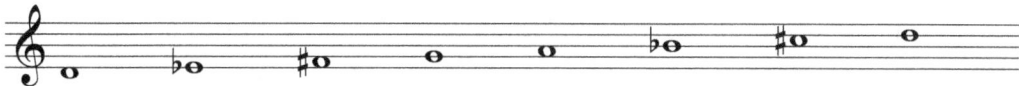

The F♯ and C♯ were a bit lower than they are on our instruments.

Figure 20-6c: Saba maqam:

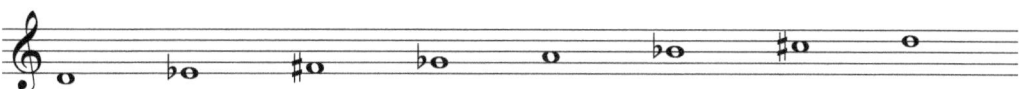

Again, the F♯ and C♯ were lower, so the F♯ and G♭ are <u>not</u> the same pitches.

Persia

In the traditional Persian *dastgah* system, several of the scales are very close to our diatonic modal scales. However, a couple of them are clearly non-diatonic. The following scale, *Homayun*, has seven pitch classes, as do our diatonic scales, but there is only one whole step between the two half steps:

Figure 20-7a: A Persian 7-tone scale.

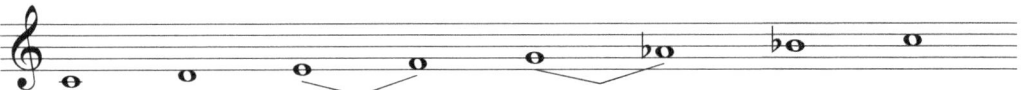

Recall that in diatonic scales there are either two or three whole steps between the half steps. In the *Esfahan*, there are four whole steps between the half steps:

Figure 20-7b: Another Persian 7-tone scale.

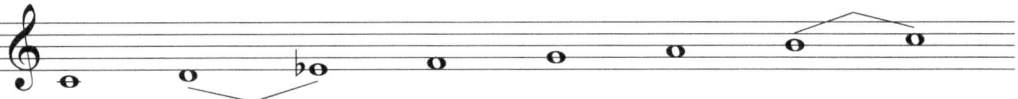

India

In early music of India the octave was divided into 22 parts called *sruti*, each being just larger than a quarter tone (half of a half step). However, there are only seven tones (pitch classes) that make up a scale, which are called *svara* and are given syllabic names that are used like our solfege to assist singing and hearing the degrees of the scale. These syllables are: *sa, ri, ga, ma, pa, dha, ni*. There were two common forms of parent scales that make up the collection of pitch classes for songs. They are shown here along with the number of svara that were used in each interval of the scale. Again, we show the pitches on a Western staff even though they are only approximate:

Figure 20-8: Systems of Indian singing syllables.

Sa-grama:

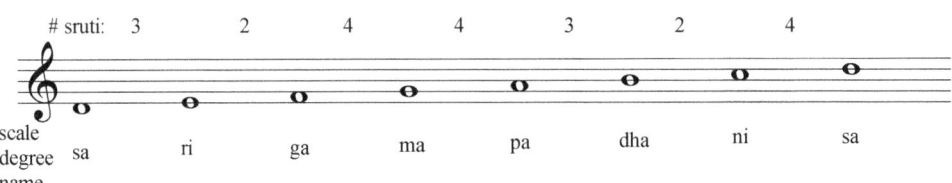

Ma-grama:

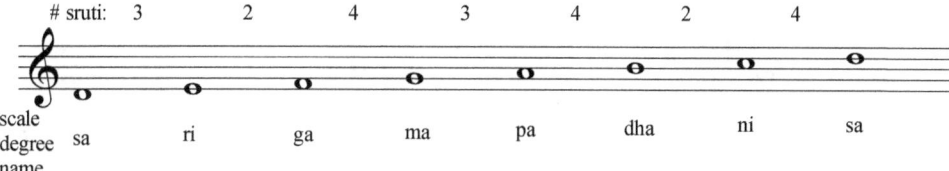

An interval of 2 *sruti* is just barely larger than our half-step; 3 *sruti*, just smaller than our whole-step; and 4 *sruti*, just larger than our whole-step. The division of the octave into 22 microtones is traditional; in today's Indian music, they use a division of the octave into 12 parts, but these vary by style and region and are complicated by numerous pitch slides and glissandi. In traditional style, there were seven scales derived from each of the two parent scales above. A *raga* is actually a particular pattern of notes used in a piece, with the notes identified by their roles: which used as the drone, which have special melodic importance. There are many *ragas* in use; theoretically, there are hundreds of them. The study of such ragas is complex and well above the scope of this treatment. There are many practical scales that can be identified in modern Indian music. Here is just one example:

Figure 20-9: A typical Indian scale usable as part of a raga.

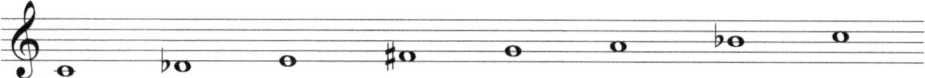

China and Korea

Pentatonic scales are used for the basis of much Chinese and Korean music, even in today's practice. A traditional Chinese scale was a pentatonic scale to which some "changing" notes would be added. So, a traditional Chinese scale might be described in the following way, with the black notes at the end identifying the changing tones:

Figure 20-10: Chinese pentatonic with changing tones.

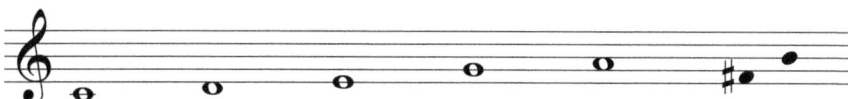

Following is a simplified transcription of a traditional Chinese tune, "Lament of the Twin Stars". It is unusual in that it starts with one pentatonic scale:

Figure 20-11a: First pentatonic scale for "Lament ..."

then, later on, it changes to a different pentatonic scale:

Figure 20-11b: Second pentatonic scale for "Lament ..."

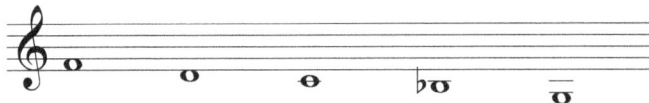

Example 5. The opening (simplified) tune for "Lament of the Twin Stars":

Taiwanese music makes use of six-tone scales, omitting either the leading tone or the 4th scale degree.

Japan

Japanese music uses pentatonic scales and also 7-tone diatonic scales. However, also important in their tradition is the interval of the perfect 4th (approximately), and how it is filled with a single note in between, leading to four possible variants:

Figure 20-12: Filling a tetrachord – Japanese practice.

Summary

In this chapter, we have studied the seven diatonic modes used in today's Western music and also have sampled pitch materials from non-Western cultures.

Next

Next, we will shift gears and deal rather thoroughly with the concepts of consonance, dissonance, and non-harmonic tones. These are concepts you must understand before doing your first exercises in writing music.

Quiz 20

1. In the Greek Classic period, a scale was made up of two tetrachords which were ___ filled in with ___ movable pitch/es.
   a. P4s; 1
   b. P4s; 2
   c. +4ths; 2
   d. +4ths; 3

2. Modern Western modal scales are all _____ .
   a. tritonic
   b. pentatonic
   c. octatonic
   d. diatonic

3. A modern Western modal scale contains ___ pitch classes.
   a. 5
   b. 6
   c. 7
   d. 8

4. Name the following modal scale:

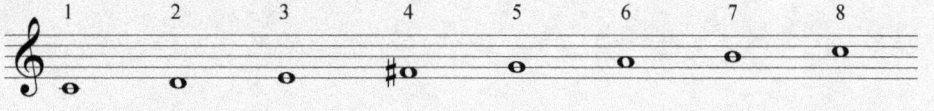

5. Name the following modal scale:

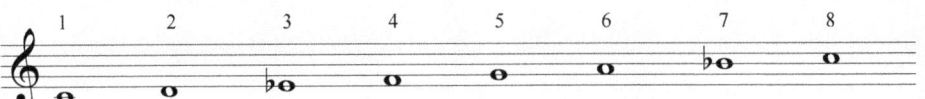

6. Name the following modal scale:

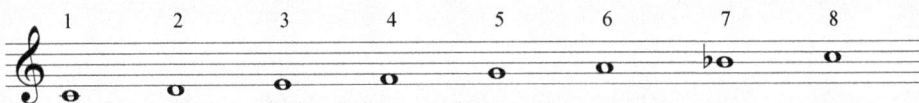

7. Name the following modal scale:

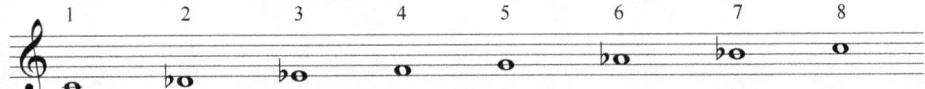

8. In Japanese music, pitch resources for a particular song are often described as a perfect 4th filled in with how many other pitches?

   a. 1
   b. 2
   c. 3
   d. 4

9. There are _____ ragas.

   a. two
   b. seven
   c. eight
   d. hundreds of

10. In the pitch resources of traditional Indian music, the octave was divided into ___ approximately equal parts.

    a. 5
    b. 7
    c. 12
    d. 22

CHAPTER 21: NON-HARMONIC NOTES

Objectives:

1. Define: voice, register, consonance, dissonance, and non-harmonic note.
2. Identify essential characteristics for the non-harmonic notes explained in this chapter (neighboring note, passing note, appoggiatura, escape note, anticipation, suspension).
3. Given a notated passage that includes a non-harmonic note, name the type of the non-harmonic note.

Consonance and Dissonance Revisited

First, we need to discuss "voices" or "lines" or "parts" in music. A *voice* can have two different meanings. (1) A voice can mean a singer's instrument (vocal cords plus resonant chambers in the mouth and sinus cavities). (2) A *voice* is also a technical term for an individual part in a piece of music, whether produced by the human voice or by a mechanical (or electronic) musical instrument. In this book, we will use the second meaning, unless we clarify that we are talking about human voices. They are often called "voices" because vocal music was the kind for which rules about how to write "parts" were written. In writings about musical structure, you may see these referred to as "voices" or as "***parts***", or as "***lines***". They are often used interchangeably. One also can find music written for a single, multiphonic instrument such as piano or organ, in which there are several, relatively separate lines (usually separated by register). ***Register*** is simply a range of pitches. For human voices, sopranos have a higher register than altos, who have a higher register than tenors. Basses sing in the lowest register. A tuba plays in a low register, whereas a trumpet plays in a high register.

Recall the following definitions from an earlier chapter. Consonance and dissonance in music are on opposite ends of a bipolar concept in which consonance is *sensed* as stable and as a condition of resolution; ***dissonance*** is sensed as unstable and needing to move toward resolution to more consonant sounds. It was also clarified that what intervals or chords are interpreted as consonant and which as dissonant depends upon the style of the music. For example, many of the intervals considered dissonant in Classical style are heard as consonant in jazz music. Usually, dissonances resolve to consonances; there is a tendency – a pull – for them to do so. However, even at the end of a composition, a composer may choose to include a dissonance in the final chord of a piece precisely for the particular quality of sound contributed by the dissonant tone, or because of the unresolved pull to move to a different note. <u>Remember this</u>: In any particular voice in a musical texture, a dissonant note has a pull to either resolve to a consonant note or become a consonant note (yes, a note can change from being dissonant to being consonant without moving – another line changes in that case).

So, let's discuss, in the classical tonal style (for now), how to determine which notes are consonant and which are dissonant. At any given instant, either a single note is sounding, or a chord is sounding. Consonance and dissonance depend upon a context of intervals and chords, so a single tone has neither consonance nor dissonance by itself. In traditional classical style, consonance/dissonance can be determined by intervals. First, let's consider the diatonic intervals of just two voices: bass and an upper voice. Consonant intervals, above the bass, are: unison, major and minor 3^{rds}, perfect 5th, major and minor 6^{ths}, and the perfect octave. Some writers distinguish between perfect consonances (unison, P5, and P8) and imperfect consonances (the 3^{rds} and 6^{ths}). The dissonant intervals include 2^{nds}, 7^{ths}, dim 5th, and all 4^{ths} (yes, even the P4th). Compound intervals – P8th plus an interval – have the same classification. Now, look at the following chord in a 3-voice texture:

The lowest note is the F. The A above this is a M3rd: consonant. The D above the F is a M6th: also a consonance. There is a P4th between the A and the D, but the presence of this 4th does not create a dissonance. The classification of consonance and dissonance depends only upon the interval of each upper voice against the lowest (the bass). So, in the following interval, the P4th of the A against the bass makes A a dissonance:

The role that each note has in a musical part (or voice) is influenced by whether it is heard as a consonance or a dissonance. Next, we address such roles in terms of harmonic notes and non-harmonic notes.

Non-Harmonic Notes

A **non-harmonic note** is a note that is not a member of the prevailing harmony. A dissonance is a non-harmonic note in traditional Tonal style. This may not always be the case with jazz, but the roles are a bit more complicated in that style. We will cover jazz structures in a later section. A note that is classified as an imperfect consonance might be a harmonic note or a non-harmonic note, depending upon context. For example, we will later study situations for which a 6th resolves to a P5th. A non-harmonic note will always have a tendency to resolve to a harmonic note (or become a harmonic note), as is the case for all dissonances in the style. In this topic, we will examine how non-harmonic notes are commonly approached and resolved.

Neighboring Notes

A *neighboring note* is approached by step and then resolves back to the same note. You can have an upper neighbor (the D below) or a lower neighbor (the B♭):

Figure 3-3-1: Neighboring notes.

Notice that the D is an upper neighbor note (nn) which forms a P4th with the bass note and the B♭ is a lower neighbor forming a half-step with the bass. (Of course, if the A is a bass voice or instrument, it will be in a lower register than shown.) You can also have accented neighboring notes:

Figure 3-3-2: Accented neighboring note.

Above, the D is on a relatively strong beat (it could even be on the first beat!). You can have two neighboring notes one after another – one in one direction and one in another – as follows:

Figure 21-3a: Double neighboring notes.

Then, the composer could leave out the extra A in the middle to produce what is called a "neighboring group":

Figure 21-3b: Neighboring group.

Example 1a. Here are two neighbor notes at the beginning of the Adagio (2nd movement) in Mozart's Piano Sonata No.2, K. 280. The first (the D♭) forms a 6th with the base (F), resolving to a P5th; the second (the A♭ in the next measure) forms a 7th with the bass, resolving to the 6th. So here you have an example of a 6th making a non-harmonic note (the D), and then just a measure later, a 6th creates (if temporarily) a harmonic tone (the G):

Example 1b. In the next measure in this same piece, we get a neighbor note in the bass (the D♭). Yes, the bass itself can have a non-harmonic note. In this case, the prevailing harmony is the C Major triad, so the D♭ is obviously not part of this chord. Also, the ear easily hears that the real bass note is C throughout this measure, so the "bass" is still C, not D♭.

Example 1c. Here are these first three measures:

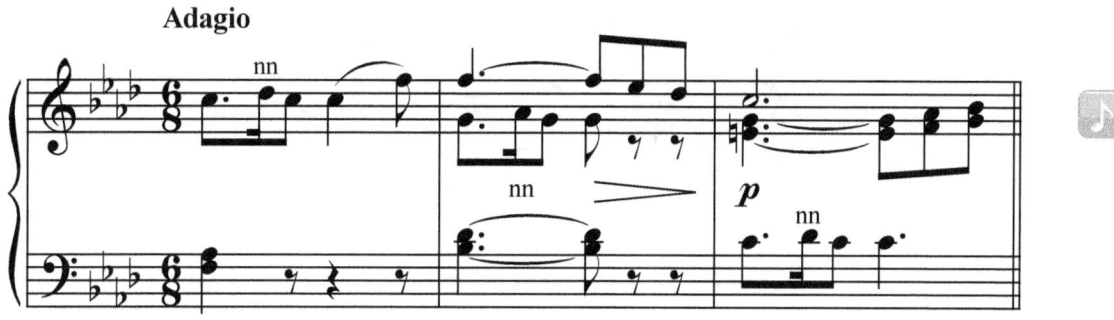

Duration and accent (metric or written) also support the distinction between harmonic and non-harmonic notes. Notice in the above example that the neighbor notes are of short duration and are not on metric accents. (They are not even on the beat subdivision, which is the 8th note.)

Example 2. Following is an example of the use of simultaneous neighboring notes: those that sound together in two different voices (top and bottom in this case). These are the first two measures in Mozart's *Sonata No. 11*, K. 331:

The prevailing harmony in the first measure is obviously the A Major triad, which is I, making the B and D non-harmonic notes. In the second measure, the prevailing harmony is the E Major-minor 7th chord, which is V^7, making the A and C# non-harmonic notes.

Passing Notes

A *passing note* is approached by step and then resolves by step in the same direction; that is, if you go up to the passing note, you would resolve to the next note a step higher. So, you can have ascending and descending passing notes.

Figure 21-4: Passing notes.

As was the case with the neighboring note, a passing note can also appear on a metric accent:

Figure 21-5: Accented passing note.

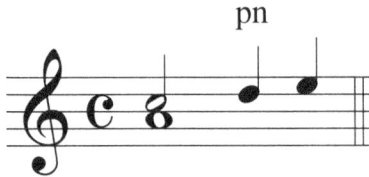

In the above cases, the passing note fills in the interval of a third in the prevailing harmony. Suppose you want to use passing notes to fill in a 4th. Here is an example of using two passing notes to do this:

Figure 21-6: Successive passing notes.

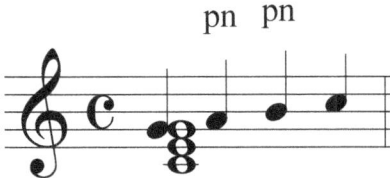

Example 3. A simple example of an ascending passing note is in the opening of *Frere Jacque*:

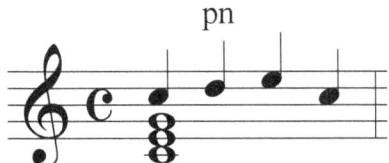

Example 4. How about a simple example of a metrically accented, descending passing note? This is the beginning of *Swanee River*, by Stephen Foster:

The first D is accented; the second, unaccented.

Example 5. Here are multiple passing notes in measures 8-10 of Mozart's *Piano Sonata No. 5*, K. 283:

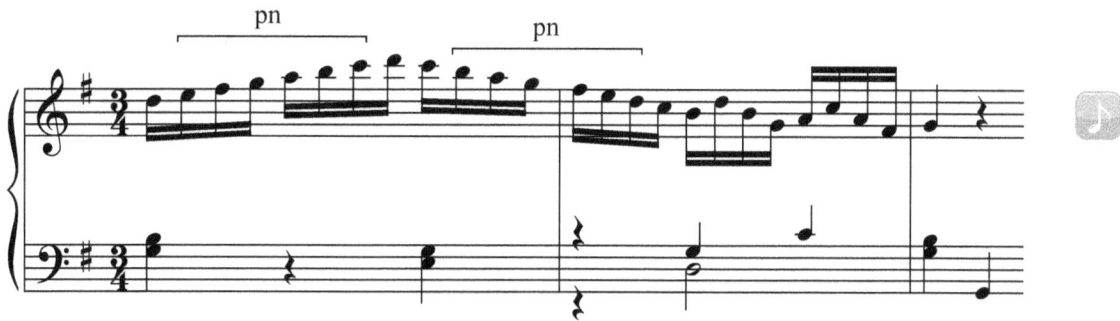

There are passing notes between two octaves: D up to next higher D; then C down to next lower C. Even though there are some consonant notes in each scalar motion, the rhythmic context and unbroken series of notes in each create the effect of all passing notes filling in the octave.

Appoggiaturas

The term "appoggiatura" has been used at different times in music history and in different sources to mean a variety of things. In this book, we will use a very common and clear definition. An **appoggiatura** is a metrically accented non-harmonic note that is approached by leap (any interval larger than a 2nd) and resolved by step, usually in the opposite direction.

Figure 21-7a: Appoggiatura.

Okay, but what if you have a non-harmonic note that is approached by leap and resolves by step but is <u>not</u> on a strong accent, as in the following?

Figure 21-7b: Local appoggiatura.

Such a pattern would be interpreted as an incomplete neighboring note – "incomplete" in the sense that it is not prepared.

Sometimes a non-harmonic note is only locally an appoggiatura or incomplete neighbor. Look at the following:

Figure 21-7c: Neighboring note, not appoggiatura.

The D in the first measure is definitely a harmonic note. The ear can clearly make the connection of the motion from this D up to the E♭ in the next measure and back to the D. Over the longer span, the neighboring note is not incomplete. Check out this example:

Figure 21-7d: Accented passing note, not appoggiatura.

Locally, the E in the second measure looks like an appoggiatura: it is approached by leap from the G, is sounded on a strong metric accent, and resolves by step to the F. However, the fact that the D in the first measure is a harmonic note on a metric beat gives it an emphasis that causes the ear to hear the E as an accented passing note between D and F. This is another important lesson in musical context: before making decisions about non-harmonic notes, look back a ways in the music to see if it makes a logical and musical connection with a non-adjacent note.

Example 6. Here is an example of appoggiaturas in *Sonata in C Major* by Joseph Haydn:

Example 7. Now let's look at just the top and bottom lines in a short segment of Beethoven's *Piano Sonata in C Minor*, Op. 13 (the "Pathetique"). This is from the second movement in A♭ Major:

In isolation, the B♭ in the last measure of the segment appears, locally, to be an appoggiatura. However, notice that there is a very clear, descending passing note motion in the top of the texture, starting from the E♭. Hear the following line in the passage:

There is a very clear passing note motion from the 5th scale degree down to tonic in the key, with consonant support for the end points of that motion. Therefore, the more correct interpretation of the B♭ is that it is an accented passing note.

Some books distinguish another kind of non-harmonic note called an *escape note*. This is a non-harmonic note that is approached by step and then followed by a leap (just the opposite of the appoggiatura). However, a leap is not a satisfactory resolution, so when this happens look for the stepwise resolution a bit later in the line.

Figure 21-8: Accented passing note, not escape note.

The resolution of the C♯ is actually to the B, which makes it an **accented passing note**, not an escape note.

Anticipations

This is the first of two similar types of non-harmonic notes that occurs because of timing the resolution of a note. With both of these, there is a change in the prevailing harmony and a note moves, by step, to fit that harmony either before or after the change of chord. In the case of the *anticipation*, the change of this note comes early, before the change of chord.

Figure 21-9: Anticipation.

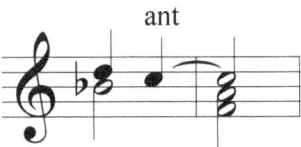

Example 8. There are many examples of anticipations in the Chorales of Bach. Here are two at the end of Chorale 357, "Warum sollt' Ich mich denn grämen?":

In the pick-up, the A is not in the prevailing harmony, I (G-B-D), but becomes a chord tone when the chord changes at the beginning of the next measure to V (D-F#-A). Near the end, the G (the 16th note) is not in the prevailing chord, V, but is a chord tone at the end when we get the I chord (G-B-D). Notice that an anticipation can be either tied over to the chord change or it can, as here, be repeated. Well now, what is the quarter note G at the beginning of the last measure? This is a good example of the next non-harmonic note: the one where the change to a chord note occurs late instead of early.

Suspensions

A *suspension* is a non-harmonic note that is prepared as a harmonic tone, then is held over or repeated at a change of chord, where it becomes non-harmonic, after which it resolves by step to a harmonic note. The suspension is thus created by three events: preparation, suspension, and then resolution. Let's break down the three events for the above example. In the following version, we have provided just the line in question plus the chord changes, along with labeling the events:

Figure 21-10: Suspension.

Preparation: the G is the root of the I chord (G-B-D);
Suspension: the G is repeated where the chord changes to V (D-F#-A);
Resolution: then that voice moves down by step to F#, the 3rd of the prevailing chord (still V).

If the suspension resolves upward by step, some books call it a "retardation", but we will just call it another form of suspension.

191

Summary

A *voice* is a separate line in music that can be played by a separate instrument or human voice or that can be separable from other lines by register.

A *consonance* belongs with the prevailing harmony and has no strong tendency to resolve to another note; a *dissonance* is a note that is not a member of the prevailing harmony and will tend to resolve by step to a note that is consonant.

Non-harmonic notes:
neighboring note: approached by step; resolves back to the approach note.
passing note: approached by step; resolves by step in same direction. There can be several passing notes in a row.
appoggiatura: approached by leap; resolves by step.
escape note: approached by step and then moves away by leap. However, most of these are some other non-harmonic note if you look for stepwise resolution further ahead in the line.
anticipation: is dissonant in the prevailing harmony and then is repeated at change of chord, where it becomes a chord tone.
suspension: prepared as chord tone, repeated at change of chord where it becomes a non-harmonic note, then resolves by step to a chord note.

Passing notes and neighboring notes can occur off a main beat (unaccented) or on a main beat (accented). Any non-harmonic note may be either a member of the prevailing diatonic scale or it may be "chromatic" (requiring an accidental). Look for what appears to be an escape note to resolve later in that voice.

Next

In the next chapter, we will turn to rules and guidelines for how to move voices with each other in a multi-voice texture, starting with only 2 voices at first. Since triads have only three notes, when we discuss 4-voice pieces, we will introduce some guidelines for which note(s) to double. You will begin your first writing assignments in this next chapter.

Quiz 21

1. A/An _____ moves back to the note from which it was approached.
   a. anticipation
   b. appoggiatura
   c. neighboring note
   d. passing note
   e. suspension

2. A/An _____ is approached by step and resolves by step in the same direction, filling in a leap of a 3rd.
   a. anticipation
   b. appoggiatura
   c. neighboring note
   d. passing note
   e. suspension

3. A/An _____ occurs because of moving a line to a note of the next chord before that next chord is played.
   a. anticipation
   b. appoggiatura
   c. neighboring note
   d. passing note
   e. suspension

4. A/An _____ occurs because of delaying stepwise motion to a note of the next chord **after** that chord is played.
   a. anticipation
   b. appoggiatura
   c. neighboring note
   d. passing note
   e. suspension

5. A/An _____ is a non-harmonic note that is approached by leap and resolved by step.

   a. anticipation
   b. appoggiatura
   c. neighboring note
   d. passing note
   e. suspension

6. Identify the type of non-harmonic note, in the top line, with the asterisk (*) above it.

   a. anticipation
   b. appoggiatura
   c. neighboring note
   d. passing note
   e. suspension

7. Identify the type of non-harmonic note, in the top line, with the asterisk (*) above it.

   a. anticipation
   b. appoggiatura
   c. neighboring note
   d. passing note
   e. suspension

8. Identify the type of non-harmonic note, in the top line, with the asterisk (*) above it.

   a. anticipation
   b. appoggiatura
   c. neighboring note
   d. passing note
   e. suspension

9. Identify the type of non-harmonic note, in the top line, with the asterisk (*) above it.

   a. anticipation
   b. appoggiatura
   c. neighboring note
   d. passing note
   e. suspension

10. Identify the type of non-harmonic note, in the top line, with the asterisk (*) above it.

   a. anticipation
   b. appoggiatura
   c. neighboring note
   d. passing note
   e. suspension

11. Identify the type of non-harmonic note, in the top line, with the asterisk (*) above it.

   a. anticipation
   b. appoggiatura
   c. neighboring note
   d. passing note
   e. suspension

12. Identify the type of non-harmonic note, in the top line, with the asterisk (*) above it.

   a. anticipation
   b. appoggiatura
   c. neighboring note
   d. passing note
   e. suspension

CHAPTER 22: VOICE LEADING: TWO VOICES

Objectives:

1. Define "voice leading" and "harmonic rhythm".
2. Identify and distinguish among the four types of motion between two voices.
3. Identify the voice leading guideline that is NOT followed in a given passage for two voices.

Recall that a "voice" is any line in the music made separable by instrument or register. There are also structural features that help voices sound separable. When we wish for the listener to be able to hear separate lines, or voices, then certain rules or guidelines about how the voices move relative to one another will aid this separation. **Voice leading** is the motion of individual voices (or parts) from one chord to another.

Harmonic Rhythm

Let's examine one more principle before we look at the guidelines for voice leading. Chords change in a passage at a relatively predictable rate. In a tune such as the following, the rate of change, called **harmonic rhythm**, is one chord change per measure.

Example 1. Here is a portion of Bob Dylan's "Hey, Mister Tambourine Man", showing one chord change per measure:

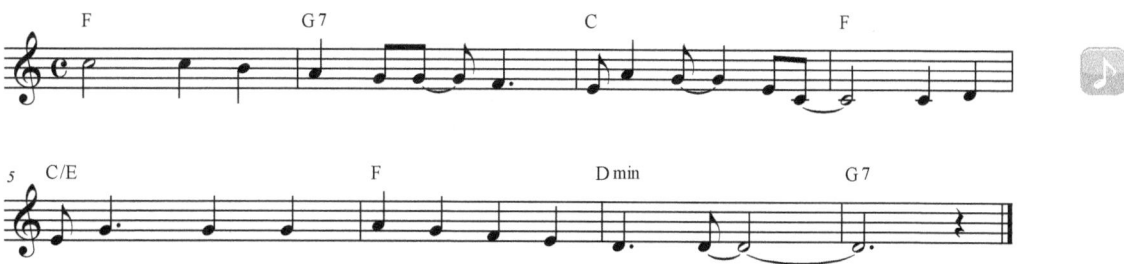

In many pieces, the harmonic rhythm speeds up right at the cadence formula.

Example 2. In the traditional English tune "Early One Morning", notice that there is one chord change per measure except right in the next to last measure of the phrase, where there are two chords. This is quite common in cadence formulas.

Notice that the same chord can be played again in the next measure without disturbing the "once per measure" change.

In other styles, there may be one chord change per <u>beat</u>. Many chorales and hymns have this characteristic.

Example 3. The traditional hymn tune "Praise God From Whom All Blessings Flow" has a chord change every beat:

Voice-leading Guidelines: Two Voices

There are four types of horizontal motions that can occur between two voices: contrary, oblique, similar, and parallel.

Figure 22-1a: <u>Contrary motion</u>: the two voices move in opposite directions.

Figure 22-1b: <u>*Oblique motion:*</u> *one voice moves and the other stays on the same pitch.*

Figure 22-1c: <u>*Similar motion:*</u> *both voices move in the same direction, but with different (numeric) sizes of intervals.*

Figure 22-1d: <u>*Parallel motion:*</u> *both voices move in the same direction and with the same (numeric) size of intervals.*

The above example is considered parallel motion because both voices move an interval of a 2nd even though the top voice moves a whole-step and the other, a half step. This maintains a 6th between the voices (minor 6th, then major 6th).

To make sure you comprehend the four types of motion, study the next example while covering up the rest of the page below the horizontal line. Label each motion between voices: c = contrary; o = oblique; s = similar; p = parallel.

Example 4. Types of motion between two voices – "Herzlich tut mich verlangen", J.S. Bach:

Here is the solution:

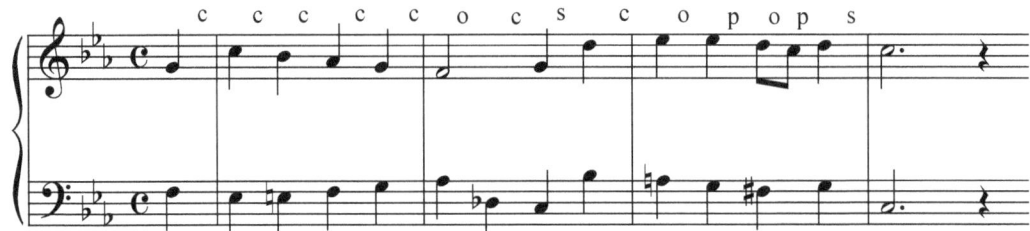

Notice the amount of contrary motion. Although we have listed every motion, look at the 8th notes in the next-to-last measure. The important motion here is that between the F♯ to G in the bass against the D in the top line, which is oblique motion. The 8th note on the C is just a neighboring tone that contributes little to the voice leading in this style because it is off the beat, and there is one chord change per beat.

All statements about voice-leading that refer to the octave, or P8th, also apply to multiples of the octave (2 octaves, 3 octaves, etc.).

Voice leading guideline #1: Use a variety of motions between voices. Contrary and oblique motions contribute most to independence of voices, whereas parallel motion contributes the least to this independence. However, all four kinds of motion are important for variety.

Voice leading guideline #2: Voices that cross each other in pitch range will confuse which voice is which. Normally avoid crossing voices. Here is an example of something to normally avoid:

Figure 22-2a: Avoid crossing voices.

On the second beat, the "lower" voice goes up above the "upper" voice. Occasionally, this might happen if the lines are played by instruments with different qualities of sound, but it is rare. However, it is okay to occasionally have two voices share a pitch for just one note.

Figure 22-2b: Shared pitch okay.

Voice leading guideline #3: Normally space higher voices closer together in pitch and lower voices farther apart. So, if you are writing two lines in the bass staff, if the bass voice is in the lower part of the staff, intervals to the next higher voice larger than a 3rd are preferred. If the bass voice is so low that it goes below the staff, the space to the next higher voice should normally be larger than a 5th. While separation by larger than an octave is common between two voices on the bass staff, it is very rare between two voices both written on the treble staff.

Voice leading guideline #4: Normally avoid parallel perfect unisons, P5ths and P8ths. (See examples below.) Parallel perfect unisons, fifths, and octaves tend to make different lines sound like just a harmonic coloring of one line; that is, they tend to blend together. So, if your intent is for the voices to be separable by the ear as different lines of music, then avoid these. However, if your intent is to combine voices or instruments in such a way that they together blend into a combined texture and should be heard as one line (with harmonic support), then you would write all such parts in mostly parallel or similar motion, and parallel unisons, 5ths and octaves would be permitted as part of creating that sound. This practice is very common in jazz ensembles where an entire section may play in parallel. Such parallel harmonization was also common in improvisational singing of early hymn tunes, where independence of lines was not desired. In these studies in voice leading, independence of lines will be one of our main goals, so parallel unisons, fifths and octaves should be avoided.

Figure 22-3: Avoid parallel P5s and P8ths (parallel 6ths okay).

Voice leading guideline #5: A "direct fifth" or "direct octave" is a leap in both voices in similar motion to a P5th or P8th. To maintain independence of voices and keep the lines moving smoothly, these should be avoided within a phrase. They are allowed at a cadence, but still it is better to fill in one of the voices (usually the top) with stepwise motion.

Figure 22-4: Direct fifths and octaves.

Voice leading guideline #6: Now we get into guidelines of voice motions that are not things to completely avoid so much as they are features that should occur relatively rarely or should not occur several times in succession. These features are likely to distract from the two main goals of voice leading practice: independence of voices, and smoothness of horizontal line in the parts. Here is the first of these: Leaps in both voices in parallel or similar motion should be rare and should normally not happen twice or more in succession.

Although there are no parallel or direct P5^{ths} or P8^{ths}, both voices leap in the same direction twice in a row, so this should normally be avoided:

Figure 22-5a: Successive leaps.

The following is better, because the leap in both voices in the same direction occurs only once, but still this should be rare:

Figure 22-5b: Simultaneous leaps in same direction.

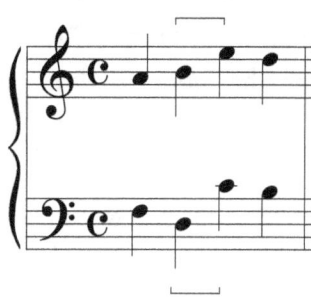

However, the next version is even better because the voicing is adjusted, so that they do not leap at the same time:

Figure 22-5c: When leap in one voice, move by step in the other.

Voice leading guideline #7: Stepwise motion is, in general, more frequent in the Tonal style than are leaps because steps help independent voices move more smoothly and linearly, which helps the ear separate the lines. It is also true that leaps are quite common in the lower voices, particularly the bass part. So, upper voices should contain more stepwise motion than leaps, but leaps should still occur to help break up the line and make it more interesting. The bass voice should contain a variety of stepwise motion and leaps, with leaps being more common in the bass than in the upper voices. If the two lines in a two-voice texture are both written in the treble staff, stepwise motion should predominate in both voices.

Summary

Voice leading is the motion of individual voices (or parts) from one chord to another. The rate at which chords normally change in a passage is called the *harmonic rhythm*. The two most common harmonic rhythms are once per measure and once per beat.

The four types of motion that can occur between two voices are:
(1) contrary;
(2) oblique;
(3) similar;
(4) parallel.

Voice leading guidelines are not hard, unbreakable rules, but are common practices that help achieve independence of voices. Here is a summary of these guidelines:

(1) Use a variety of the four types of motion between the lines.
(2) Normally avoid crossing voices (in pitch range).
(3) Normally space upper voices closer together and lower voices farther apart.
(4) Normally avoid parallel motion at a unison, P5th or P8th between the voices.
(5) Normally avoid leaping in the same direction into a P5th or P8th, except for a rare such motion at a cadence point.
(6) Normally avoid parallel or similar leaps in both voices two or more times in succession.
(7) Prefer stepwise motion in upper voices, but break it up with some leaps. Leaps are more common in the bass voice, but it should also contain plenty of stepwise motion.

Next

We have not finished with voice leading. Next, we will apply these principles plus some guidelines for "doubling" (at unison or octave) for four-voice passages.

Quiz 22

1. The following is an example of _____ motion.

   a. contrary
   b. oblique
   c. parallel
   d. similar

2. The following is an example of _____ motion.

   a. contrary
   b. oblique
   c. parallel
   d. similar

3. The following is an example of _____ motion.

   a. contrary
   b. oblique
   c. parallel
   d. similar

4. The following is an example of _____ motion.

   a. contrary
   b. oblique
   c. parallel
   d. similar

5. Referring to the summary of voice leading guidelines, which guideline "rule" is broken in the following?

6. Referring to the summary of voice leading guidelines, which guideline "rule" is broken in the following?

7. Referring to the summary of voice leading guidelines, which guideline "rule" is broken in the following?

8. Referring to the summary of voice leading guidelines, which guideline "rule" is broken in the following?

9. Referring to the summary of voice leading guidelines, which guideline "rule" is broken in the following?

10. Referring to the summary of voice leading guidelines, which guideline "rule" is broken in the following?

CHAPTER 23: VOICE LEADING: FOUR VOICES

Objectives:

1. Name the four conventional "voices" of a four-voice setting.
2. In a given four-voice passage, locate (by circling the associated notes) where a doubling guideline is NOT followed and describe what is "wrong".
3. In a given four-voice passage, locate (by circling the associated notes) where a voice leading guideline is NOT followed and describe what is "wrong".

Because today's practices of motion between voices were first developed for vocal traditions of the Medieval and Renaissance periods, it has been customary to refer to the "voices" of a four-voice setting as "soprano", "alto", "tenor" and "bass" even when band or orchestral instruments play the parts. One evidence of this is reflected in the names of band instruments. For example, saxophones are categorized as "soprano", "alto", "tenor", "baritone", and "bass" because their pitch ranges approximate those of human voices with those identifications. Guidelines developed for two-voice passages apply to the outer voices – soprano and bass – in a four-voice setting: soprano-alto-tenor-bass (SATB). Therefore, our main concern in the present chapter will be to discuss guidelines for what notes and motions apply to the inner voices and to the four-voice setting as it differs from a two-voice setting.

Doubling

One of the most obvious differences is that, in a four-voice texture, we are now dealing with chords instead of just two-note intervals. In a four-voice context, most of the chords in traditional Tonal style are triads, which need only three pitch classes each. However, a four-voice setting contains four, not three, notes. So, when we have triadic harmony, one of the notes of the triad will have to be "doubled" at the octave or unison. Even when we are voicing a seventh chord, we have the option of omitting the 5th and doubling one of the other notes of the chord. As is the case with the motion aspects of voice leading, which note to double follows conventional guidelines. Again, these are not hard rules, but are flexible guidelines based on observations from excellent examples that typify the style of a period and a culture (18th through early 21st C. Tonal music of the affluent Western cultures).

Following are the most common doubling guidelines.

1) Root position consonant triads (does not include diminished triads): double the root (the bass). (See exception in #7.)

Figure 23-1: Doubling for consonant triads in root position.

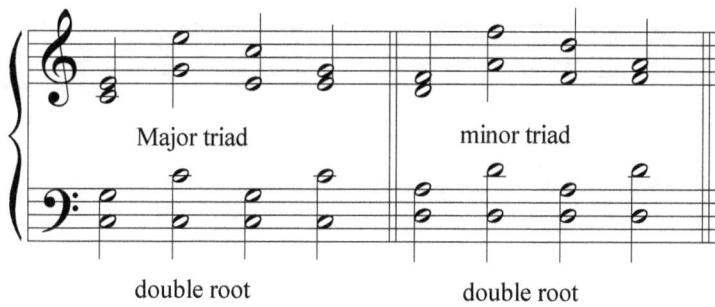

2) I6, IV6, V6 – in either a major or minor key: double the soprano. (I, IV and V are sometimes referred to as the "primary triads" in the key.)

Figure 23-2: Doubling for I⁶, IV⁶, V⁶.

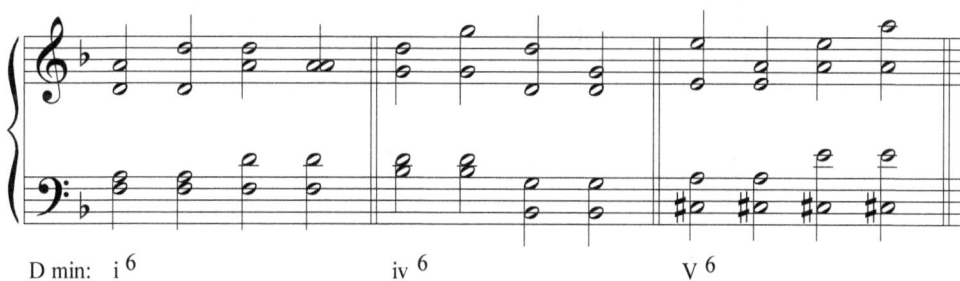

3) ii6, III6, VI6 – in either a major or minor key: double the bass, sometimes the soprano. (But don't double the 5th of a iii chord, which is the leading tone: see #9 below.)

Figure 23-3: Doubling for ii⁶, III⁶, VI⁶.

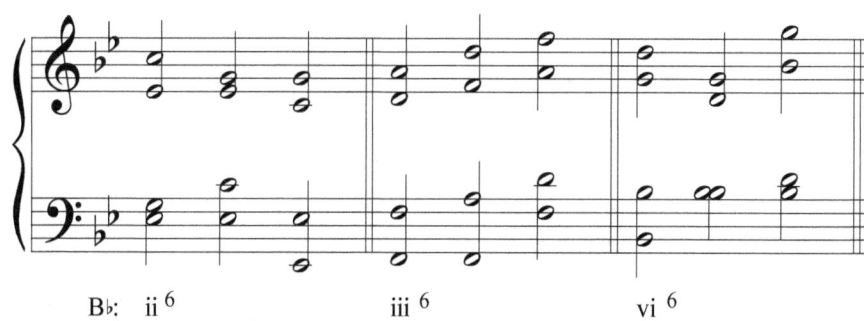

4) Second inversion, consonant triads (not diminished): double the bass.

Figure 23-4: Doubling for second inversion, consonant triads.

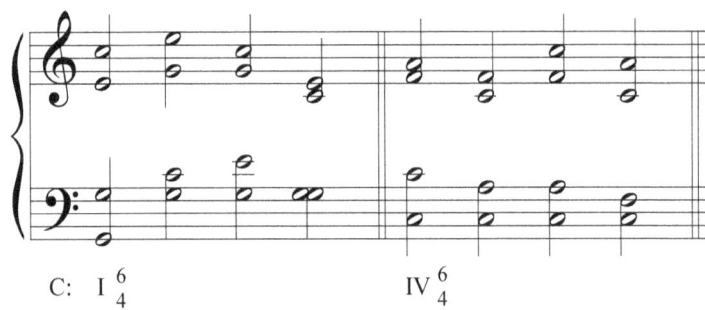

5) Diminished triads ii°, vi°, vii°, regardless of position: double the 3rd of the triad.

Figure 23-5: Doubling for diminished triads.

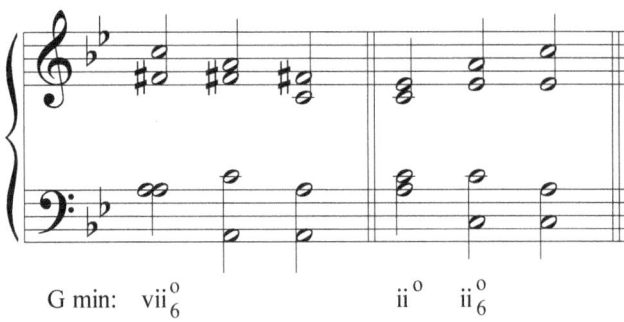

6) Occasionally, a triad is represented by only its root and 3rd (no 5th). Most frequently, this happens at the end of a cadence and results in tripling the root. Occasionally, you may see root and 3rd doubled at such points where the 5th of the triad is missing. Here are two cadential motions showing this result:

Figure 23-6: Doubling for incomplete triads.

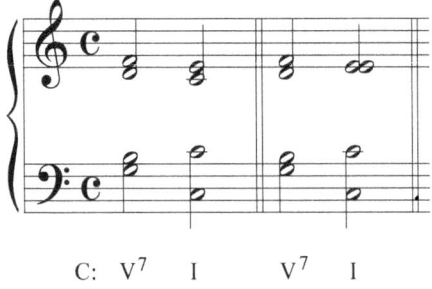

7) V – VI in a minor key: double the 3rd of the VI chord instead of the root.

Figure 23-7: Doubling for V – VI in a minor key.

8) A 7th chord can be written with a missing 5th, in which case the root is normally doubled.

Figure 23-8: Doubling for incomplete 7th chord.

9) Normally avoid doubling the leading tone, regardless of the chord in which it appears.

10) Normally avoid doubling a chromatically altered note.

Now let's look at a passage of music, identify the chords, and pick out all of the doublings, by guideline number.

Example 1. Bach Chorale "O Herzensangst" (simplified to remove ornamental non-harmonic notes). The numbers above the chords are the guideline numbers followed. A zero (0) is used to indicate no doubling (7th chord with all chord tones present); an "x" indicates a guideline was NOT followed.

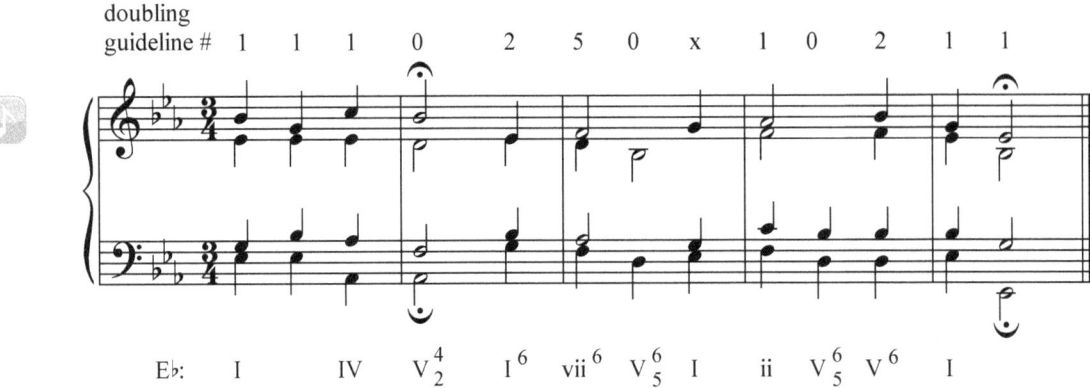

1) The first two chords are I (E♭, G B♭), a consonant triad in root position. The root is doubled (guideline #1).
2) The next chord, IV (A♭, C, E♭), is also a consonant triad in root position and the root is doubled (#1).
3) At the beginning of the 2nd measure is the dominant seventh (in 3rd inversion) with all notes present, so there is no doubling.
4) Then comes the I6 chord, a consonant, primary triad in 1st inversion. The soprano note is doubled (guideline #2).
5) Then comes the vii chord (D, F, A♭), which is a diminished triad in 1st inversion (F in the bass). The 3rd of the chord is doubled (#5).
6) Then a dominant seventh chord in 1st inversion, with all four notes present; no doubling.
7) At the "x", Bach chose to double the 3rd of a consonant triad in root position (instead of the root). His choice avoided the possibility of creating parallel octaves between alto and bass lines when moving to the next chord (e.g., if he had doubled the E-flat in the alto voice). His voice leading between tenor and bass lines also provided a natural resolution for the dissonant diminished fifth in the previous chord (to a 3rd in the chord at the "x"). So, voice-leading considerations often determine the best doubling.
8) The next is a ii chord (F, A♭, C) in root position, with the root doubled (#1).
9) After this is a V⁷ chord in 1st inversion, with all notes present (no doubling).
10) The next chord is a V chord (B♭, D, F) in 1st inversion, with the soprano doubled (guideline #2)
11) Finally, we get I again, in root position with the root doubled (#1).

Voice Leading Guidelines: Four Voices

All of the voice leading guidelines shown for two-voice settings apply, when practical, to even the inner voices of a four-voice passage, but particularly to the outer voices.

For review, here are the guidelines already provided in the previous section:

1) Use a variety of the four types of motion between the lines.
2) Normally avoid crossing voices (in pitch range).
3) Normally space upper voices closer together and lower voices farther apart: no greater than a P8th between adjacent voices, except between bass and tenor.
4) Normally avoid parallel motion at a unison, P5th or P8th between the voices.
5) Normally avoid leaping in the same direction into a P5th or P8th, except for a rare such motion at a cadence point.
6) Normally avoid parallel or similar leaps in both voices two or more times in succession.
7) Prefer stepwise motion in upper voices, but break it up with some leaps. Leaps are more common in the bass voice, but it should also contain plenty of stepwise motion.

Following are some additional guidelines that apply to four-voice passages.

8) Rarely allow adjacent voices to overlap. When a voice moves, if it changes to a pitch that overlaps the pitch of the just previous note of an adjacent voice, this is voice overlap and is generally avoided. In the following example, the alto voice is on the A on the first beat; then at the second beat, the soprano moves down below this A to the G.

Figure 23-9: Overlapping voices.

 ← generally avoid

Plus, this sample creates direct P5ths, which are also usually avoided.

9) The leading tone should normally move to tonic in the next chord, but this is especially important when the leading tone is in the soprano.

Figure 23-10: Voice leading for leading tone.

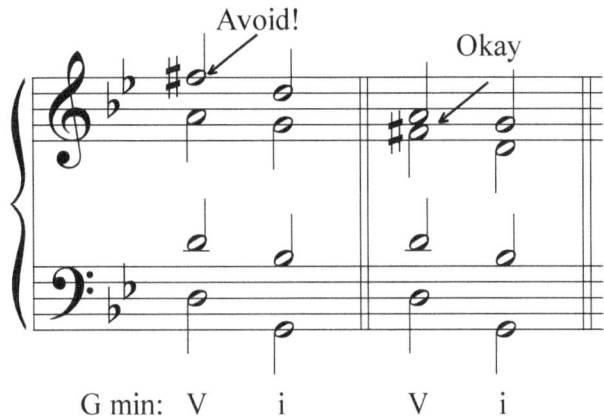

In the first sample, the leading tone in the soprano has no resolution to tonic. In the second sample, the leading tone in the alto voice can be heard to resolve to tonic in the soprano in the next chord, so this is an example of good voice-leading.

10) Here is an extension of #4. Normally avoid parallel motion from a diminished 5th to a perfect 5th between two voices. However, it is okay to go from a P5th in parallel motion to a dim 5th.

Figure 23-11: P5th to dim 5th, and vice versa.

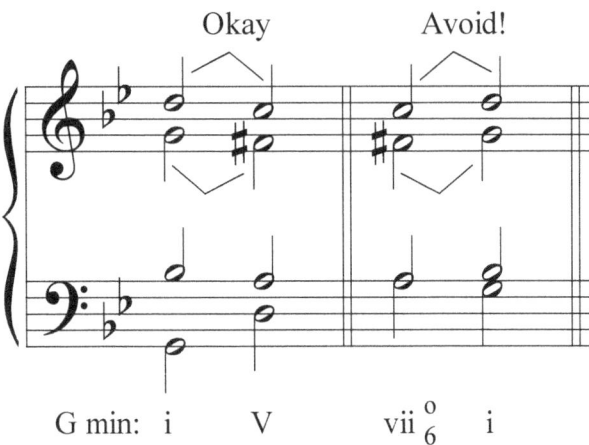

11) Normally avoid consecutive P5ths, P8ths, and unison-to-P8 or P8-to-unison motions between two voices. "Consecutive" here means you leap in contrary motion from one such interval to the other. <u>Avoid</u> all of these, regardless of which two voices are involved:

Figure 23-12: Consecutive P5ths and P8ths.

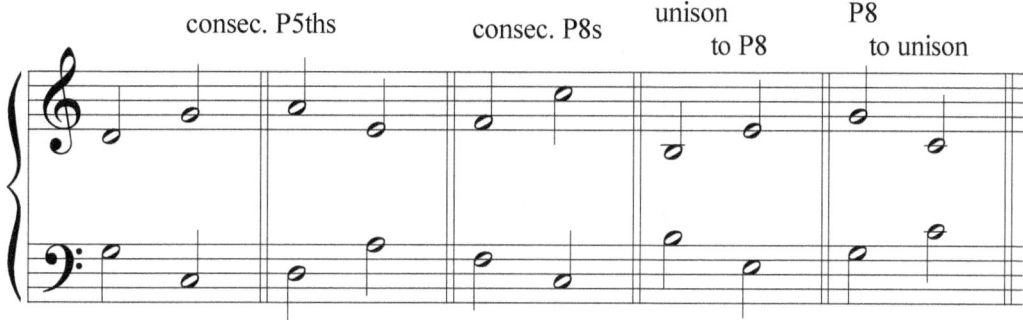

12) The 7th of a dominant 7th chord should resolve downward by step in the same voice. This even takes precedence over moving the leading tone to tonic unless the leading tone is in the soprano.

Here is a V⁷ – I with the leading tone skipping down a 3rd in an inner voice. Notice that the 7th of the V⁷ resolves down by step. This is okay:

Figure 23-13: Resolving the 7th of V⁷.

However, if the leading tone is in the soprano, both the leading tone (the 3rd of the chord) and the 7th of the chord would have to resolve by step. These motions would necessitate leaving out the 5th of the chord of resolution (I, in this case). Otherwise, we would end up with parallel or consecutive P5ths. The 7th of the chord must resolve downward by step, while the leading tone must resolve upward by step. In the progression shown in Figure 23-14, this will cause the augmented 4th between soprano and alto to expand to a 6th. (Augmented intervals normally expand outward to resolve; diminished intervals normally contract inward to resolve.) In the following example, this results in a tripled root and no 5th in the I chord:

Figure 23-14: Tripling the root for V⁷ – I.

If the dominant 7th chord is inverted, this provides an opportunity to resolve normally and also have a complete triad in the next chord.

Figure 23-15: Resolving inverted dominant 7ths.

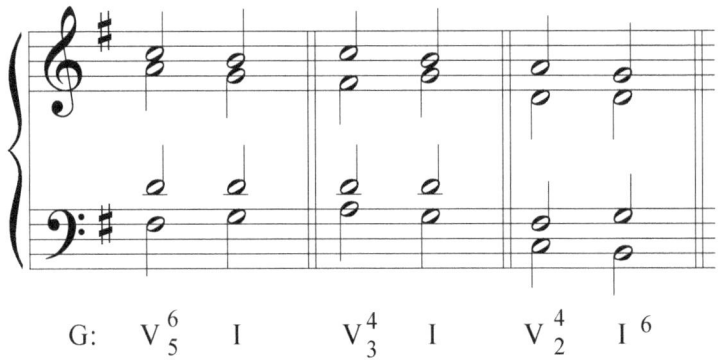

13) In resolving a diminished 7th chord, both the 5th and 7th must resolve downward by step. Be careful to avoid creating a parallel motion into a P5th interval between voices.

Figure 23-16a: Resolving dim 7ths – parallel 5ths.

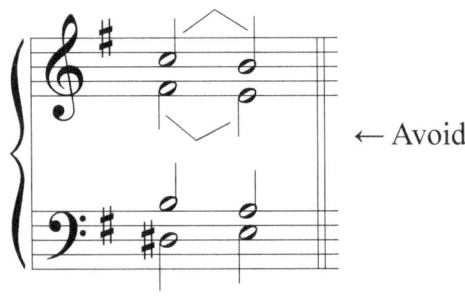

To prevent the above from happening, you will need to double the 3rd of the tonic triad.

In this case, avoiding the parallel 5ths takes precedence over the doubling guidelines.

Figure 23-16b: Resolving dim 7ths –a correct resolution.

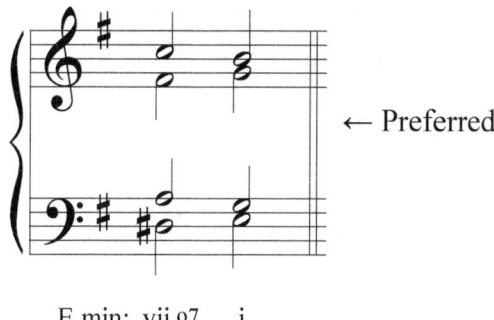

← Preferred

E min: vii o7   i

Notice that both diminished 5ths contract to resolve to 3rds.

Look at the following example, where the 3rd of the diminished seventh chord is in the soprano:

Figure 23-16c: Resolving dim 7ths – another correct resolution.

E min: vii o7   i

In such a case, the parallel 4ths between soprano and alto are okay. In fact, between upper voices, a 4th is not considered an unstable interval.

14) Notes common to consecutive chords are normally repeated if in the inner voices. This does not apply if the common notes are in the bass and the bass needs to change pitch for reasons of clarifying harmony; it would also not apply to the soprano if it is carrying the main melody, and if the melody cannot be changed to repeat at that point in its line. What do we mean by "common notes" between two chords? The F Major triad (F, A, C) and the C Major triad (C, E, G) have one note in common: the C. The F Major triad (F, A, C) and the A minor triad (A, C, E) have two common notes: A and C.

Example 2. In this example, there are notes in common between successive chords. Where these appear in the inner voices, they are repeated:

F: vi   ii   IV   V⁷   I

Here are the common notes:
- vi → ii: D; this is repeated in the alto.
- ii → IV: B♭, D; these are repeated in alto and tenor.
- IV → V7:   B♭; this is repeated in tenor.
- V7 → I: C; not repeated because the only place it occurs in V is in the bass, where the note must change.

15) This one more guideline is a very loose one. Certain intervals may be difficult for the musician to hear and are thus normally not preferred over other intervals. They are not taboo, but should occur only where there are no better alternatives. Thus, in successive notes in a single voice, normally prefer other melodic intervals to these: augmented or diminished intervals; leaps greater than an octave, except in the bass; leaps of a 7th in upper voices (soprano, alto, tenor) unless followed immediately by one or more notes that fill in the gap.

SUMMARY

Doubling:
1) Root position consonant triads: double the root.
2) 1st inversion primary triads (tonic, subdominant, & dominant): double the soprano.
3) 1st inversion secondary triads: prefer double the bass; sometimes soprano.
4) 2nd inversion consonant triads: double the bass.
5) diminished triads: double the 3rd of the triad.
6) triad without a 5th: triple root, or double both root and 3rd.
7) V – VI in a minor key: double the 3rd of the VI chord.
8) 7th chord with missing 5th: prefer doubling the root.
9) Normally avoid doubling the leading tone.
10) Normally avoid doubling a chromatically altered note.

Voice leading:
1) Use a variety of the four types of motion between the lines.
2) Normally avoid crossing voices (in pitch range).
3) Normally space upper voices closer together and lower voices farther apart: no greater than a P8th between adjacent voices, except between bass and tenor.
4) Normally avoid parallel motion at a unison, P5th or P8th between the voices.
5) Normally avoid leaping in the same direction into a P5th or P8th.
6) Normally avoid parallel or similar leaps in any two voices two or more times in succession.
7) Prefer stepwise motion in upper voices.
8) Normally avoid overlapping voices.
9) Leading tone usually goes to tonic; always if in the soprano.
10) Avoid parallel motion from a dim 5th to a P5th.
11) Normally avoid consecutive P5ths, P8ths, and unison-to-P8 or P8-to-unison.
12) The 7th of a dominant 7th chord should resolve downward by step.
13) Both the 5th and 7th of a diminished 7th chord must resolve downward by step.
14) Repeat common notes between two chords if these common notes exist in the inner voices.
15) In a single voice, normally avoid melodic augmented or diminished intervals and leaps greater than an octave (except in the bass). A leap of a 7th should normally be filled in by a change in melodic direction following the leap.

Next

In a previous chapter you were introduced to secondary dominants. In the next chapter, you will conclude the study of harmony by examining additional chords and harmonic structures.

Quiz 23

Each of the following items contains an example. In each example, there is a guideline of doubling or voice leading that is not followed. Identify where this occurs by circling the note or notes involved and then briefly describing what is "wrong" – that is, what occurs that should have been avoided. Some examples may exhibit more than one problem.

1.

2.

C:

3.

C:

CHAPTER 24: FUNCTIONAL HARMONY, PART 4

Objectives:

1. Describe or identify distinguishing characteristics of each of the following types of chords: borrowed chords, Neapolitan sixths, augmented sixths, and augmented triads.
2. Given a chord on a staff and the key, identify it, with the proper functional symbol for that chord, as one of the chords described in this chapter.
3. Distinguish among the different types of augmented sixth chords, naming each.
4. Report the chord sequence to which a Neapolitan sixth will most commonly resolve.
5. Report the chords to which an augmented sixth will most commonly resolve.

Before we make the next step toward the process of writing, we need to add to our arsenal of harmonic materials.

Borrowed Chords

Composers and arrangers sometimes wish to temporarily make a short passage seem like it is in a different mode. A piece in a major key may temporarily sound minor, or vice versa. This can be accomplished by "borrowing" a chord from the parallel key. A ***borrowed chord*** is a chord built on a particular scale degree that has the structure and quality of the corresponding chord in the parallel key. Two triads cannot be "borrowed" because they are identical in major and minor (due to using the raised 7th scale degree in minor to create a leading tone): V and vii°. Likewise, the dominant 7th, V7, is the same.

The tonic and subdominant triads have the same root and 5th. Compare these chords in C Major and C minor:

Figure 24-1: Borrowed chords – tonic and subdominant.

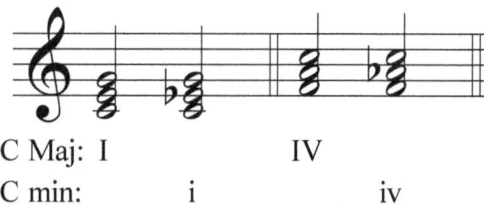

C Maj: IIV
C min:iiv

Example 1. In this short phrase in *Sonatina in C Major* by Joseph Haydn, there is a borrowed tonic from the parallel minor, created just by using the E♭ instead of E♮.

C: V   V   7   i (borrowed from minor) - - - - - - - - - - -   V

Example 2. When in a minor key, one can borrow the major tonic at the end of an authentic cadence. This was so common, it had a special name: the "Picardy Third". From J.S. Bach's chorale, "Our Father, Thou in Heaven Above":

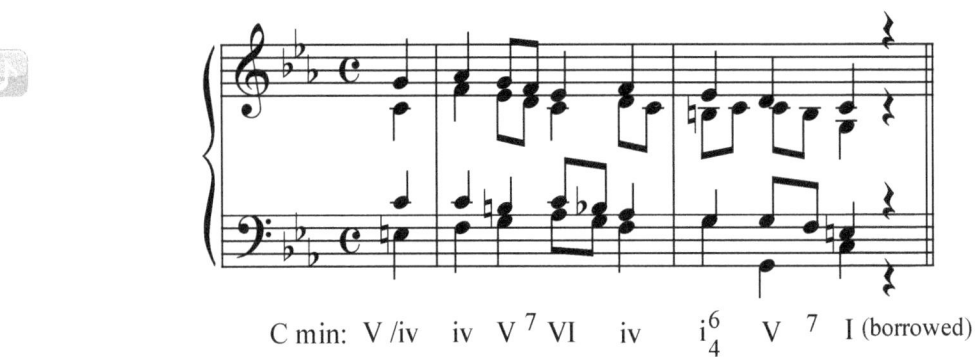

C min: V /iv   iv   V ^{7} VI   iv   i$^6_4$ V ^{7} I (borrowed)

Notice that the first chord is interpreted as a secondary dominant, not a "borrowed" chord. This is because it resolves to iv, making it clear that the C Major triad at the beginning of the phrase is functioning as the V of the F minor triad, iv. When in a minor key and you find a triad made major by one or more chromatically altered notes, check first to see if its root is a P5th above or a P4th below the root of the next chord. If so, it is a secondary dominant, not a borrowed chord.

The supertonic triad and 7th chord also differ between the modes by only one note. In this case, it is the 5th of the chord.

Figure 24-2: Borrowed chords – supertonic.

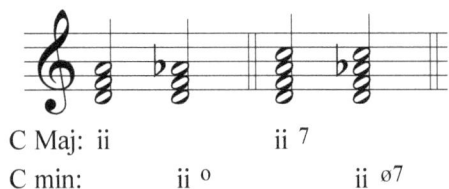

C Maj: ii   ii ^{7}
C min: ii ^{o} ii ^{ø7}

In a major key, it is not too unusual to borrow mediant or submediant triads from the minor, but this requires two altered notes: root and 5th. Notice that when the root is altered, an accidental is placed before the Roman numeral to indicate the chromatic alteration of the root.

Figure 24-3: Borrowed chords – mediant and submediant.

C: iii   ♭III   vi   ♭VI

Although the vii triad is identical between the two modes (major and minor), the seventh chord built on the leading tone differs by one note and is often borrowed in the parallel key:

Figure 24-4: Borrowed chords – leading tone chords.

C Maj: vii ø7
C min: vii o7

Neapolitan Sixth

The Neapolitan 6th chord is a major triad in first inversion, built on the flat-2 scale degree: ♭II6. (Instead of labeling the chord ♭II6, you can also label it just N6.) It can exist in a major or minor key. However, in a major key, it requires two chromatic alterations, and in minor, where it is by far more common, only one chromatic alteration is needed. It is the same chord in either major or minor:

Figure 24-5: The Neapolitan 6th.

C: ♭II6

The Neapolitan 6th most often resolves as shown here:

Figure 24-6: Resolving the Neapolitan 6th.

C min: ♭II⁶   i$^6_4$ V

or

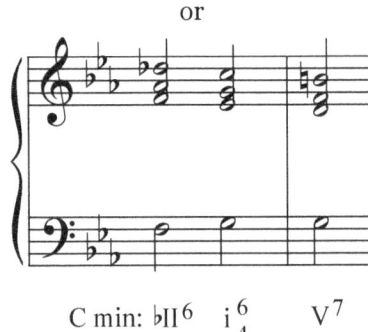

C min: ♭II⁶   i$^6_4$ V⁷

So, it can be seen that it functions as a kind of dominant preparation. The tonic 6-4 chord serves to smoothly connect the Neapolitan 6th to the dominant.

Example 3. There is a good example of a Neapolitan Sixth in Beethoven's *Moonlight Sonata* (measure 50):

V$^6_5$ i   N⁶   V⁷   i   V/iv

(We know that the last chord is V/iv, not a borrowed I, because the next chord after the sample shown is F♯ minor, which is iv.)

Augmented Sixth Chords

An augmented 6th chord is one built on the flat-6 scale degree, contains a note at the interval of an augmented 6th above this (a raised 4th scale degree), and functions as a dominant preparation chord. The distinctive characteristic of this chord is that the bass note is a half-step <u>above</u> the dominant scale degree (^5), and another note in the chord is a half-step <u>below</u> ^5, creating a strong pull to the dominant.

Figure 24-7: The +6th interval and its resolution.

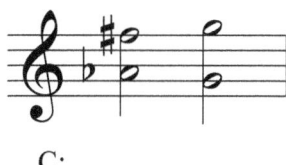

There are three forms of the augmented sixth chord, named after the countries in which they were in common early practice: Italian (It+6), German (Gr+6), and French (Fr+6). Following is the structure of each of these chords:

Figure 24-8: The three conventional types of augmented sixth chords.

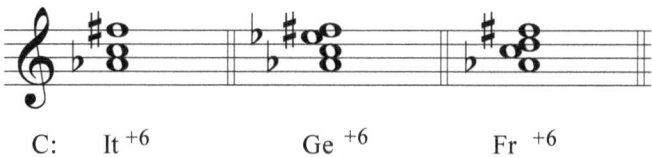

They all have the following in common: they are built on the ♭6 scale degree; they all contain a note that is a Major 3rd above the bottom note (happens to be ^1); and all of them contain a note at an augmented 6th above the bottom note. Here is where they differ:

- It+6:   no other pitch classes are in the chord. In a four-voice setting, the 3rd of the chord (^1) is doubled.
- Ge+6: another note is a P5th above the bottom note (the E♭ in the sample).
- Fr+6:   another note is a +4 above the bottom note (the D in the sample).

Following are the most common resolutions for each of these in a four-voice setting. (Examples are shown in C minor, but they may occur in any key.)

Figure 24-9: Italian +6th:

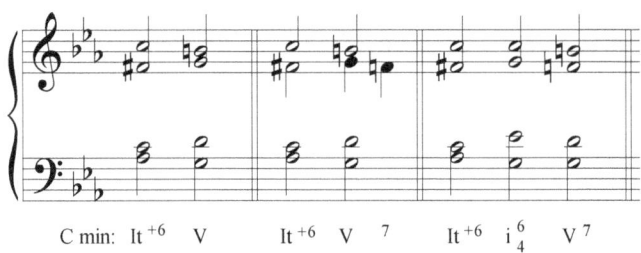

C min: It^{+6} V   It^{+6} V^7 It^{+6} i$^6_4$ V^7

 Example 4. The second movement of Beethoven's *Piano Sonata 24*, Op. 78, begins with an Italian augmented sixth:

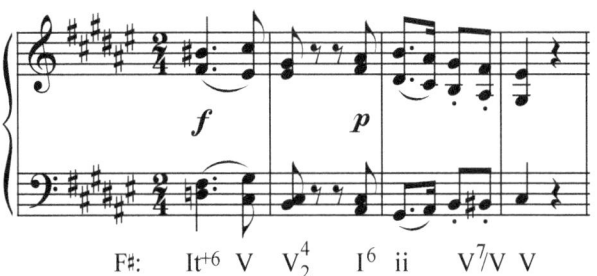

F#:   It^{+6} V V$^4_2$ I^6 ii V^7/V V

Figure 24-10: German +6th:

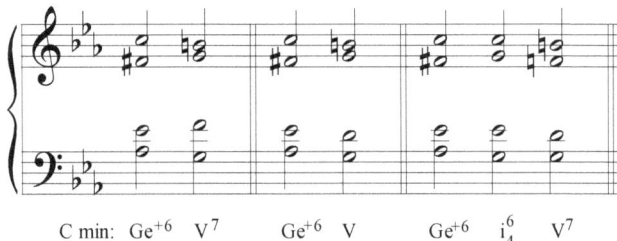

C min: Ge^{+6} V^7 Ge^{+6} V   Ge^{+6} i$^6_4$ V^7

(The parallel 5ths in the second sample above are allowed in this case. However, in the third sample, this is avoided by interposing the I$^6_4$ chord.)

Look at the last sample above. There is a slightly different-looking resolution if this progression is done in major, with a consequent enharmonic respelling of the E♭ to a D♯:

C: Ge^{+6} I$^6_4$ V^7

Some books call this a French +6 with a doubly augmented 4th. The result is the same regardless of the name of the chord.

Figure 24-11: French +6th:

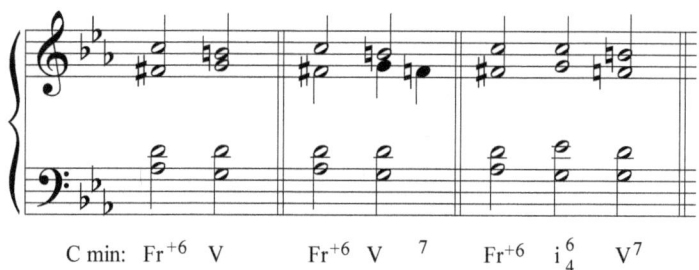

The "Tristan" chord:

Here is one more type of augmented 6th structure:

Figure 24-12a: Tristan chord.

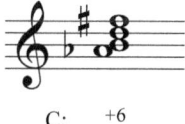

This is a type of +6th chord that is called the Tristan chord because it was popularized by Richard Wagner in his opera *Tristan und Isolde*.

Figure 24-12b: One way to resolve the Tristan chord:

Figure 24-12c: This is how Wagner resolved the Tristan chord:

Other chords formed by Chromatic Alterations

<u>Augmented mediant in minor key</u>

The III chord is formed with scale degrees ^3, ^5, and ^7. In a minor key, when ^7 is raised to provide a leading tone to ^1, the result is an augmented triad:

Figure 24-13: The augmented mediant.

<u>Augmented dominant in major key</u>

If you raise the 5th of the dominant triad, you get an augmented 5th that is just a half step below the 3rd scale degree in a major key. This chromatic alteration gives a kind of leading tone effect to this note, as shown here:

Figure 24-14: The augmented dominant.

> ## Summary
>
> In this last chapter on functional harmony, you have been introduced to several chord structures that contain chromatic alterations: borrowed chords, Neapolitan sixths, augmented sixths, and augmented triads.

> **NEXT**
>
> With a more complete knowledge of harmonic resources, we will next analyze some passages to determine chord function. We will identify all of the non-harmonic notes and label the chords with Roman numeral symbols to identify how they function in the key of the passage. There will be examples, guided practice, and exercises.

Quiz 24

1 – 8. Identify the given chord with one of the following symbols:

B for borrowed from the parallel major or minor,

N6 for Neapolitan 6th,

It+6 for Italian augmented 6th,

Ge+6 for German augmented 6th,

Fr+6 for French +6th,

Tr+6 for the Tristan chord,

III+ for augmented mediant triad, or

V+ for augmented dominant triad.

1.
E min:

2.
G maj:

3.
D min:

4.

   A min:

5.

   G min:

6.

   A min:

7.

   C Maj:

8.

   C min:

9. An augmented sixth chord normally resolves directly to one of which two chords?

10. The most common resolution of a Neapolitan chord is directly to ___ and then to ___ .

CHAPTER 25: IDENTIFYING CHORD FUNCTION

Objectives:

1. Given a progression of two or three chords in a four-voice texture, write the functional symbol for the first chord.
2. Given a complete phrase from a four-voice chorale or hymn tune, identify, by writing functional symbols, all chords, and circle all non-harmonic notes.

Now that you have completed the study of the basics of harmonic function and non-harmonic notes, it is time to tie all of this together by closely examining such features in real Tonal examples. You will begin by looking at just melody and chord symbols. Then you will closely examine the other voices in a musical context that includes four voices.

Review Chord Identification

1) Name the letter names of the notes of the chord, starting from the bottom note and going upward.
2) Rearrange these notes in 3rds, unless the chord contains an augmented 6th.
3) Identify the bottom note of this stack of 3rds as the root of the chord.
4) Note the specific intervals of the other notes, as they relate to the root.
5) Based on the root note and the intervals of the other notes above the root, name the chord.
6) Identify the position of the chord (root position or an inversion) by noticing which note of the chord is in the bass.

Now we will add functional notation:

7) Assign a Roman numeral based on which scale degree the root of the chord lies. Don't forget that some chords may have special functional symbols based upon the structure of the chord and how it resolves (e.g., secondary dominants, N6, borrowed chords, augmented 6ths, etc.).
8) Affix numbers beside the main symbol to reflect the position of the chord.

Demonstration: Here are some chords in the key of D minor. Let's go through the entire process, one step at a time, for each chord.

Figure 25-1a: Chords in D minor to identify.

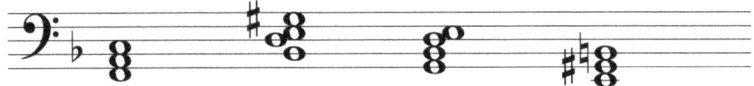

1) Notes for each chord
   F, A, C
   B♭, D, E, G♯
   G, B♭, D, E
   E, G♯, B♮
2) Arrange in 3rds
   F, A, C
   contains a +6th interval (B♭ to G♯)
   E, G, B♭, D
   E, G♯, B♮
3) Roots: F; B♭; E; E

Note that the second chord has the bottom note of the structure identified as "root" even though the chord is not stacked in 3rds; this is a special exception for augmented sixth chords.

4) Intervals above root:
   M3, P5
   M3, +4, +6
   m3, °5, m7
   M3, P5
5) Name of chords:
   F Major triad
   B♭ French +6th
   E half-diminished 7th
   E Major triad
6) Positions:
   root; "root"; 1st inv.; root

Note that we identify the +6 chord as "root" merely because the bottom note of the +6 interval is in the bass.

7) Functional symbols:

   III; Fr+6 (no Roman numeral for this chord); ii; V/ V

8) Functional symbols including inversion, if any:

Figure 25-1b: Chords in D minor identified.

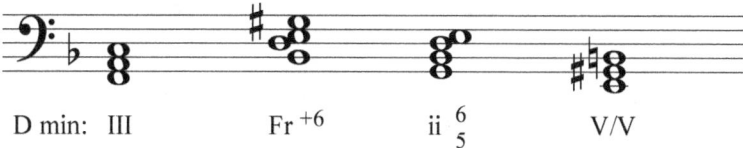

D min: III   Fr +6   ii $^6_5$ V/V

(**Note:** The above is not a functional progression; these are just random chords in the key.) We know the last chord is a secondary dominant even though we are not supplied with its resolution: the chord built on E in D minor is not a Major triad (it would be e diminished); it is not borrowed from the parallel major because that triad is a minor triad (ii); and it cannot be the Neapolitan triad because it is built on ^2, not ♭^2. Thus, through the process of elimination, it must be a secondary dominant. Identifying secondary dominants will not usually be possible without seeing the chord of resolution. One more sample:

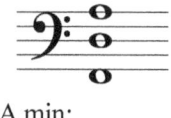

A min:

Notes: F, D, A
In 3rds: D, F, A
Root: D
Intervals: m3, P5
Chord: D min triad
Position: 1st inv. (3rd in bass)
Functional symbol: iv6 (root, D, is on 4th scale degree)

Practice: Try these yourself. Answers are provided below the horizontal line after the samples.

Figure 25-2: Chord identification practice examples.

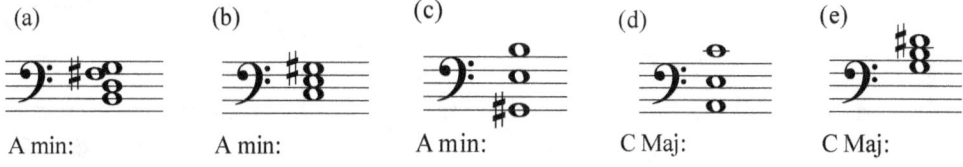

(a)   (b)   (c)   (d)   (e)

A min: A min: A min: C Maj: C Maj:

Exploring Musical Structure

- - - - - - - - - - -

Answers (Don't look until you try them!):
(a) vii$^6_5$ (b) III+   (c) V^6 (d) vi   (e) V+

Chord Functions in Context

Example 1a. Mozart's *Piano Sonata No. 4*, K. 282, "Menuetto I":

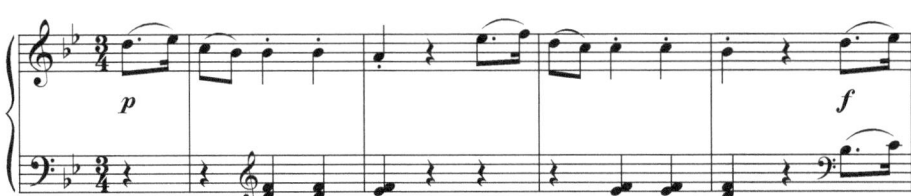

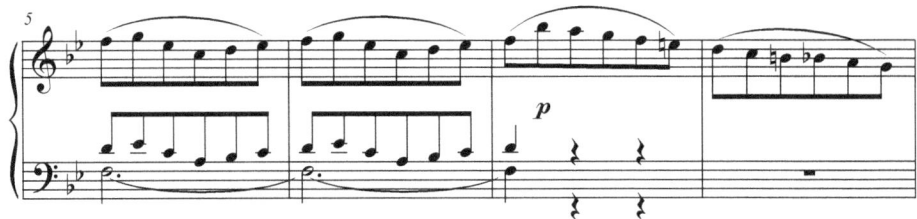

Listen to the passage first; then we will take it four measures at a time. If you wish to clearly identify what key a section is in, look at the cadence at the end of the section. This minuet ends (ending not shown here) with an authentic cadence on the B♭ Major triad, so the section is in the key of B♭ Major.

Example 1b. Now, let's look at the first four-measure phrase:

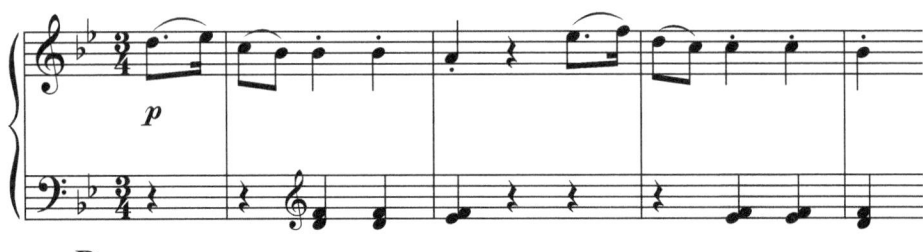

B♭:

The measure **after** the pick-up (anacrusis) is measure 1 (ms.1). We get our first chord on the 2nd and 3rd beats of ms.1: a B♭ Major triad in 1st inversion: I^6. At the beginning of ms.2, the chord changes to E♭-F-A, which is an F dominant 7th chord with a missing 5th and the 7th of the chord in the bass: V$^4_2$. The dominant chord is repeated at the end of ms.3, except the 3rd (A) is missing instead of the 5th; then we again get the I^6 at the end of the phrase. In the melody line, the non-harmonic notes are labeled (en = escape note). Also shown is the pick-up to the next phrase.

Example 1c.

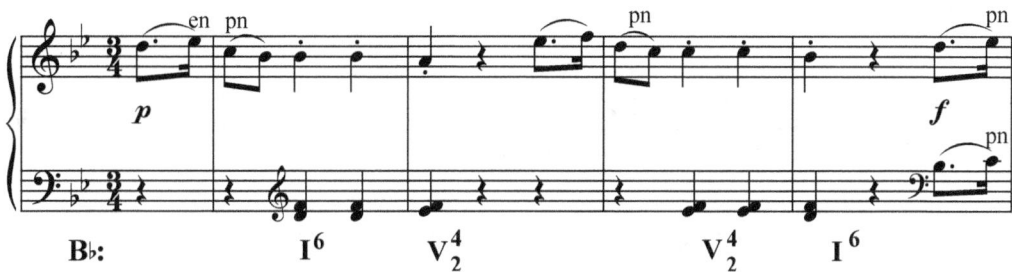

Example 1d. Now examine the next phrase (pick-up notes shown above), ms. 5 – 8:

Measures 5 and 6 are identical. Where a melody successively outlines a chord is called an arpeggio. The top line contains an arpeggio on the notes C, E♭, and G; the bottom line, on A, C, and E♭. Below this is a very long F in the bass. Spelling notes upward from the bass, we have: F-A-C-E♭-G, which is a V^9 chord. It is not uncommon for the dominant chord to be a tertiary chord extended to a 9th, or even 11th or 13th if the stack of 3rds is made clear in the context. Then, starting in measure 7, we get a descending run of steps and half-steps starting from the high B♭. Of particular interest is the effect of going through the E♮ instead of E♭. More about that later. At the beginning of ms. 7, we have the F and D in the left hand and a leap from F to B♭ on top, clearly indicating that the chord at this point is the B♭ triad in second inversion, I$^6_4$.

Example 1e.

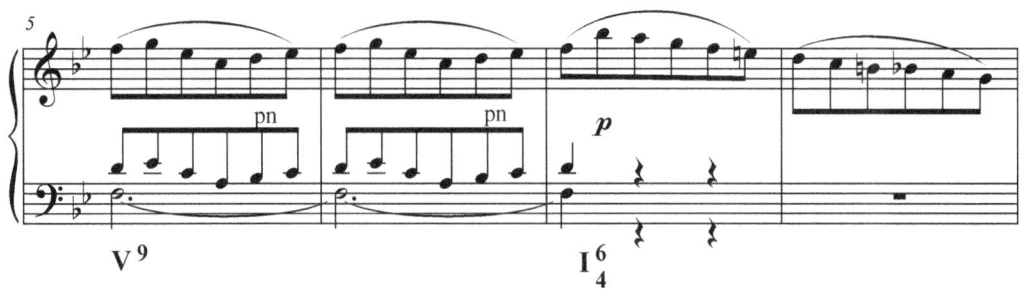

Example 1f. Now for the last phrase in this passage, ms. 9 – 12:

The first chord is the F Major triad, in 2nd inversion; then C dominant 7th; followed by F Major, now root position at the beginning of ms. 10. The C^7 is V^7/V. Here is the rest of the chord analysis, with non-harmonic notes identified for this last phrase:

Example 1g.

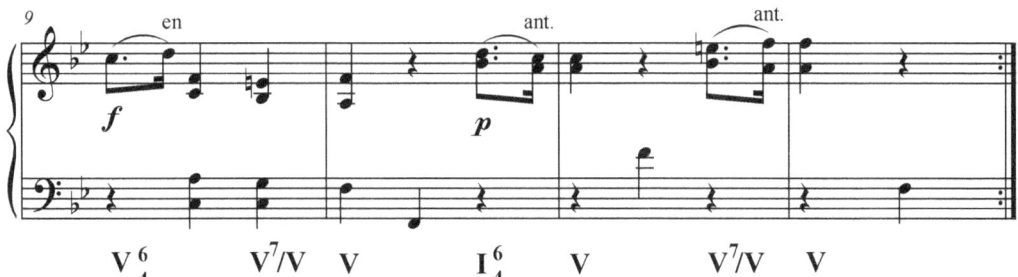

Remember the E♮ instead of E♭ in measure 7? It was a melodic foreshadowing of the later role of the V/V chord, where the E♮ was needed to form a temporary leading tone for the root of the V chord. It is quite common for a composer to forecast a chromatic alteration by having it play a subtle role in a melodic passage before making it part of harmonic progression. (Note: The V^6_4 chord could also be labeled a I^6_4 of V, but we have not yet studied chords with secondary function except for the secondary dominant.) Notice that since the C^7 chord has already been solidly expressed in ms. 9, Mozart uses only the 3rd and 7th of this chord on the third beat of ms. 11 to recall its function (very efficient!).

Example 2. Now let's look at the chorale "Nun danket alle Gott", by J. S. Bach. It will be enough at this point to analyze just the last two phrases:

Establishing the key and harmonic rhythm are the first things to do. The key signature implies that the passage is in either A Major or F♯ minor; the ending on an A Major triad confirms the key is A Major. As we analyze the chords and non-chord tones, go back and play the passage as many times as needed to hear the dissonances, chords, and chord progressions. Listening to or playing the passage will confirm for you that the normal harmonic rhythm is one chord change per quarter-note beat. The first chord is obviously I (A, C♯, E), the tonic triad. On the first beat of the first full measure of this phrase, you have D (doubled), A, and F♯: the D Major triad, IV. The 8th note C♯ in the bass and B in the alto are passing notes. Let's look closely at the 2nd and 3rd beats of this measure (remember that you often need to look at the next chord to determine current chord function).

Example 2b.

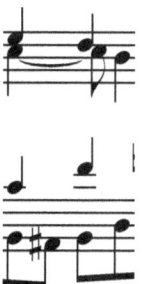

The C♯ at an octave in alto and tenor identify this as a chord note; the E in the soprano forms a consonant 3rd with this C♯. We need one more chord tone to make a triad. The B in the bass makes a 2nd (plus one and two octaves) with tenor and alto, so this is a non-harmonic passing note. The bass then moves on down to the A♯. The A♯ forms a diminished triad with the notes in the upper voices (A♯, C♯, E). Notice two things: the A♯ is a chromatic alteration of the prevailing scale in the key, and it moves upward a half-step to the B on the next beat. Thus it looks like a momentary leading tone. The chord on the next beat is B-F#-D (a B minor triad). This triad is built on the 2nd scale degree in A Major, and is therefore the ii chord. If the B minor triad can be heard as a temporary tonic, the A# diminished triad would function as a secondary dominant substitute, the viio of B. Therefore, it is analyzed as viio/ ii. The C# in the alto is a suspension: it has consonant preparation, dissonant suspension, and consonant resolution by downward step-wise motion to the B. On the last beat of that measure, the chord is F#-A#-C#: the V/ ii. Non-harmonic notes (marked with the arrows, below): The E in the bass is a passing note; the G♮ in the tenor voice is a chromatic neighboring note; and the B in the alto is suspended into its resolution to A#.

Example 2c.

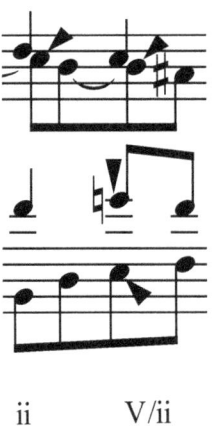

ii   V/ii

The phrase then ends on the ii chord.

Now let's examine the last phrase. First chord, from bass up: C#-E-A-C#. This is a I6 chord. Then passing note D in bass to E-E-G#-B: V. Next is A-E-A-C#: I. Then an interesting thing happens just after the beat. The bass skips down to F# while the tenor moves up to F#, both under still sounding A and C# in alto and soprano, forming the vi chord in the middle of the beat. Then during the 3rd beat of the measure, we get the base and tenor skipping through D and B in bass and F# and D in tenor. There is also a B in the soprano. These form the ii chord. You could say that this is the ii7 chord, but the A is obviously a non-harmonic tone: the suspension, which resolves down to the G# on the next beat. The last chord in this measure is V (E-G#-B), with the 8th-note A in the soprano being an anticipation. The last chord is I, completing the perfect, authentic cadence one expects at the end of a piece in this style.

Here is the last phrase with chords (non-harmonic notes are circled):

Example 2d.

I⁶   V   I   vi   ii   V   I

Practice

Analyze two phrases from this same Bach chorale. Write Roman numerals under the chords and circle all non-harmonic notes. Don't look below the horizontal line until you are ready to see the answer. Play it first so you can hear the chords and dissonances.

Example 3a.

Example 3b.

V - - - - - - - I - - - - - V   V   I   iii   vi   V/V   V

Notice that the suspended E in the soprano in the next-to-last measure does not resolve to a consonant chord note until the next chord. This is quite common for suspensions. Also notice that the use of the temporary leading tone D♯ is forecasted as a passing note before it appears as a chord note in the V/V chord (the B Major triad).

Exploring Musical Structure

SUMMARY

In this chapter, we have applied our knowledge of harmony and non-harmonic notes by identifying all chords and non-chord notes in passages of real compositions by masters.

NEXT

You are nearly ready to start writing. We will next deal with a few principles of melodic form. Most writing starts with melody, and then we examine this melody to determine what the melody tells us that will be useful when we later complete the other parameters of a musical passage.

Quiz 25

1. Write the functional symbol for the first chord in the given progression.

C: ?

2. Write the functional symbol for the first chord in the given progression.

C: ?

3. Write the functional symbol for the first chord in the given progression.

C: ?

4. Write the functional symbol for the first chord in the given progression.

A min: ?

Identify all chords with functional symbols and circle all non-harmonic notes:

Example 4. A phrase from a chorale by J.S. Bach:

G:

CHAPTER 26: MELODIC STRUCTURE

Objectives:

1. Define or describe the following: motive, sequence, arpeggio.
2. Given a short motive, identify each of the following alterations: transposition,
3. inversion, retrograde, retrograde inversion.
4. Given a melodic passage notated on a musical staff, provide the following information:
   - Describe the phrase structure, including the types of melodic cadences used.
   - Mark motives with brackets and numbers. Describe any treatments of these.
   - Identify and describe sequences, if any.
   - Circle any arpeggios you find and name the chords outlined by them.
   - Describe melodic shapes and tell where they are located by the range of measure numbers.
   - Report the most likely harmonic rhythm implied by the structure of the tune.
   - Mark notes that are given special emphasis by writing an asterisk above each.

Review Phrase Structure

A phrase is a segment of music that expresses one complete gesture longer than a measure. Phrases are frequently 2, 4, or 8 measures in length, although it is not too unusual in today's music to find phrases of other lengths. A melody is a line of music that carries listener interest as the main focus of attention. Some musical passages do not have melodies. However, a composer might choose to write one line before adding other parts, so the issues of melodic form will often still apply to such a line. Division of a line into phrases is usually apparent in a single-line melody. Antecedent and consequent melodic phrases form a period.

Example 1. Here is an example of antecedent and consequent phrases in a melody in Mozart's *Symphony No. 38*:

Melodic cadences: Recall that each phrase ends with one of two kinds of melodic cadence. In the above example, the antecedent phrase ends on the 3rd scale degree, which makes it a terminal melodic cadence, but the melody does not rhythmically pause there. The consequent phrase ends on scale degree ^2, which makes it a progressive melodic cadence, where there is a pause in the motion of the piece. The cadence at the end of an antecedent phrase is not as important (is not as emphasized to the listener) as is the one at the end of a period. The cadence at the end of the above period being progressive means that the piece is tonally not yet stable and can not end there: the listener will expect more to come.

Melodic Treatments

Motives

In addition, the above passage includes an example of the use of *motives*: short melodic fragments that are repeated in order to form a longer melodic element. A motive may be altered in several different ways. One or more intervals in the motive can be contracted or stretched, a device used by Mozart in the first phrase. The first phrase is shown below with the motive marked. First it includes a leap of a 6th; then a 7th; finally, an octave.

Example 1b.

In the second phrase, the entire motive appears on different pitch levels.

A motive can also appear inverted (upside-down).
Play or listen to the first 12 measures of this piece:

Example 2. Bach's "Two-Part Invention in D minor":

This piece contains motive inversions. The inverted pattern contains a larger leap, but it is still recognizable as a version of the original motive, but upside-down.

Example 2a.

A motive can also be played backwards, called **retrograde motion**. Although he did not do so in this piece, Bach could have retrograded the motive and produced another musically effective variant:

Example 2b.

Sequences

A passage comprised of repeating a melodic pattern at a different pitch level is called a *sequence*. The repetition at different pitch levels can occur several times as in the second phrase from the Mozart symphony above:

Figure 26-1: Example of sequence from Mozart.

The Bach example also contains many sequences such as:

Figure 26-2: Example of sequence from Bach.

The two-measure pattern of the motive plus the inverted version of the motive is repeated in the next two measures, one step lower.

Arpeggios

An arpeggio is formed by playing the notes of a chord one after another instead of simultaneously. A melody can contain one or more arpeggios, which will facilitate selecting the accompanying harmony.

The opening measure of "Have Yourself a Merry Little Christmas" (by Hugh Martin) contains an arpeggio:

Figure 26-3: An arpeggio.

Melodic Shape

Although melodies can be pretty static and lack melodic shape, most melodies exhibit a shape, or contour, that can be identified aesthetically as a kind of extended musical gesture. Such "shape" may be created by pitch pattern or by rhythmic pattern or, very often, both.

Example 3. Here is the complete opening melody for "Have Yourself a Merry Little Christmas":

Notice that the opening gesture in the first two measures is repeated in measures 5 and 6. Although the composer could have just followed the first gesture immediately with the second, he achieved a much more interesting melody by breaking it up with the contrasting gesture in measures 3 and 4. The middle piece also provides a rhythmic contrast. All three of these small two-measure gestures have a simple pitch pattern of rising and then falling. Notice also the effect of the third gesture in rising higher than the previous ones: it creates an overall rise-and-fall gesture for the entire eight-measure melody, which helps to bind them all together.

Another important pitch concept that is realized in melodic shaping is the emphasis given to pitches important in the prevailing key of the melody. The melody above is in C Major. The melody starts on C, the root of the tonic triad; then there is a clear emphasis on G, the dominant, in the middle part; then the melody ends on the third of the tonic triad. Hence all three notes of the tonic triad are emphasized, with special attention given to the dominant in the middle. Such emphasis on tonic and dominant harmonies are an important feature of a melody that clearly establishes the key of the passage. We will deal with this concept in more detail in the topic called "Tonal Emphasis" later in this chapter.

Implied Harmonic Rhythm

A given melody will place restrictions on what the harmonic rhythm can be. This is determined by both the style in which it is written and by the melodic structure. In some melodies, the harmonic rhythm is easy to determine by examining just the melody; for others, you would need to look at other voices as well. In Example 3 above, it is easy to hear a harmonic rhythm of one chord per measure. Measures 1, 3, and 5 have arpeggios on the tonic triad (I):

Figure 26-4: Role of arpeggios in harmonic rhythm.

The melodic pattern in measures 2 and 6 are very similar and both emphasize notes of the dominant triad or dominant 7th chord. Measure 4 is a single note (^5):

Figure 26-5: Chords emphasized by melodic pattern.

Whether or not you actually choose dominant harmonies for all of these, the point here is that the melodic patterns can easily support a harmonic rhythm of one chord per measure.

As indicated above, style also helps determine reasonable options for harmonic rhythm. A popular song, such as "Have Yourself a Merry Little Christmas", most commonly has a harmonic rhythm of one or two chords per measure, sometimes even slower. A Bach chorale or a hymn tune usually has a chord change every beat.

Tonal Emphasis

Another thing we should notice about a melody is which notes are particularly emphasized and recall that there are two types of accent (emphasis): rhythmic and agogic. Some notes are emphasized because of extreme position, in either time or pitch range. So, the first and last notes of a phrase or period receive emphasis by extreme time position; the highest and lowest notes of a phrase or an entire melody receive emphasis by extreme pitch position. If we look again at Example 3, we can see special emphases on the notes marked:

Figure 26-6: Identifying emphasized notes.

The C in the first measure is emphasized by the following ways: C is the beginning note of the melody; the first C has metric accent, and the pitch class is repeated at the octave, which is filled in, outlining the C. Then there is a special emphasis on D because it ends a melodic gesture and is followed by a rest. In measures 3 and 4, the G is given special emphasis by agogic accent (duration) and by occurring on metric accents (beat 3 and beat 1 in the meter). Finally, E is emphasized in the following ways: Like C was at the beginning of the piece, E is the beginning note in measure 5, has metric accent, and is repeated at the octave (which is again filled in); also E is the final note of the melody and is given metric and agogic accent. You could also say that the D at the beginning of measure 6 is emphasized by metric accent. Noticing the scale degrees of the notes that receive special emphasis reveals the tonal emphasis of the melody: in this case, notes of the tonic triad (^1, ^3, ^5) are given the greatest emphasis, and a secondary emphasis is placed on two of the scale degrees of the dominant triad (^5 and ^2, the root and 5th of that triad).

Melodic Tendencies

Another fact that influences the listeners' expectations is that in Western Tonal style, the harmony leans toward and resolves to the tonic triad. This means that all other notes of the scale in the key will have a tendency to move (eventually) to scale degrees in this triad: ^1, ^3, or ^5. Here are the most natural melodic tendencies in a <u>major</u> key:

Figure 26-7a: Melodic tendencies in major keys.

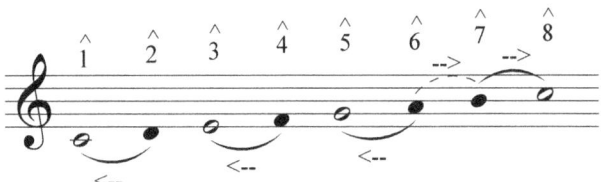

Notice that there is an alternate tendency for scale degree 6: it can tend toward 7, which, of course, will then eventually move on to 8.

Melodic tendencies for a melody in a <u>minor</u> scale naturally will conform with the expectations for the two forms of the melodic minor scale.

Figure 26-7b: Melodic tendencies for minor keys, ascending form.

Figure 26-7c: Melodic tendencies for minor keys, descending form.

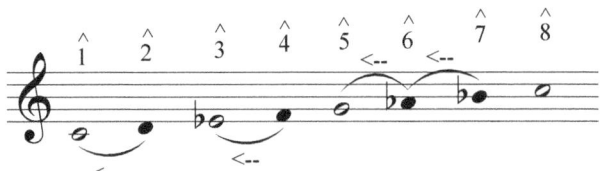

Keep in mind that any of these notes could move by step to notes other than those shown above, but they "eventually" move to their natural goals. For example, consider the following passage:

C:

Even though the B (^7) goes first to ^6, the passage later returns to ^7, where it resolves to ^1, where it naturally "wants" to go. Similarly, sometimes ^2 will go immediately to ^3 even though its most natural resolution is to ^1; or ^4 may move immediately to ^5 and then later resolve to ^3.

Example Melodic Analysis

Let's examine the first 16 measures of a popular tune.

Example 4. Following are the first two 8-measure phrases of "The Best Things Happen While You're Dancing", by Irving Berlin, made famous in the movie classic *White Christmas*:

(**NOTE:** When you listen to this, you will notice that the 8th notes sound like triplets, not equally spaced notes; this is because the tune was written in the "swing" style popular in the 1940s and 50s. In this style, 8th notes were performed as you hear them in this sample.)

Phrase structure

There are two, 8-bar phrases, antecedent-consequent. Notice that the second phrase is a repetition of the first, up one step, except for a very few notes. It is important when a sequence differs by very few notes to pay attention to what is different. Notice that the leap down a 6th in measures 1 and 3 is replaced by a leap of a 4th in measures 9 and 11 in the second phrase, placing a special importance on the note G. Also notice that at the cadence, the first phrase ends with a motion up a 2nd to the E♭ (^4); however the second phrase ends with a motion down a third to the note D. If it had gone up a step, it would have ended on G. Why is that important? Because D is ^3, which makes the second cadence a terminal cadence, giving more of a sense that the period of two phrases has reached a goal. Ending on G would have made it a progressive cadence.

Motives

Motive 1 covers the first two measures:

It is immediately repeated with no changes. In the second phrase, this motive is played up one step and altered slightly by just one note; otherwise it is identical with its first appearance:

It is also immediately repeated without modification.

Motive 2 is first found in measure 5:

It is then repeated a 3rd lower in the next measure. The downward, stepwise motion in the motive is maintained everywhere it appears.

The next time motive 2 is played, it starts up one step, but the immediate repetition of the motive is down one step instead of down a 3rd.

Notice that this creates a strong support for C, which has been emphasized in the last few measures, to move on down to B♭ (tonic).

Sequences
Motive 2 is written in two sets of sequences: ms. 5 to ms. 6; and ms. 13 to ms. 14. In addition, the entire first phrase is repeated up one step, except for a few notes.

Arpeggios
Motive 1 is an arpeggio of a triad, except for a single passing note. The triad arpeggiated by motive 1 in the first phrase is B♭ Major (I).

In the second phrase, motive 1 outlines the C minor triad (ii).

Melodic Shape
The first two measures have a rather abrupt down and up shape, spanning an entire octave, which is repeated in the next two measures. Then there is a gradual descending motion in the last half of the phrase. These shape patterns – down-up → down-up → gradual descent – are repeated in the same manner in the second phrase, supporting the similarity of these phrases.

Possible harmonic rhythms

Since a chord can be repeated at the harmonic rhythm, it is best to start where it is obvious that you have chord changes. Therefore, let's examine measures 5, 6, and 7:

While you could play this entire passage with an E♭ Major triad, the result would be relatively static. That leaves two good options: one chord per measure or two chords per measure. The final decision should be kept open until you can examine an arrangement showing harmonies, or until you get to the point of writing the chords yourself (something we will do in a later chapter).

Tonal emphasis

Here is the tune with numbers above the notes that receive special emphasis:

(1) and (8) begin a phrase;

(2), (3), (7), (9), (10), and (14) receive metric accents and have long durations;

(4) and (11) receive metric accent and outline an octave that is filled in;

(5), (6), (12), and (13) receive metric and/or rhythmic accent and are immediately repeated;

(7) and (14) receive metric and agogic accents and end a phrase.

These notes draw listener attention to two chords important in this melody: B♭ Major and C minor.

Melodic tendencies

Since the segment we are examining is near the beginning of the piece, it is not surprising that melodic motions sometimes resolve in directions opposite to those of their "natural" tendencies or are even left hanging by leaping away from them. Going away from natural tendencies early in a piece is a way of opening up the composition, moving away from "home", so that it can resolve back to the stability of home base (tonic) near the end. Notice, for example, that the first phrase ends on E♭, ^4, then leaps away from it at the beginning of the next phrase. It is also important to hear that the ear makes a natural connection between this E♭ at the end of the first phrase, and the D at the end of the consequent phrase. In a sense, this provides a long-term resolution of ^4 moving to ^3. However, if this were the last phrase of the song, there would likely be another E-flat in the next-to-last measure moving down to the D in the last measure, resolving the natural tendency for ^4 to move down to ^3.

Well, you have a lot of information about this melody now. This information will be useful if you wish later to write harmony and parts for it.

SUMMARY

Melodies are grouped into **phrases**, and phrases, into **periods**. Each phrase ends with a cadence. Arriving at a **terminal cadence** (one that ends on ^1 or ^3) does not necessarily mean you are at the end of a composition or section, but it does gives a sense of at least touching home base (I). A **progressive cadence** always gives a sense of leaning onward through the melody.

Motives are short fragments of a melody that make a small internal gesture that is repeated, although not always immediately, and are usually altered in any of a variety of ways: **transposed** up or down in pitch, written with one or more **intervals altered**, turned upside down (**inverted**) or written backwards (**retrograde**).

A motive or an entire phrase may be immediately repeated at different pitch levels two or more times in succession, called a **sequence**.

Another common characteristic of a melody is that three or more notes in succession can leap to notes of a chord. Outlining the notes of a chord in this manner forms a pattern called an **arpeggio**.

Every relatively complete melodic gesture has a simple **melodic shape**, or pattern.

A complete melody can have several of these. Also, the entire melody may have a simple, overall shape.

The motion of a melody through its pitches forms patterns that imply some practical options for a **harmonic rhythm**.

Tonal emphasis: Certain notes in a melody receive special emphasis in a variety of ways:

- metric or written accent
- duration (agogic accent)
- immediate repetition
- extreme pitch position: highest or lowest note of a complete melodic gesture (usually when combined with other factors that also emphasize that note)
- leaping away from a note, when combined with other factors that emphasize the note

It will be important to notice which notes receive such emphases when one writes chords or other parts to go with a melody.

In melodies written in the Tonal style, notes outside of those in the tonic triad have natural **melodic tendencies** to move by stepwise motion into members of the tonic triad. There is a "most natural" resolution for each of these, reviewed here:

Major keys:

Minor keys, ascending form:

Minor keys, descending form:

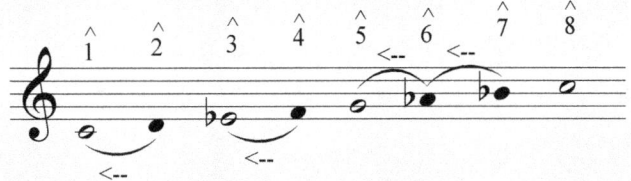

In any melody, it is important to understand that these tendencies may be realized or not near the beginning of a passage, but these tendencies are particularly strong at the end of a piece or section.

Next

The next chapter will guide you through your first writing exercises. Writing music is a fun and creative activity. We will begin the process with writing chords for a given melody.

Quiz 26

Here is a melody for you to analyze.

Example 5. "The Glow Worm", by Paul Lincke – first 8 measures of opening melody:

1. Describe the phrase structure, including the types of melodic cadences used.

2. Mark motives with brackets and numbers. Describe any treatments of these.

3. Identify and describe sequences, if any.

4. Circle any arpeggios you find and name the chords outlined by them.

5. Describe melodic shapes and tell where they are located by the range of measure numbers.

6. What is the most likely harmonic rhythm implied by the structure of this tune?

7. Mark notes that are given special emphasis by writing an asterisk above each.

CHAPTER 27: HARMONIZING A MELODY

Objectives:

1. Analyze a given melody using methods shown in this chapter.
2. Harmonize a given melody by providing chord symbols above the staff and Roman numerals below.

Even if you have no plans to be a composer or arranger, writing music is one of the best ear-training activities. Also, later on in your career, if you are asked to lead or direct a musical ensemble, you will probably have to write arrangements for the group – or reductions. A reduction is a piece in which you rewrite a composition, originally composed for a larger group, so that a smaller ensemble can play it. So you never know when you may want to write something even if you do not major in composition.

One of the earliest tasks is to find chords for a melody. We will work with the melody for "The Best Things Happen While You're Dancing", the Irving Berlin tune analyzed in the last chapter. Here are the first 16 measures:

Figure 27-1: Melody for "The Best Things Happen When You're Dancing".

Structure of the Melody

The first thing to do is to analyze the melody, which we did in the last chapter and thus discovered it has the following characteristics.
- Two phrases (antecedent-consequent).

- First cadence is progressive, ending on ^4; second is terminal, ending on ^3.
- The melody in the second phrase is a copy of that in the first phrase and is written a step higher; only a few intervals differ.
- There are some arpeggios that will make identifying the supporting chord easier.
- The most natural harmonic rhythm is two chords per measure.
- Certain notes receive special emphasis.

<u>Identify arpeggios</u>
We will begin by identifying all of the arpeggios. They are shown in the following copy by dotted slurs drawn to point to each note of the arpeggiated chord.

Figure 27-2: Finding the arpeggios.

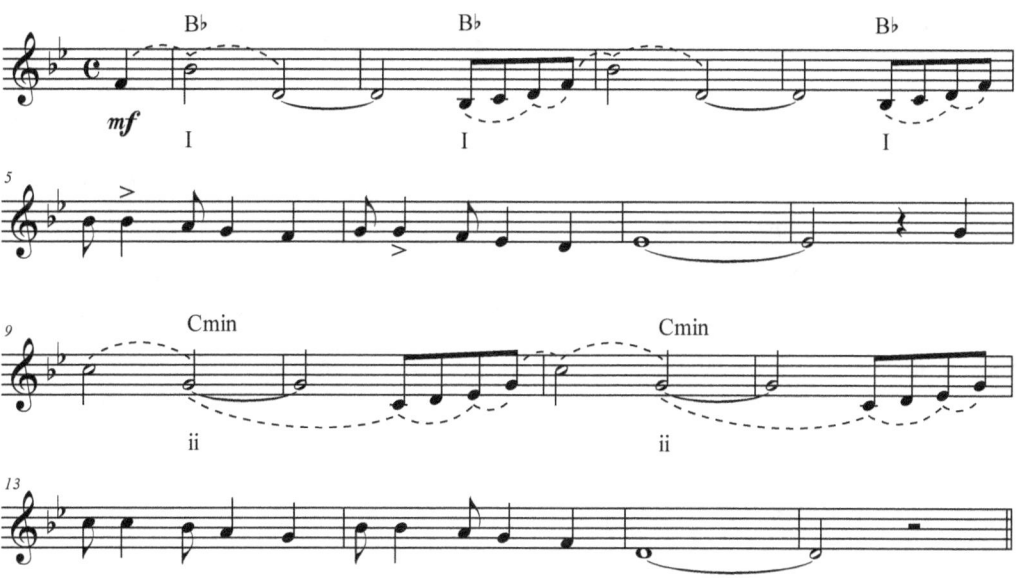

<u>Identify scale degrees at cadences</u>
First cadence (ms. 6-8): ^3 → ^4 (D to E♭);
Second cadence (ms. 12-14): ^5 → ^3 (F to D)

<u>Sequences?</u>
Second phrase is a copy of the first phrase a step higher, except for a few notes. Those few emphasized notes in the second phrase that are **not** a direct copy of the first phrase (up a step), are circled in the example below:

Figure 27-3: Sequences: What differs from the established pattern?

The change to G emphasizes C minor since this is the 5th of the C minor triad (or dominant in C minor). Notice that the entire motive in measure 14 is up a 3rd instead of a second. The most important effect of this change is that the emphasized note at the beginning of the measure receives special attention: the tonic note. To the ear, this signals an obvious change back to emphasizing B♭ Major instead of C minor.

Emphasized notes

Figure 27-4: Mark emphasized notes.

In the first four measures, the emphasized notes outline the B♭ Major triad (I). Notice that the emphasized G and E♭ in ms. 6 and 7 forecast the upcoming emphasis on C minor in the second phrase.

Okay, you now have a lot of information obtained by examining just the melody. Next, let's look at all of the logically musical possibilities for finding a chord for a note.

Chords Possible for a Given Note

For each note of the melody, there are the following possibilities. The note can be:

- the root of a chord
- the third of a chord
- the fifth of a chord
- the seventh of a chord
- a non-harmonic note

If it is a 7th, it also can be a non-harmonic note since it is dissonant with the bass, or it can be considered a chord tone. A non-harmonic note would normally have a stepwise resolution to a chord note. If a melody note has a duration that lasts through the length of time taken by one chord (or more) in the harmonic rhythm, it would be rare (though not an impossibility) for it to be a non-harmonic note. While these facts will eliminate some options, they still leave a wide range of possibilities.

Review "Normal" Chord Progressions

There is a "most natural" chord progression in the Tonal style. This progression leads into the cadence in each phrase. Following is a brief chart that lists the most normal progression of chords for chords built on diatonic scale degrees. Keep in mind that the tonic triad can appear (often in inversion) between any two chords in the chart. We will show this for major keys and then explain exceptions for minor keys.

Figure 27-5: Chart of normal chord progressions.

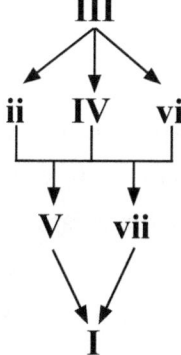

Keep in mind the following facts:
- Any chord can be repeated at the harmonic rhythm.
- The tonic triad, in any position, can go naturally to any of the other chords in the chart (i.e., can point back up the chart to any other chord).
- ii can also go immediately to IV, and vi can go immediately to ii or IV, prolonging dominant preparation before moving to the dominant.
- You can have a secondary dominant immediately precede any chord in the chart except vii° or I. (Recall that vii° is a form of V^7.)
- Chromatically altered chords: Remember that in addition to using ii, IV or vi as dominant preparations, you also have chromatic options of Neapolitan and augmented 6th chords.

Exceptions for minor keys:
- Dissonant triads do not usually have secondary dominants, so the ii° or vi° chord would not normally have a V/ii° or V/vi°, but the ii (minor triad) or ♭VI (major triad) quite frequently are preceded by a secondary dominant.
- You have the possibility of a ♭VII (major triad) chord in minor. It could also be preceded by a V/♭VII.
- If you write a ♭VII chord in a minor key, it can resolve naturally to: vi°, ♭VI, or (as V/III) to III.

That still leaves a lot of options, but we have narrowed the possibilities a bit. There is one more guideline that is absolutely the **most important**: your musical ear. An experienced musician will use his/her ear to determine what notes to write at every stage of the creative process, often without conscious recognition of what rules or guidelines are being followed. This happens because to a highly experienced musician, there is only a barely perceptible difference (or none) between musical structure and musical sound. His/her training is sufficiently complete that she/he can "see what she/he hears" and "hear what she/he sees". So that you also can reach this stage, always listen critically to the musical effects of what you write and let your musical sense be your own best and worst critic. Know the structure of what you are writing and listen to the sound created by that structure.

Order of Attack

There is no one place you <u>must</u> to start when you wish to harmonize a tune. You could start at the beginning; you could look for arpeggios and do those first; or you could begin at the end. All of these are legitimate approaches. However, it is always a good idea to fix where you are going – your intermediate and final goals – before you get too far along. It is a good practice in each phrase to start at the cadence. That way, you will know where you have to end-up. Frequently refer to your melodic analysis. After choosing chords for cadences, you might then look at how each phrase begins. Then start back at the cadence and complete chords backwards until you reach the beginning of the phrase. Pay particular attention to what chord options might be implied by specially emphasized notes and melodic structure. Melodic leaps within the range of a chord in the harmonic rhythm will give extra help in narrowing the options; normal chord progression will also assist. So, here is a suggested order of approach – at least until you gain further experience:

1. Choose chords of each cadence.
2. Choose a chord (or maybe two options) to begin each phrase.
3. Go back to a cadence and work backwards toward the beginning of the phrase, choosing chords at the harmonic rhythm. (**NOTE:** You might wish to consider whether or not it "sounds like" the harmonic rhythm speeds up in the last two or three chords at the cadence.)
4. Repeat 3 for each phrase.

This is not an inviolable procedure. As you gain more experience, you will use a variety of routes through the task of harmonizing a melody. The above algorithm is just a good way to begin learning how to do this. Many experienced arrangers will write a bass first and then begin determining chords. Such preferences may also depend upon what instrument you play: bass players may wish to write the bass line first; guitar (not bass guitar) performers will probably wish to write chords first. We will demonstrate applying the steps above.

<u>Cadence Chords</u>
Our melodic analysis has already determined the key, B♭, so we start with the cadence at the end of the first phrase. To aid the process, scale degree numbers are provided:

Figure 27-6: The first melodic cadence.

ms. 7 E♭: We can rule out a non-harmonic note due to the length of this note. The possible chords are:

E♭ as root: E♭ Major triad (IV);
E♭ as 3rd: C minor triad (ii);
E♭ as 5th: A dim triad (vii°);
E♭ as 7th: F⁷ (V⁷).

263

We can rule out A dim because it is a dissonant triad; not likely the goal of a phrase. We can also conclude that using F^7 would not be best because moving to the dominant (of B♭) would imply that we are going back to tonic right away. This is not the case; from your analysis, you know the beginning of the second phrase emphasizes C minor, not B♭. So, the best choice seems to be C minor, since that is where we will be going next.

For the chord in the last half of ms. 6, either the E♭ is a passing note, or the D is a neighboring note. One of these two notes will be a chord note. You could go through all of the logical possibilities, but that would be the long way around. If you play that cadence, you can hear how strongly the chord should lead to Cm, ii. Therefore, is either the E♭ or the D a chord member of V/ii? Yes! V/ii is G-B♮-D, so D is the 5th of that chord. One more thing to check: Is there a B♭ in the second half or the ms. 6 melody that would conflict with (create a dissonance against) writing a B♮ in one of the parts? No, there isn't. So, let's choose V/ii. Here's what we have so far:

Figure 27-7: The first harmonic cadence.

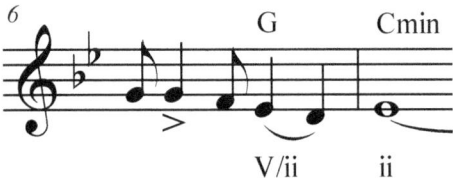

Completing the Chords in a Phrase

Now that we know where the phrase is headed, let's see where it starts.

Figure 27-8: The beginning of the first phrase.

A phrase that begins with scale degree 5 pickup to an emphasized scale degree 1 will have the I chord harmonizing that first emphasized note. So, for at least the first half of ms. 1, we will write the B♭ triad (I). So, the first phrase begins with I and ends with a V/ii → ii cadence.

From this point, the easiest way to continue is to start back at a cadence and work backwards to the first chord of the phrase.

Figure 27-9: First phrase – beginning and ending chords.

First half of ms. 6 – possibilities:
G a chord tone: E♭ Major (IV); G minor (vi); G⁷ (V⁷/ii); C minor (ii).
F a chord tone: B♭ Major (I).

We will rule out G⁷ and C min because we would like a B♭ in the harmony to make a chromatic ascent from B♭ → B♮ → C in some voice through measures 6 and 7. Let's choose the B♭ Major triad, even though the note G is emphasized in the melody. You could also choose G min⁷ if you wanted to include the G as a chord tone.

Ms 5:
For the second chord, B♭ or D min would be good choices here, choosing F as the chord tone. The D min has a more interesting color, so let's choose that chord.
In the first half of ms. 5, an excellent choice would be a B♭ triad.

Look at ms. 3 and 4:

Figure 27-10a: Measures 3 – 4 melody.

While you could choose B♭ for the entire motive, you would want to vary it somehow so that the other voices are not too static. In fact, at this point, since the melody skips around so much, it would be good to see if some voice could move in stepwise motion against it. So, look at and listen to the following two voices moving against one another for these two measures:

Figure 27-10b: Adding a line against melody in ms. 3-4.

Sounds good! Whenever you see the melody skipping around through more than one chord in the harmonic rhythm, you should see if you can write a second voice that moves in stepwise motion against it. Also, if you compare this to the first two measures, you see that they are identical, so whatever we work out here will be good harmonization for measures 1 and 2 also. You recall that we already chose the B♭ triad (I) for the first chord. The next chord has an A and D in it, so the D minor triad (iii) will work well here. Where does a iii normally lead? – to a dominant preparation, and the next chord should contain both G and D, so we choose a G minor triad (vi). Then for the last chord in this progression, you see that the B♭ triad is clearly outlined in the melody. One thing you can also decide at this point is that since vi is a dominant preparation, the second inversion of I would work best here because it has more of a dominant sound (since ^5 is in the bass). So, we will write I → iii → vi → I$^6_4$.

Figure 27-10c: Ms. 3-4 completed.

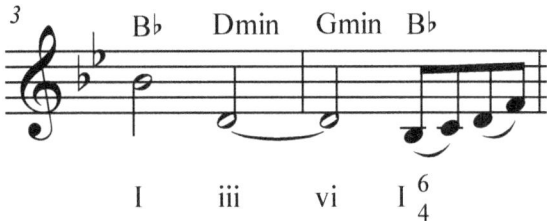

So, following is the entire first phrase with chords:

Figure 27-11: First phrase harmonized.

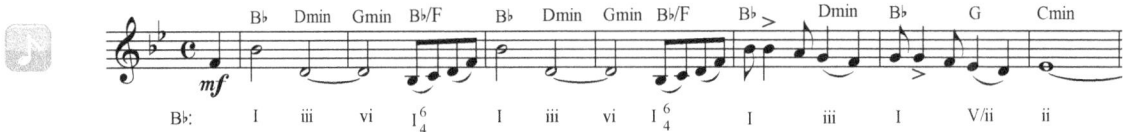

Finding chords for the second phrase will be left as an exercise.

Summary

In this chapter, we have looked at our analysis of a melody to see what it tells us that can help in choosing chords. In particular, you should pay attention to scale degrees, cadences, repetitions or sequences of motives or phrases (as well as what is different when something is repeated), implied harmonic rhythm, arpeggios, and notes that receive special emphasis.

Sometimes you have to look for all possibilities for a given note: chord note root, 3rd, 5th, or 7th; or non-harmonic note. Often, there are clues that help you to not have to examine all of these possibilities for each note, including the most important guide: your ears.

Memorize and keep in mind the chart of normal chord progressions:

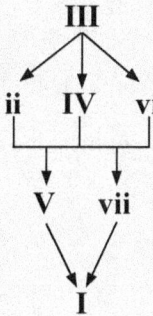

Finally, we presented a recommended order for choosing chords for each phrase: cadence first, then phrase opening, then the rest (normally working backwards from the cadence). Occasionally think about other voices during this process; they often can help narrow down the possibilities. In particular, you learned that if the melody is skipping around, some other voice is likely moving against this with stepwise motion.

Next

In the next chapter, it will be time again for a review of the unit. After that, the last unit will deal with four-part writing, transposition, jazz harmonies, modulation, and musical forms.

Quiz 27

Choose chords for the second phrase of the melody studied in this chapter. It is given below with a tenor line to help narrow the options:

Figure 27-12: Exercise to harmonize.

Notice that in the first four measures of this phrase, the tenor voice does exactly what it did in the first phrase, just up a step. The rest of the tenor line was written to create an ascending stepwise motion against the descending motion in the melody. You don't have to write any other voices, just supply the chord symbols above the staff and Roman numerals below.

CHAPTER 28: FOUR-VOICE WRITING

Objectives:

1. Write bass line and chords for a given melody.
2. Given only the soprano part and the key for a phrase of a chorale or hymn tune, write the other three parts.

Naturally, you cannot expect to learn all you will need to know about part writing in a single introductory course. However, this chapter will give you guidelines and practice for writing four parts given a soprano line. We will designate the four voices as soprano, alto, tenor, and bass (SATB) even though instruments other than human voices may be used on such parts. The best context for learning to write a four-voice passage is a hymn tune or chorale for which the assumed harmonic rhythm is one chord change per beat, and the voices are to be written in such a manner as to support independence of voices.

Voice Leading with Examples

Following are, again, the voice-leading guidelines. You have seen these before, but this time we tell you what you need to know in order to use them to write parts. They are ordered, below, **roughly** from the most stringent to the most flexible. Thus, the guidelines presented first should take precedence over those listed later on, in case you run into situations in which it is difficult or impossible to abide by both of two different "rules". Therefore, you should comprehend the purpose of following a "rule" and thus the consequences (in the sound produced) of **not** following it.

Most of the guidelines are there to improve the degree of independence and balance of voices or to support natural melodic tendencies. You might find any of these rules "broken" in works of experienced composers, but not without an understanding of the consequences. Such purposes are reviewed for each. Also, you are supplied with some examples, for the more critical guidelines, so that you can hear the consequence of following or **not** following the guideline. Some of these are subtle effects, so it may require some critical listening.

1. **Between any two voices, avoid parallel unisons, P5^{ths}, or P8^{ths}.** Reason: parallel motion at these intervals causes the combined sound of the two voices to merge and sound like one voice instead of two.

Figure 28-1: Parallel octaves.

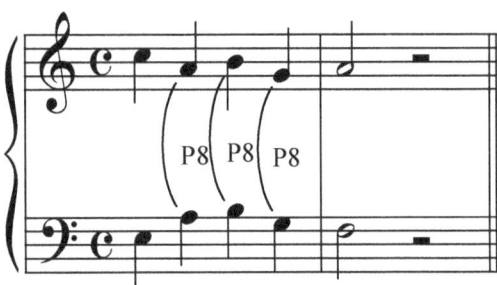

Hear how the lines tend to merge into one because of the parallel octaves.

2. **Normally avoid crossing voices.** Crossing voices makes it difficult for the ear to separate one voice line from the other; the ear has a tendency to jump from one voice to the other at the place where they cross unless the tone qualities of the voices or instruments are very different.

Figure 28-2a: Crossing voices.

On the second beat, it sounds like the soprano line takes the A instead of the F. One way to fix this is to move the alto line to the tenor:

Figure 28-2b: A fix for crossing voices.

Now it is easy to hear the correct soprano line.

3. **Normally avoid leaping in the same direction into a P5th or P8th**, except for a rare such motion at a cadence point. For just that moment when the leap to the perfect interval occurs, it would be more difficult for the ear to keep each of the two lines separate, particularly if another voice provides stepwise motion to one of the lines from which you leap.

Figure 28-3: Leaps in same direction to P5ths (+ fix).

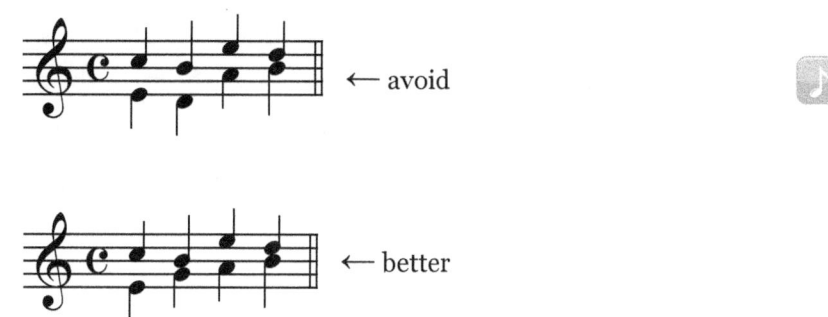

Can you hear that the second version is smoother? In general, between upper voices, when one leaps, try to move the others by step (or repeat common note).

4. **Normally avoid consecutive P5ths, P8ths, and unison-to-P8 or P8-to-unison** motions between two voices. "Consecutive" here means you leap in contrary motion from one such interval to the other. Although not as severe as "rule" #1 above, there is a danger, to some degree, of the sounds merging.

Figure 28-4: Consecutive P5ths.

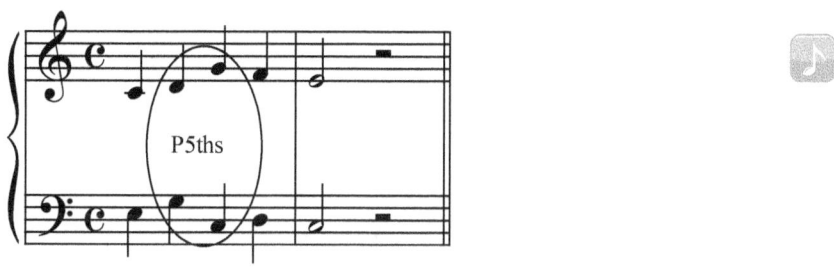

Can you hear the sounds subtly merge on the third beat? It is jumping from one P5th to another, even if not by parallel motion.

5. **Rarely allow adjacent voices to overlap.** There is some danger of the ear switching voices at such a point instead of being able to easily track each voice independently.

Figure 28-5: Overlapping voices.

Can you hear that the ear may track the alto voice to the G on the second beat instead of the E?

6. **The 7th of a dominant 7th chord should always resolve downward by step in the same voice.** The 7th of V⁷ is the 4th scale degree. It should take its normal resolution to ^3. The 7th of the dominant 7th always forms a tritone (recall this is the aug4th or dim5th interval) with the 3rd of the chord, which is scale degree ^7, the leading tone. This tritone is a dissonance which has a strong tendency to resolve into a more consonant interval.

Figure 28-6: Resolving the 7th of a V⁷.

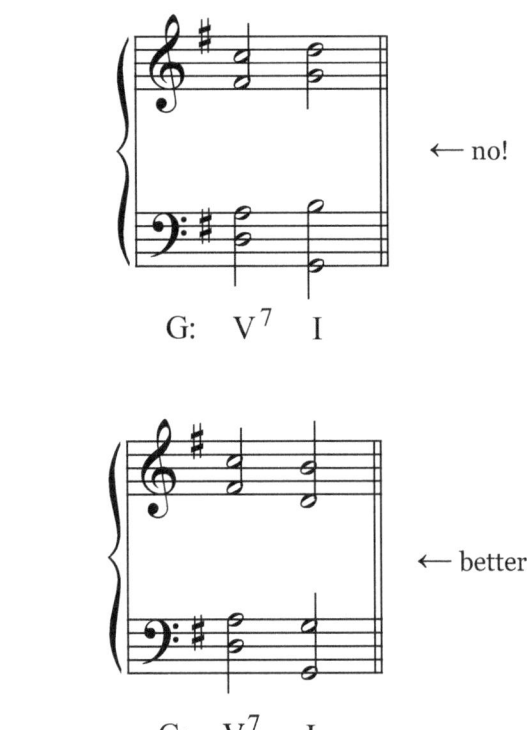

There are two problems: The first is that the 7th in the V⁷ does not resolve naturally to B; the second problem will be addressed in (8) below.

7. **A leading note in the soprano voice must resolve to tonic**, in that same voice. A leading tone in other voices also has a strong tendency for its natural resolution to ^1 if the prevailing harmony is dominant or a dominant substitute.

Figure 28-7: Resolving leading tone in soprano.

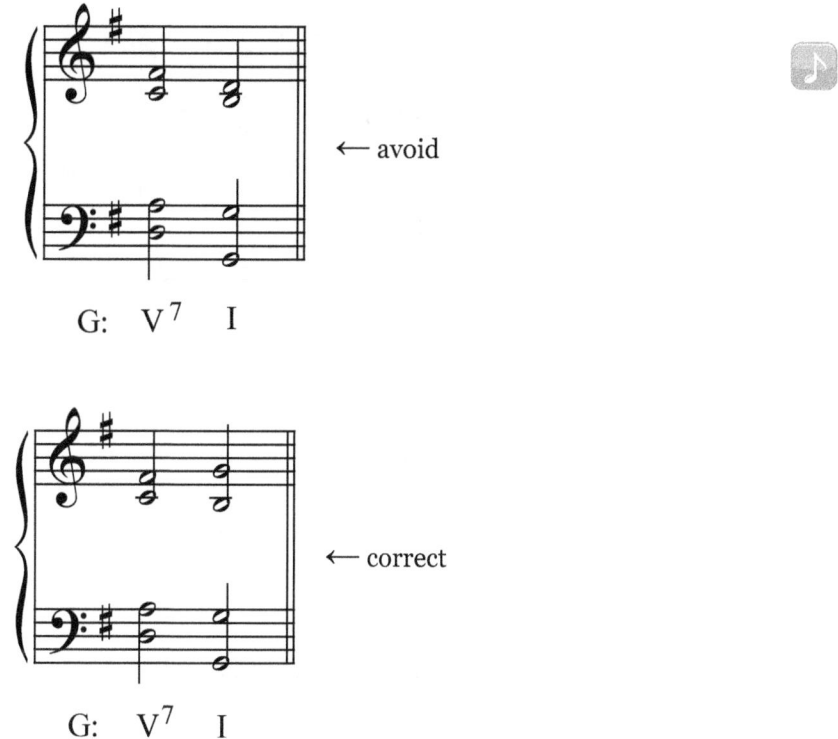

Can you hear in the first sample that the F♯ "wants" to go to G and does not? Notice in the correction, that you are forced to write a tonic triad without its 5th, but this still sounds better.

8. **Normally avoid parallel motion from a diminished 5th to a perfect 5th between two voices.** However, it is okay to go from a P5th in parallel motion to a dim 5th. Look at the example in 6 again and notice the dim 5th going to a P5th. This contributes to thinning out the texture at the second chord.

9. **For a diminished 7th chord, both the 5th and the 7th of the chord must resolve downward by step.** The most natural resolution for this chord is for each of the two dissonant tritones to resolve normally: contracting to a 3rd if it is written as a dim 5th, expanding to a 6th if it is written as an aug 4th. If you do not follow this guideline, you could create the situation you are told to avoid in #8 above.

Figure 28-8: Resolving a diminished 7th chord.

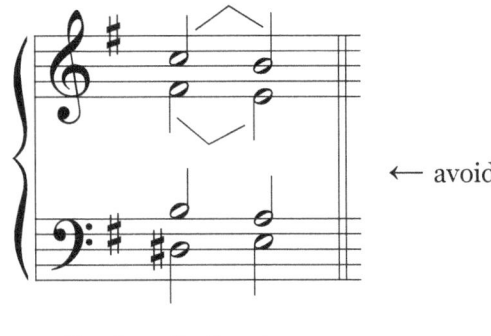

← avoid

E min: vii o7   i

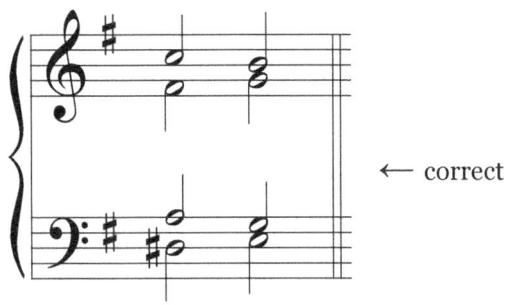

← correct

E min: vii o7   i

10. **Normally avoid parallel or similar leaps in any two voices two or more times in succession.** This simply makes it more difficult for the ear to track each line separately.

11. **Use a variety of the four types of motion between the lines.** Independence of lines is most easy to maintain with contrary motion, is quite easy with oblique motion, is more difficult with similar motion, and is most difficult with parallel motion. However, all four types are needed to maintain a pleasant balance of relative importance between the voices.

12. **Move the inner voices** – alto and tenor – **as little as possible to get to notes of the next chord.** However, they should move enough to be interesting; a voice that repeats or stays on the same note too long will fade from the listener's attention. (It's not much fun for the performer either!)

13. **Normally space upper voices closer together and lower voices farther apart**: no greater than a P8th between adjacent voices, except between bass and tenor, where larger intervals are quite common. This has to do with the nonlinearity

of human hearing: small intervals in a low register just sound like a kind of "growl" instead of the more pleasant sound we hear when they are played in a higher part of the pitch range.

14. **Notes common to consecutive chords should be repeated in the same voice if they occur in alto or tenor.** This just helps to achieve the smoothest motion from one chord to the next (if that is your intent).

15. **In any single voice, normally avoid consecutive augmented or diminished intervals, or interval leaps greater than an octave** (except bass, which can sometimes leap a 10th). This is a very loose guideline and the restriction about augmented and diminished intervals is based simply on the fact that it may be more difficult for the performer to hear the interval.

Review Doubling

Doubling guidelines are not as important as are voice leading "rules", but will help avoid many problems in voice leading and help produce a better sound.

1. Root position consonant triads: double the root.
2. 1st inversion primary triads (tonic, subdominant, & dominant): double the soprano.
3. 1st inversion secondary triads (other consonant triads): prefer double the bass; sometimes soprano.
4. 2nd inversion consonant triads: double the bass.
5. diminished triads: double the 3rd of the triad.
6. triad without a 5th: triple root, or double both root and 3rd.
7. V – VI in a minor key: double the 3rd of the VI chord.
8. 7th chord with missing 5th: prefer doubling the root.
9. Normally avoid doubling the leading tone.
10. Normally avoid doubling a chromatically altered note.

(The reason for the last two is that these notes have strong, natural melodic tendencies, so if you double such a note you will either have to choose to not resolve one naturally or you will end up with parallel octaves.)

Roles of Non-harmonic Notes and Timing

For the purposes of these exercises, we will assume simple meters in which the quarter note takes one beat and the harmonic rhythm is once per beat. In this context, it would produce rather boring results if there were no 8th notes. Therefore, consider using a variety of note durations: 8th, quarter, dotted quarter, and half notes (an occasional dotted half or whole note at a cadence would be okay). Tied note values are also found frequently in the chorale style. For these exercises, we will not insert rests into individual voices (sometimes done by students in an attempt to avoid voice leading problems); keep the sound going in each voice all the way to the final cadence.

A passage without non-harmonic notes is also not nearly as interesting as one that contains some. We will complete the chord notes first, and then look for ways to improve the musical momentum of the piece by making subtle alterations to add non-harmonic notes. The exception will be if we immediately hear an opportunity to treat a given soprano note (or a portion of it) as a non-harmonic tone.

Writing a Bass Line

We will supply a soprano voice and then have to write the other three parts. First, begin by doing a brief analysis of the soprano line and writing a bass line against it.

Example 1a. "O Herzensangst", last phrase of chorale tune from a chorale by J. S. Bach:

Identify the key: This is the last phrase; the piece ends on E♭; and the key signature has three flats. Conclusion: the chorale is in E♭.

Major.

Example 1b. Add scale degrees for the given part:

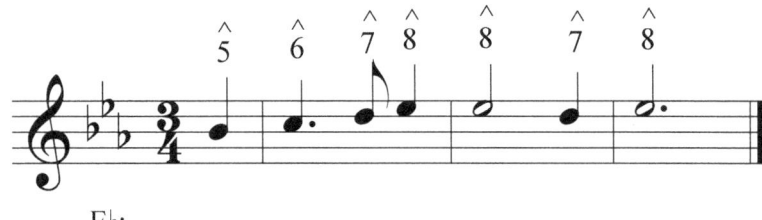

E♭:

Characteristics of melody: completely stepwise motion from dominant upward to tonic; specially emphasized notes are ^5 and ^8 (^1), with some emphasis on ^6. The cadence is terminal with a leading-tone to tonic motion at the end. One more characteristic of the melody near the cadence is that the E♭ in the next-to-last measure is a repetition of the same pitch in the previous measure and then moves downward by step; this looks like it could be treated effectively as a suspension.

First, write simplest bass and harmony: Even though the harmonic rhythm is one chord per beat, we can at first choose the main chords for the overall motion, and then improve them and the bass sine at the same time. So, you know the most common harmonic motion in such a piece is one of dominant preparation to dominant to tonic. For the purposes of this example, we will number the measures 1 through 4. You can anticipate an authentic cadence at the end, so measures 3 and 4 will contain a V→I motion. Since the E♭ in ms. 3 may be treated as a suspension, let's choose V as the main harmony for this measure. We will write bass notes and indicate chord at the same time.

Example 1c.

Then, a V is preceded by a dominant preparation, so we need a ii, IV, or vi chord that can be used to harmonize the C in ms. 2. Actually, any of these will work.

ii: F, A♭, C;
IV: A♭, C, E♭; or,
vi: C, E♭, G.

The IV will be a good choice:

Example 1d.

Eb: IV   V   I

There are several good bass notes and chords we could choose for the first chord to lead smoothly into IV. I (with E♭ in the bass) or I⁶ (with G in the bass) would work well. However, let's see if the secondary dominant would work here. The V/IV is identical with I, so to make it sound like a secondary dominant, we would need to use the 7th chord, V⁷/IV (E♭, G, B♭, D♭). We can deal with the D♭ later. For now, we observe that the B♭ in the soprano is a chord tone, so it can work. The motion in the bass works out well to use the G there, so we will write the chord in first inversion. Here is what we have for the main chord progression and its bass line.

Example 1e. Listen to the bass against soprano:

E♭: V⁷/IV IV   V   I

Notice the consonant parallel motion between these lines. Sometimes you may prefer contrary motion between soprano and bass; other times, consonant parallel motion will sound musically effective, as it does here.

<u>Improve bass and harmonic progression</u>: Now let's see if we can't make the bass a bit more interesting so that it provides a better motion with and against the soprano, and add some chords so that our harmonic rhythm of once per beat is more clearly stated. Look at the last beat of ms. 2 and notice that the soprano has ^1. You know we can put an inversion of a I chord between dominant preparation and dominant, so let's do

that and throw in some 8th notes to give the bass line a bit more motion. Notice the interesting interplay between the 8th note in the soprano line followed right after that with the 8th note motion in the bass.

Example 1f. Add some 8th notes to the bass.

Let's now provide a chord change in the second measure by switching to another dominant preparation. We can go to the ii chord in first inversion and keep the bass as it is; the 8th note in the soprano is a non-harmonic passing note.

Example 1g. Complete first measure after pick-up.

Now let's speed up the harmonic rhythm in ms. 3. We want this entire measure to be a prolongation of V. The second inversion of I can do this as well as going from V as a triad to V as a 7th chord just before the end. Will I$_4^6$ V V^7 work? They all have the same bass note, B♭. The suspension works very well because the E♭ is clearly a non-chord tone against the V chord on the second beat, and it resolves to a chord tone (D) on the 3rd beat. We have now completed choosing bass notes and chords. (Don't forget you can always change them later on if you run into problems filling in the other two lines.)

Example 1h. Bass and chords completed.

E♭:   V⁷/IV   IV   ii⁶   I⁶   I⁶₄   V   V⁷   I

Before going on, you should probably look back at bass against soprano and make sure that the voice leading guidelines for two voices are followed.

- There are no parallel unisons, 5^{ths} or octaves.
- There are no leaps in both voices; there is only one leap, in the bass, and it is set against stepwise motion in the soprano.
- The leading notes in the soprano move immediately to tonic.
- There are a variety of types of motion: parallel, oblique, and contrary.

So, we are okay to move onward.

Complete the Inner Voices

For this task, we will need to pay close attention to voice-leading and doubling guidelines. We will stick strictly to the first ten voice-leading guidelines and adhere to the doubling guidelines wherever possible. We start at the cadence. For the last chord, there are three octaves between bass and soprano, so we will get the best sound by stretching out the other notes a bit, but remembering that a wide space can separate Bass and tenor. Here's a good solution for the last chord (we need a G and a B♭):

Example 1j. Inner voices on last chord.

I

For the next chord to the left (V⁷), we have the root (B♭) and the 3ʳᵈ (D), so we need, as a minimum, to supply the 7ᵗʰ. Remember that the 7ᵗʰ of a dominant 7ᵗʰ must resolve downward by step, so if we put it in the tenor, we would have to change our minds about the distribution of the notes in the final chord. Let's leave the final chord alone and see if we can put the 7ᵗʰ in the alto voice.

Example 1k.

I$^6_4$ V V⁷ I

But what will we put in the tenor? The note that provides the closest motion to the next chord would be the B♭, following the guideline that we should, when possible, try to repeat notes common between two chords in the same voice. Recall that when you omit the 5th in a V⁷ chord, you double the root. So,

Example 1m. A solution for the last two chords:

$$\text{I}_4^6 \quad \text{V} \quad \text{V}^7 \quad \text{I}$$

For the next chord to the left, V, we will write the complete triad: B♭, D, F, but the D has not yet arrived because of the suspension, so it will be delayed into the next chord. That means that for alto and tenor, we need another B♭ and an F. Either way will work, but let's maintain the common note of B♭ in the tenor voice:

Example 1n.

$$\text{I}_4^6 \quad \text{V} \quad \text{V}^7 \quad \text{I}$$

Now the I_4^6 (B♭, E♭, G): Recall from the doubling rules that we should double the bass of a 2nd inversion consonant triad. The E♭ is already there in the soprano, so in the other two voices, we need B♭ and G. Let's maintain the common tone in the tenor again, which gives us a smooth step motion in the alto voice.

Example 1p.

I_4^6 V V^7 I

Back up one more chord to the I^6 (E♭, G, B♭). The G is in the bass against E♭, in the soprano. First, we need a B♭ somewhere. We will then need to double one of the notes of the chord. Bach chose to repeat common notes between chord in the alto and tenor even though this meant not following the most common doubling practice. For a I^6 chord, the soprano is most commonly doubled, but Bach chose to double the bass instead so that common notes could be maintained.

Example 1r.

IV ii^6 I^6 I_4^6

For the ii6 chord, there is already A♭ (3rd) in the bass and C (5th) in the soprano. So, we need an F and a note to double. However, before we do this, notice that we are coming from a IV chord, which is closely related to the ii, varying from it by only one note (E♭ in the IV chord must become F in the ii chord; the other two notes, A♭ and C, are in both chords). Let's put the changing notes in the alto, giving us a pleasant stepwise motion on up to the G in the next chord:

Example 1s.

IV   ii⁶   I⁶   I$^6_4$

The IV and ii triads are now complete; it is only a matter of what note/notes to double in the tenor voice. The doubling guidelines suggest the A♭, which is the root of IV and the bass of ii6. However, Bach decided to double the C instead. Why? We will find out when we look at the chord that leads into this one. You cannot always choose the best voicing by looking at only the next chord; often, you must also consider the chord that leads into it.

Example 1t.

IV   ii⁶   I⁶   I$^6_4$

Now we have just the first chord. The secondary dominant has the following notes: E♭, G, B♭, D♭. The critical note is the D♭ which, as the 7th of the chord, must resolve downward by step, which means to the C, so it must go in the tenor voice. Now we know why the tenor had to contain a C: the only other C is in the soprano, and we did not have the option of changing the soprano line to provide a D♭. G is in the bass, B♭ in the soprano, and D♭ in the tenor. This leaves E♭ for the alto – happily a good choice!
Here is what we have now:

Example 1v. All voices written.

Eb: V7/IV   IV   ii6 I6   I$_4^6$ V   V7   I

Listen to it. However, Bach did not stop there, and neither should you. Look for ways to add interest. Some embellishments containing non-harmonic notes? Adding some variety to the rhythmic sound? We need to do something about that rather boring succession of quarter note B♭'s in the tenor line.

Example 1w. Here is what Bach came up with:

Eb: V7/IV   IV   ii6 I6   I$_4^6$ V   V7   I

Notice that tying the G's together in the alto and changing two of the quarters in the tenor line help to add rhythmic variety. Notice how the 8th note activity gets passed around from one voice to another. This helps to draw listener attention to different voices, helping to create a balance among them. It says, "We are each important". Notice what he does in the alto voice just before the last chord. The 8th notes provide rhythmic activity, but he also cleverly solves the problem of the V^7 chord missing a 5th: he gives you both the 5th and the 7th of the chord in one voice by leaping from one to the other (F to A♭).

Quiz 28

It is your turn to try your hand at writing four parts for a chorale tune.

Example 2. "Now Let Us Come Before Him", first phrase only, by Nikolaus Seinecker (ca. ~1590):

G Major:

Since this is not the last phrase of the chorale tune, we give you the key. (Make sure you listen to what you are doing by playing the passage as you add notes. If you have the ability, play it yourself on a keyboard instrument; if not, use a music program such as Mozart, Sibelius, or Finale to enter the notes and have the program play it back for you.) HINT: There are two passing notes in this tune; treat the C in the last measure as a non-harmonic escape note.

CHAPTER 29: TRANSPOSITION & INSTRUMENTATION

Objectives:

1. Transpose a short, melodic passage at a specified interval and direction.
2. Given the concert key and the name of an instrument (e.g., F horn, B♭ clarinet, etc.), report the key in which music should be written for the instrument.
3. Report the instrumental family to which a specified instrument belongs.
4. Given the score for a short passage as it has been written for a given transposing instrument, rewrite the passage as it will sound in concert key, or identify which of several passages is the correct one for the concert key.

Transposition

We have discussed transposition as a passage repeated at a different pitch level. Another meaning of **transposition** is to write a passage in another key or to change the key of a passage. If you have written a passage in a certain key for a soprano singer and find that an alto wishes to sing the passage, you may need to transpose the passage to a bit lower key, so that it will be in a comfortable range for alto voice (see example below). When you transpose a passage, you keep all of the intervals exactly the same sizes; you just shift everything up or down. For example, we can transpose the following passage (which may have been written for a soprano singer):

Figure 29-1a: Passage for soprano.

Figure 29-1b: Transposed down a major 3rd (for an alto singer):

Notice that the succession of intervals between the notes is identical: ↑M3, ↑m2, ↑M2, ↓m6. We could write the first passage with an A Major key signature, and the second with an F Major signature, effectively changing the passage from A Major to F Major:

Figure 29-2: *Changing key signatures for the transposition.*

When you change key, a given passage may end up higher or lower than originally written. Consider the example above originally written in A Major. If you change to D Major, the passage may end up:

When you change keys with a passage, it is not enough just to make the intervals the same. You must transpose the entire passage up or down by the same interval that is between their key centers (tonics). For example, the distance between A Major and D Major is either a P4th up or a P5th down.

An equivalent and more useful way to accomplish the transposition is to keep all of the scale degrees the same, even to the way chromatic notes are written. Below, we will look at another passage. This time, we will show the scale degrees. First however, we need to examine a convention followed for indicating chromatically altered scale degrees.

If we wish to indicate that scale degree 4 is raised a half step, it will be written as ♯^4; if we wish to indicate that the 4th scale degree is lowered a half step, it is written as ♭^4. It does not matter whether you raise the note a half step by adding a sharp or changing a flat to a natural or changing a sharp to a double sharp – in all such cases, the alteration would be indicated the same: ♯^4. Likewise, lowering a note by a half step can be done by flatting a note, changing a sharp to a natural or by changing a flat to a double flat; all such alterations indicated by ♭^4.

Figure 29-3a: Using scale degrees to transpose: initial passage.

C min:

Suppose we wish to transpose this passage up one step and put it in D minor. We change to the D minor key signature and write each note a M2nd higher, keeping the same succession of scale degrees: $\hat{5}\ \hat{\sharp 7}\ \hat{8}\ \hat{6}\ \hat{4}$

Figure 29-3b: Transposed to D minor (using scale degrees).

D min:

Transpositions for Musical Instruments

At one time, all instruments were written in concert pitch: that is, they all produced tones at exactly the pitches written. With many modern instruments, this is no longer the case. What?! You mean there are instruments on which if you write a middle C, it will actually play some other pitch? Yes! To show how this works and why, let's look at a practical example: the family of clarinets.

There are actually five different sizes of clarinets: the smallest play relatively high pitches, and the largest play relatively low pitches. The average range of pitches for one clarinet is different from that of another clarinet. Thus, each particular position of your fingers on the holes and keys produces one pitch on one clarinet and a different pitch on another. Now, all of the clarinets have the same arrangement of holes and keys (with very few exceptions). The performer would like to know that if she/he places the fingers in a particular position, this would be the correct position for only one note. If this is not to be the case, what is the consequence for the performer? She/he would go to the trouble to learn scales in all of the keys on one instrument and then when she/he picks up another clarinet, the performer would have to learn a whole new set of scales: C Major would no longer be played the same way; in fact the note C would no longer have the same finger position on the different clarinets. Therefore, so that the clarinetist will have to learn only one position for a given note, the arranger or composer writes the note the player wants to see in notation, but understanding that this is not the pitch that will sound, the note is written on that note that will cause the desired pitch. An example is given in the next paragraph.

How does this work? Let's start with the B♭ clarinet (the most common clarinet used for solo melodies). This instrument sounds a M2 lower than written. Calling it a B♭ instrument means that if the player plays a written C, what will sound is actually a B♭; for the B♭ instrument, this is actually the B♭ that is a M2nd lower. So, if we want, for example, the instrument to sound the following pitch: 𝄞o , we would write: 𝄞o in order to get the G we want. What does this look like on the instrument?

Figure 29-4: A graphic showing the holes and keys on a clarinet.

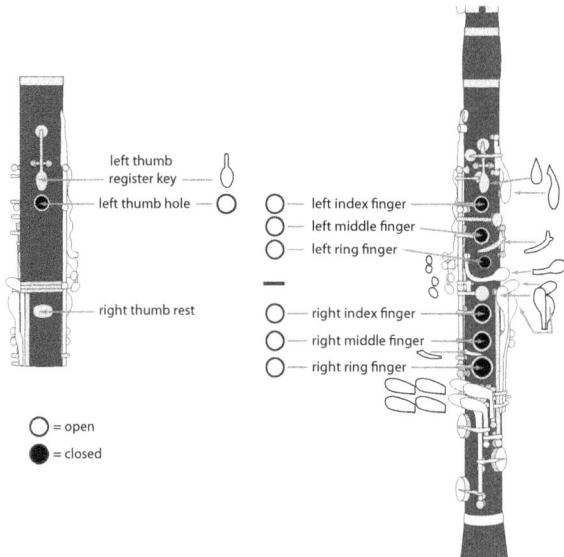

This is what would be pressed down to play the note A:

Figure 29-5: Fingering for written note "A".

In fact, we would write every note a M2nd higher than the sounding pitch. This means that we would write all passages for this B♭ clarinet in the key that is a M2nd higher than the key in which the pitches sound as written, called the ***concert key***. A piano is played in the concert key, so it sounds exactly where written. So do violins, violas, cellos, and many other instruments. If you have written a piece for piano in the key of F Major and wish the B♭ clarinet to play the top line, you will have to transpose the line up one step and write the clarinet part in the key of G Major (a M2nd up from F).

Several other instruments exist in families that include transposed instruments: trumpets, saxophones, flutes, horns, double reed winds. These transpositions are shown in Appendices, along with instrument ranges. In some cases, the transposition may indicate "8vb" (written below the note/s) meaning that the instrument will sound pitches an octave lower than written, or "8va" (written above the note/s) meaning that the pitches will sound an octave higher than written. This is done because the ranges for these instruments are so low or so high that the player would have to be reading many ledger lines below or above the staff on a continual basis. So, the notes are written within the staff range but sound lower or higher. For an instrument that sounds an 8ve lower, the arranger would write an octave higher. Of course for these instruments, the key would be the same. For example, a double bass sounds an 8ve lower than written. If you wish a double bass player to play this pitch: 𝄢, you must write: 𝄢 .

When writing a score that contains instruments of various transpositions, it is convenient to write the score in concert key (writing all notes on the sounding pitches). This practice facilitates seeing what chords you are writing and following voice-leading and doubling guidelines. Then when you break out the parts, you write a part for each instrument in the transposed form (for transposing instruments).

Additional Instrumentation Basics

Families of instruments

Instruments are grouped into families that have similar characteristics. Following are the conventional families of instruments with examples of some of the most common instruments that belong in each.

<u>Woodwinds</u>: piccolo, flutes, clarinets, saxophones, English horn, oboe, bassoon.
<u>Brass</u>: trumpets, French horn, trombones, euphonium, tuba.
<u>Percussion</u>: drums, cymbals, triangles, bells, xylophone, marimba, vibraphone.
<u>Keyboard</u>: (many of these are considered to be percussion instruments): piano, harpsichord, celesta, organ.
<u>Strings</u>: violins, violas, violoncellos (cellos), double basses, guitars, harps.

Woodwinds are further grouped by **single reed** (clarinets & saxophones), **double reed** (oboe, English horn, & bassoon), and **cross-blown** (piccolo and flutes).

Percussion are grouped by whether they are **pitched** (such as the xylophone) or **unpitched** (such as the drums – except for some, like the timpani, which are pitched). Strings are grouped by whether they are normally bowed (e.g., violins) or plucked (e.g., guitar).

Instrument ranges and registers

The *range* for an instrument is the span of pitches that can be played on that instrument from the lowest to the highest. Following is the practical range for a B♭ clarinet, shown for both concert (sounding) pitch and for transposed notes. While some players may be able to play higher notes than indicated, you should keep within the practical ranges unless you are writing for a particular performer who can and desires to play notes outside of that shown.

Figure 29-6: Range for B♭ clarinet.

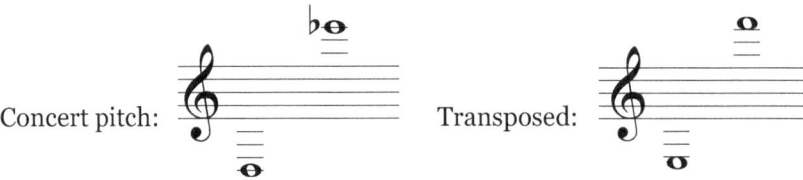

In this book, we refer to the "B♭ clarinet" to mean the one with this range.

The clarinet we refer to as the "bass clarinet" is also a B♭ instrument, but it is a much larger instrument and it sounds a major 9th below written. Following are the concert and transposed ranges for the bass clarinet.

Figure 29-7: Range for bass clarinet:

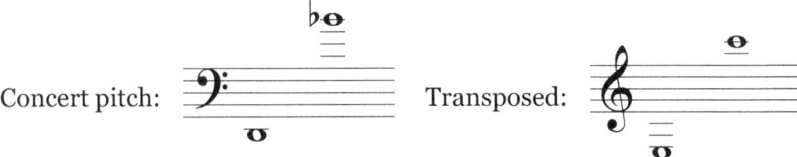

Notice that when you are writing for the bass clarinet in concert pitch, it is best to use the bass clef, whereas the transposed part is always written in the treble clef.

Not only do you have a range for each instrument, this range is normally broken up into two or three registers (sub-ranges). A register for a particular instrument is a portion of its range characterized by quality of sound (tone color). A performer must learn to alter technique needed to produce a "good" tone for different registers. Let's look at the clarinet again for an example. The B♭ clarinet has three registers. The bottom register covers the lowest octave and has a very rich, dark, open quality; its notes are very easy to produce. The middle register covers the following approximate range of notes (transposed):

Tones produced in this middle register are rather neutral and a bit weaker in quality; they are also a little bit more difficult to produce. In fact, the instrument has a "break point" around the note B♭ where the performer has to switch from closing nearly all of the holes to opening nearly all of the holes on the instrument concurrent with a change in reed pressure. Although the keys on a modern instrument help make the transition, playing a fast tremolo on notes on either side of this break point are very difficult and best avoided. In the high register, the sound quality is clear and bright; producing a good tone in this register requires greater lip pressure on the reed and a tightening of muscles around the lips. The overall range of all instruments, including the human voice, includes registers with similar differences in tone quality and technique.

Refer to Appendices for a chart of transpositions and practical ranges for the most common band and orchestral instruments.

Additional considerations
Breathing: For wind instruments – whether woodwind or brass – you should always be careful to give the player a short rest break periodically. If the passage is particularly demanding, make sure you insert some written rests; if not, use slurs to indicate passages to be taken with one breath so that the player knows she/he can take a quick breath between slurs.

Balance: For any given ensemble, pay attention to how well the instruments sound together and how each complements the sound of the total. Balance should be good enough for all parts to be heard. It is quite possible to write a passage in which the rather soft sound of a flute playing in a low part of its register gets completely masked (covered up so completely you can't hear it) by horns playing in the same pitch range.

There are special effects that can be considered when writing for orchestral or band instruments. Most of these concern the attack of a note, like a written accent, grace note, or mordent. Others affect the body of the sound, such as trills. A flute can produce a special shimmering effect with a technique called "flutter tonguing". A bowed stringed instrument has a number of such special effects that affect the character of the sound: tremolo, playing near the bridge, pizzicato (plucking the string). It is beyond the scope of this book to go into details of these effects. The best advice anyway is to get to know your performers. If you want to write a really interesting and fun piece for clarinet, get together with a clarinetist and do some workshops with the performer to learn what all she/he can do, what she/he likes to do, and how to notate such things. Write some short passage segments and have the performer play them so that you do some ear training regarding how the instrument sounds when your directions are followed.

The best advice we can give you: Write for performers, not just for instruments. Also, go to lots of live concerts and listen for how the instruments sound and are used together. How is balance achieved for a solo clarinet playing with a full orchestra? Sometimes the orchestra has to play rather softly in order for the solo instrument to be heard. Notice that whatever is on top of the pitch range or is rhythmically busy draws listener attention. Notice that for a large ensemble, not everyone is playing all of the time. Many instruments may have several **measures** of rest before coming back in.

Try your hand at reading a score while listening to a recording. Many publishers sell study scores which are perfect for this practice. Following a score will require quite a bit of practice; make sure you know where all of the instruments are located on your score. Woodwinds will be on top, then brass, then percussion and keyboard instruments, and finally strings at the bottom. Tap the beats and keep up with how fast the measures are going past; that way, you can keep up with where you are in the score even if you have trouble following an individual line. Follow only one line at a time; try to pick the line for an instrument that stands out in the body of sound.

SUMMARY

Naturally you cannot cover the entire topic of instrumentation in a single section or chapter of a book. On the college level, there are entire courses devoted to instrumentation or orchestration. We have given you only a taste of this discipline in this chapter. Refer to Appendices whenever you need to know instrument transpositions or ranges.

Chapter 29: Transposition & Instrumentation

NEXT

Next you will examine some introductory principles of jazz harmony: jazz scales and chords. You will find that each chord has a scale or set of scales associated with it. This facilitates jazz improvisation: when a jazz musician reads a particular chord symbol, she/he knows which scale tones can be played with that chord.

Quiz 29

1-3. The following passage is to be transposed by the prescribed interval:

1. Transpose the given passage <u>up</u> a **minor 3rd**.

   a.

   b.

   c.

   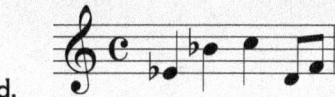
   d.

2. Transpose the given passage <u>down</u> a **Major 9th**.

   a.

   b.

   c.

   d.

3. Transpose the given passage <u>down</u> a **Perfect 5th**.

a.

b.

c.

d.

4. Concert key for a given passage is G minor. The key in which an F horn (sounds note F when a C is played) should be written is:

   a. F minor
   b. C minor
   c. D minor
   d. B♭ minor

5. Concert key for a given passage is E♭ Major. The key in which an E♭ clarinet (sounds note E♭ when a C is played) should be written is:

   a. G♭ Major
   b. C Major
   c. E♭ Major
   d. G Major

6. Concert key for a given passage is F Major. The key in which a B♭ saxophone (sounds note B♭ when a C is played) should be written is:

   a. G Major
   b. B♭ Major
   c. F Major
   d. E♭ Major

7. Concert key for a given passage is G Major. The key in which an A clarinet (sounds note A when a C is played) should be written is:
   a. E Major
   b. E♭ Major
   c. B♭ Major
   d. C Major

8. A violin is in the _____ family.
   a. woodwind
   b. brass
   c. percussion
   d. string

9. A trombone is in the _____ family.
   a. woodwind
   b. brass
   c. percussion
   d. string

10. A cymbal is in the _____ family.
    a. woodwind
    b. brass
    c. percussion
    d. string

11. An oboe is in the _____ family
    a. woodwind
    b. brass
    c. percussion
    d. string

12. Here is a passage written for the performer of an E♭ saxophone, which sounds a M6th below written.

Which of the following shows the passage in the concert key, where it would sound?

a.

b.

c.

d.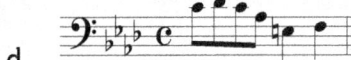

CHAPTER 30: JAZZ HARMONY

Objectives:

1. Explain similarities and differences between classical harmony and jazz harmony.
2. Identify which note/notes of an extended tertian chord (7th, 9th, 11th, or 13th) could be omitted.
3. Explain the structure of the sixth chord in jazz; write the notes for a specified (jazz style) sixth chord.
4. As practiced in jazz, name the scale to be used with a given chord in a specified key.
5. Given a scale written on staff, identify with which one of several chords the scale would commonly be used.

Some Fundamentals in Jazz Harmony

In Classical Tonal theory, you learned that certain intervals above the bass were dissonant, and that such dissonances would eventually resolve into consonances. An example of this fact in Classical music is that the final chord in such a piece will be a consonant triad, not one that includes a dissonance above the bass note. In Jazz style, this is not the case. It is very common in a jazz piece for it to end on a seventh chord, or even ninth. Seventh chords are more frequent in many jazz pieces than are triads. It is very important in jazz music to be aware that some notes are more dissonant than others; that is, some will have a strong tendency to resolve, and others, though still dissonant, will have a weak or practically nonexistent tendency to resolve.

Voice leading in jazz is different. In a jazz ensemble, an entire section or the entire band may be playing in mostly parallel and similar motion. The effect is that the voices will no longer sound independent, but this is what the jazz composer or arranger wants. She/He wants to create the impression of a single line, the melody, which has a rich harmonic texture. The precautions against parallel octaves or 5^{ths} do not apply in this style because independence of individual voices is no longer a goal. Where one does want a line to stand out independently of another line, the same classical voice leading rules do apply. The bass line must sound the succession of pitches that clarify harmony, so the bass line often does not move in parallel or similar motion with the other instruments. In a small jazz combo (say three or four instruments), independence of lines is important, so the classical voice leading guidelines are followed, including special attention to rhythmic independence.

Another feature of jazz that is important in a study of jazz harmony is the practice of improvisation. In such practice, it is essential that when a performer reads a particular chord, she/he immediately knows which scale notes will sound natural when played with that chord. Therefore, jazz musicians associate full scales with each chord in a key.

Jazz has undergone many stylistic transitions, from ragtime, to blues, to swing, and on to modern jazz. The foundational concepts of jazz harmony apply to a lot of popular music even for popular pieces that are not written in a jazz style. It is not our purpose to study all of these stylistic transformations, but the result in today's jazz and popular idioms is a set of structural characteristics of jazz harmony and its relation to improvised melody.

Harmonic Structures

<u>7th, 9th, 11th, and 13th chords.</u>
Although secundal and quartal chords are part of the harmonic resources in jazz, most of the chords are tertian. Among tertian chords, the 7^{ths} of seventh chords are considered chord tones. Although they add a certain tense interest that the triad does not have, the 7^{ths} in jazz do not create a strong tendency to resolve. The 9th, 11th, or 13th of a chord does carry a relatively strong tension and has a greater tendency to "want" to move and propel the line forward, in whatever part it appears.

Also, recall from our study of tertian chords in an earlier section that these chords often do not contain all of the notes in the stack of 3^{rds}. To review, here are some common structures for 7th, 9th, 11th, and 13th chords:

Figure 30-1: Structures for extended tertian harmonies.

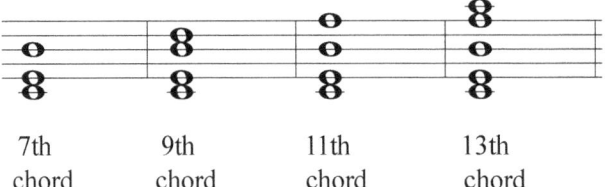

7th chord   9th chord   11th chord   13th chord

Notice that the 5th is missing from all of these, and that the 9th is missing from the 11th and 13th chords. These are common omissions. There are several reasons why one may wish to omit some of these notes: voice leading may dictate doubling of some notes instead of having a full chord; the number of instruments playing may limit the number of pitches that can sound at one time; the arranger or composer may want the richer sound of one of these chords but may not want the denser texture that would result from so many different pitch classes sounding together. Notice that for the 13th chord, the 11th gives consonant support for the 13th. By forming the interval of a third, the 11th gives the 13th the consonant anchor it needs to be heard as a part of the chord. Without such consonant support, the 13th would be treated as a non-chord tone and would be resolved as such (passing note, neighbor note, suspension, etc.).

Giving consonant support to non-harmonic notes

Even notes that are clearly non-harmonic notes at the harmonic rhythm of a jazz piece are frequently given consonant support. Such support does not detract from their function as non-harmonic notes, but such tones add a harmonic richness to even these non-harmonic tones. Notice in the following passage that the second melodic note is given harmonic support even though it is clearly just a passing note, and this does not distract from hearing the chord during the first half of the measure as the D minor 7th chord.

Figure 30-2: Giving consonant support to a passing note.

If you spell the chord on the second 8th note, you might refer to it as the E minor 7th chord, but it is just a way of giving diatonic consonant support to the passing note, adding a richness to its sound that is like the same sound (minor 7th sonority) as the rest of the passage. This is very common practice in jazz.

Sixth chords in jazz

In jazz, one can add to the richness of a triad by adding the 7th to the chord. For example, the tonic triad in F Major could be enriched by adding the major 7th:

Figure 30-3: Major 7th chord.

Also, consonant (major or minor) triads in jazz and popular music can be enriched by adding a note to the triad at an interval of a major 6th, without changing the chord function. Here is the tonic triad in F Major enriched by adding the sixth:

Figure 30-4a: The 6th chord in jazz.

Wait a minute! Isn't that the D minor 7th chord in first inversion? In <u>classical</u> theory that is certainly the way we would interpret it. Whether it is interpreted in jazz or popular music as a sixth chord or the first inversion of a seventh chord depends upon the key you are in and how the harmony progresses. If the bass note is tonic, as in the example above, it would function as I6. However, suppose the key for the above chord were C Major and this chord progressed on to the dominant chord. In such a case, interpreting the chord as the first inversion of ii7 would be appropriate; in A minor, it could also function as the iv7 chord in first inversion. In both of these latter cases, the chord symbol would be as follows:

Figure 30-4b: Same chord interpreted as a 7th chord (1st inversion).

With regard to chord progressions, the same expectations exist in jazz as in classical music. The same chart of root progressions apply: the mediant leads to a dominant preparation, dominant preparation to dominant, and dominant to tonic. Secondary dominant chords function as with classical music. There are a number of dominant preparations that are formed with chromatic alterations, such as augmented 6th chords. All of the expectations with regard to root progressions still hold.

Relating Scales to Chords

Improvisation is at the foundation of jazz. Every jazz musician must learn improvisational techniques. Part of this technique concerns the need to answer the question: What notes can one play with a given chord? For an improvisational solo passage, the composer or arranger provides only the main chord progression and a series of slashes to indicate the passing of beats. Here is what a portion of such a passage might look like:

Figure 30-5: Slash marks in improvised passage.

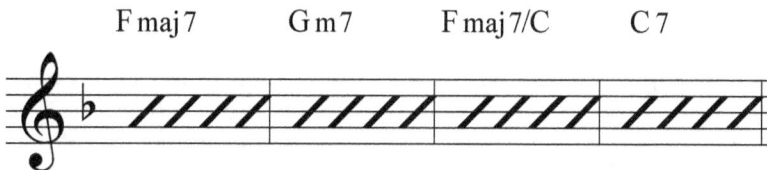

Each slash mark indicates one beat. The performer improvises notes that fit the style of the piece, often borrowing motives from the main melody, and plays notes that fit with the indicated chord.

Well, she/he knows that the chord notes can be used. For example, with the first chord, FM7, the performer could play any or all of the following notes: F, A, C, E. However for non-harmonic notes and other notes that might fit with the chord, what could be played? The general answer is that for every chord, there is a scale that sounds good with it. There are many chords in jazz, and each different type of chord could have a different scale. In classical music, we build scales on the tonic in a given key. In jazz, the musician thinks of a scale in relation to a chord, building the scale on the root of that chord. It is beyond the scope of this course to introduce a comprehensive list of all such chords and scales, but we will introduce you to some of the most common so that you can begin to get some experience with jazz harmonies.

Case 1: Use diatonic notes in the key.
To determine what scale goes with a chord, the first step is to write the notes of the given chord. For example:

Figure 30-6a: Write chord notes.

There are three notes missing. For those, we will need to know what key we are in. If the key is B♭ Major, with the Cmin7 functioning as ii7, then we use the diatonic notes for the key to fill in the rest of the notes:

Figure 30-6b: Scale in key of B♭.

Now we have the scale of notes that will go with a Cmin7th chord in the key of B♭ Major. A jazz musician will further classify this scale by the positions of the half- and whole-steps in it. In the above case, it is the C Dorian scale (half steps between 2&3 and 6&7).

If the key were E♭ Major, with the Cmin7 acting as vi7, the scale would use the notes of the E♭ key, which would require the note A♭:

Figure 30-6c: Scale in key of E♭.

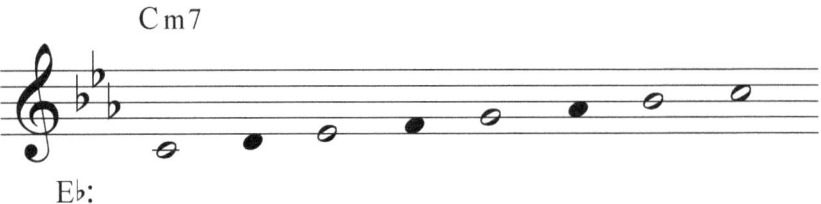

Now the half steps are between 2&3 and 5&6, making this the C Aeolian scale (or the natural minor scale).

<u>Case 2: A melody already written contains chromatic alterations.</u>

If the musician knows what notes are already written for a different instrument for that same place in the score, she/he can get scale notes from that passage. This is especially needed if there are chromatic alterations in the written part. For example, suppose you must play notes to go with a Cmin7 chord and the following is a passage to be played at that same time by another instrument (shown in concert pitch):

Figure 30-7a: Chord with passage in another instrument.

In this case, you know that the other notes should be the same as in the passage above so that your part will not clash with the one already written. So, now the scale, regardless of what key you are in, should be:

Figure 30-7b: Correct scale for Case 2.

For this situation, the scale is C Phrygian (half steps between 1&2 and 5&6).

Case 3: The given chord contains chromatic alterations.

How would one decide what scale to choose if the given chord itself contains chromatic alterations? Use diatonic notes of the key you are in except where it would produce an augmented 2nd with another note. For example, if you are in C major and need a scale for the D♭ Maj7 chord, first write down the chord notes:

Figure 30-8a: Chord containing chromatic alterations.

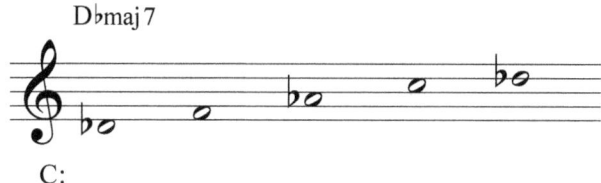

C:

In C Major, the E would make a +2 with the D♭; the G would make a M2 and a m2 with the F and A♭, and the B would form a +2 with the A♭. So, the only note diatonic in C Major that would form normal half- or whole-steps, would be the G:

Figure 30-8b: Add the note diatonic in the key (G).

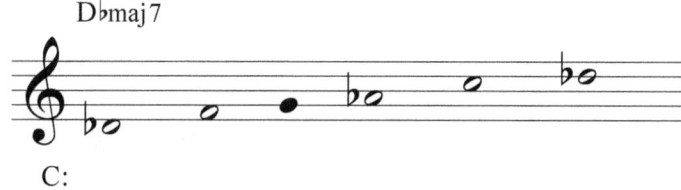

C:

For the other two notes of the scale, choose notes in C Major that would form only whole steps with the notes on either side.

Figure 30-8c: The completed scale for Case 3.

which is the D♭ Lydian scale. (Review modal scales from Chapter 20 if you do not recall these.)

The above procedures work for 6th or 7th chords built on consonant triads. How about 7ths built on a diminished triad? Half-diminished 7th chords (the diminished-minor 7ths) will generally use the diatonic collection of notes from the prevailing key.

Case 4: the diminished 7th chord.
The fully diminished 7th chord is a special case. It usually shows up as the vii7 in a minor key. Here are the chord notes for vii7 in C minor:

Figure 30-9a: The diminished 7th chord.

The scale that goes with a fully diminished 7th chord is the octatonic scale that includes the chord and the tonic note in the key. The only octatonic scale that fits those criteria for B dim7 in C minor is:

Figure 30-9b: The scale for a dim 7th (an octatonic).

Case 5: the augmented triad.
For an augmented triad, the most common scale to use is the whole-tone scale. For example, the G+ chord could support a melody made up of notes from the following scale:

Figure 30-10: The augmented triad and scale (whole-tone)

Case 6: The augmented-Major 7th.

The augmented triad with the major 7th added is also a special case. This chord can result from building a 7th chord on III in a minor key, using the melodic minor form:

Figure 30-11a: The augmented-major 7th chord.

The scale that goes with this chord is a Lydian scale with a raised 5th, called the Lydian augmented scale:

Figure 30-11b: The Lydian augmented scale.

This places a half step between 5&6 instead of 4&5 (as it is in the pure Lydian mode).

There are many more chord structures and variations of scales. The general guidelines are to (1) use all of the chord notes, (2) choose from the rest notes that are part of the key you are in, and (3) avoid forming augmented 2nds in the resulting scale. Remember that in a minor key, you have the possibility of chromatically changing some scale notes in the key due to alterations for melodic and harmonic minor forms.

SUMMARY

Similarities between classical and jazz harmony:
- Root progression expectations are the same.
- The bass is the foundation for establishing the harmony.

Differences between classical and jazz harmony:

In jazz, the 7^{ths} in 7th chords are usually treated as chord notes, not non-harmonic tones.
- In jazz, several parts may be written in parallel style, giving harmonic texture to a single line. Independence of voices is more important in classical styles.
- In classical style, all of the music is written out, with only occasionally some minor ornamentation not notated. In jazz, improvisation is common practice.

Jazz chords

Jazz and popular music styles make frequent use of extended tertian chords: 7ths, 9^{ths}, 11^{ths}, and 13^{ths}. In fact, 7th chords are more frequent in jazz music than are triads.

Non-harmonic notes are frequently given consonant support even though the prevailing chord is different from that used to support the non-harmonic note.

A sixth chord in jazz has the same structure as does the 1st inversion of a seventh chord in classical music. Whether it functions as a 6th chord with the bass as root or as an inverted 7th chord will depend upon the harmonic progression.

Jazz scales

Jazz scales are formed in relation to the root of the chord, with scale degree 1 being the note of the chord's root. Only for a chord built on the tonic would such a scale correspond with how a scale is identified or formed in classical theory. You were introduced to forming jazz scales for six different cases. These cases, while covering the most common situations, are not comprehensive; there are many more chord and scale structures than those introduced in this book.

Case 1: Use diatonic notes in the key. This case is used under two conditions: the chords contain only diatonic notes, and there are no other parts that use chromatic alterations.

Case 2: A melody already written in another part contains chromatic alterations even though the chord itself uses only diatonic notes.
Case 3: The given chord itself contains chromatic alterations.
Case 4: A special scale (octatonic) to be used for fully diminished 7th chords.
Case 5: a special scale (whole tone) that can be used with augmented triads.
Case 6: a special scale (Lydian augmented) that can be used with augmented-major seventh chords.

Next

Next we will go into techniques for changing the key in the middle of a passage of music, a process called "modulation".

Quiz 30

1. Describe two similarities between classical harmonic practice and jazz harmony.

2. Describe three differences between classical music and jazz that affect harmonic and melodic practices.

3. In jazz, the 7th of a chord is usually treated as a:
   a. chord note
   b. non-harmonic note

4. Write the notes for a D6 chord in jazz (functioning as tonic).

5-10: All of these are in relation to jazz practice.

5. In the key of C Major, the scale used with the D min7 chord is:
   a. C Ionian
   b. D Dorian
   c. D Locrian
   d. D Aeolian

6. In the key of C Major, the scale used with the E min7 chord is:
   a. E Locrian
   b. E natural minor
   c. E Phrygian
   d. C Major

7. In the key of C Major, the scale used with the B min7♭5 chord is:
   a. B Locrian
   b. B diminished Phrygian
   c. B natural minor
   d. B octatonic

8. The following scale would be used with which chord?

   a. F min7
   b. F+
   c. C♯ dim
   d. C♯ m7♭5

9. The following scale would be used with which chord?

   a. G Maj6
   b. G dim7
   c. B♭ min7
   d. G min7

10. The following scale would be used with which chord?

    a. D♯ min7
    b. E min7
    c. D♯ dim7
    d. B♭ Maj7

CHAPTER 31: MODULATION, PART 1

Objectives:

1. Define and distinguish between modulation and tonicization.
2. Explain the three conditions that must occur, in order, in the process of changing keys.
3. Given two keys, identify whether they are closely or distantly related.
4. Identify which of several given chords could be used as a pivot chord between two specified keys.
5. Given a short, four-voice passage on a grand staff, provide each of the following:
    a. the original key and the key to which the passage changes;
    b. the position of the pivot chord by measure and beat;
    c. each Roman numeral the pivot chord has for each of the two keys;
    d. the Roman numeral (+ inversion numbers, if applicable) and prevailing key area for at least one other specified chord in the passage.

Modulation is the process of changing keys within a piece. There are several ways to get to the new key from the current one. Some of these techniques are rather simple; others more obscure or lengthy. Sometimes the piece barely hints at a new key and then goes back to the original without clearly establishing the new key. We have seen some very short examples of this in the use of secondary dominants.

Tonicization

Tonicization is a process of making some scale degree other than ^1 sound like a <u>temporary</u> tonic. Unlike a full modulation, the passage does not continue in the key of this new tonic. Following is an example of this process.

Example 1. Two phrases from J.S Bach chorale, "O Be Glad, My Soul, Be Cheerful":

While you could analyze the A Major chords as V/V secondary dominants, we show the new temporary tonal area of D in order to clarify that all four of those chords in measures 3 and 4 can be heard relative to D Major. After that brief tonicization of ^5 (I in D is V in G, the prevailing key), the piece goes right back into G Major. So, the above is an example of tonicizing D, the 5th scale degree in G Major, making that note sound like a temporary tonic. Let's look at one which tonicizes the 4th scale degree.

Example 2. "Unto Us Today a Child is Born", first two phrases, J. S. Bach chorale:

How does one locate such tonal areas? Look for the accidental. In this case, the F♮ at the beginning of the second full measure is not in the key of G Major. When do you know for sure that it has gone back into the original key? Look for the accidental to be cancelled. This happens when the F goes back to F♯ on the first beat of the 3rd measure (tenor voice). Notice that we have identified two chords that can be heard to have dual functions. The C Major triad at the end of the first full measure is the IV chord in G and the I chord in C; likewise, the G Major triad just after the first fermata is V in C and I in G.

In the above and similar cases, a note (other than tonic) in the scale of the prevailing key is given special emphasis by tonicizing it. Sometimes this involves only the secondary dominant of that note and the consonant triad built on that scale degree. Other times, it involves a longer chord progression in the temporary tonal area, involving dominant preparation followed by V-I progression. Such changes are only temporary, immediately moving back to (or toward) the prevailing key of the piece.

Overview of Modulation

Whereas tonicization is temporary, modulation establishes the new key and continues in it for some time. Whether the result is very temporary (tonicization) or more long-term (modulation), there are **three conditions** that occur with the process of changing key:

1) The first key must be clearly established through functional chord progression to a cadence.

2) One or more chromatic alterations will be included in one or more chords, signaling a shift away from the previously established key.

3) The new key is confirmed by a functional chord progression establishing the new tonic.

Techniques of modulation are simpler in some cases and more complex in others. Modulations are traditionally classified by how close is the relationship between the old and the new keys. For **closely related keys**, the modulation process can be relatively simple; for **distantly related keys**, the process is usually more involved. How close or how distant is this relationship depends upon how many chromatic alterations are required to effect the change from one to the other. For example, the relationship between C Major and F Major is close because there is only one chromatic alteration needed: Changing from C Major to F Major, the B♮ would have to be changed to B♭; to go from F Major to C Major, the B♭ becomes B♮. The keys C Major and D♭ Major are distant: there are five notes different between these two keys. When the key signatures differ by not more than one sharp or flat, the keys are **closely related**; keys whose signatures differ by more than one sharp or flat are **distantly related**. In this section, we will describe modulation techniques that are most commonly used for changing between closely related keys. Let's bring back the Circle of Fifths to examine these:

Figure 31-1: The Circle of Fifths – Keys.

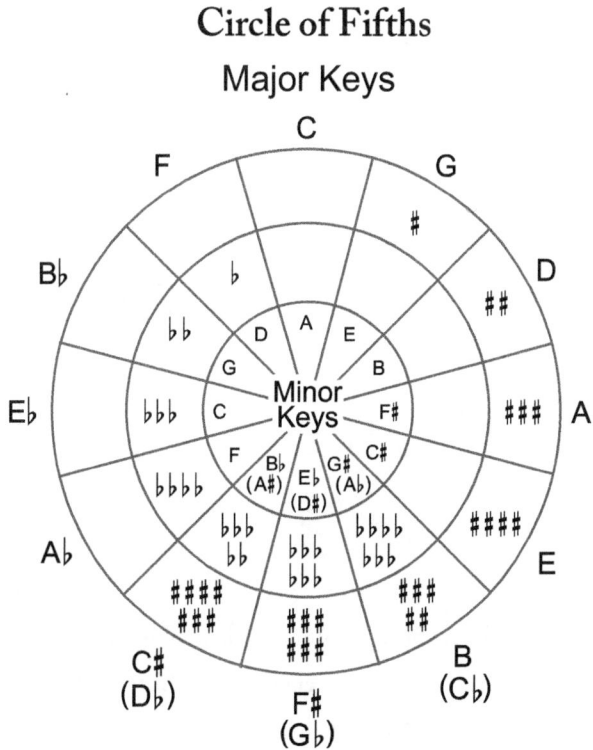

Keys, both Major and minor, that are adjacent on the circle (or have the same signature)

are closely related. All other pairings are distant. For example, looking at the circle, the Key of G Major has five keys closely related to it: C Major, D Major, A minor, E minor, and B minor. Modulation to a relative minor or Major key is close; modulation to a parallel minor or Major is distant.

Common (Pivot) Chord Modulation

The diatonic scales of closely related keys have at most one note different between them. This also means that there are several triads that are the same. To discover what they are, build consonant triads on scale degrees, placing them one below the other on the notes common to both. Here is an example for comparing C Major with F Major:

Figure 31-2: Comparing chords: C Major with F Major.

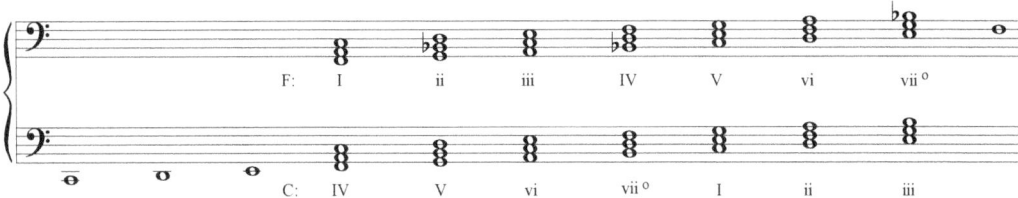

Comparing the chords, we can see that the following triads are the same in both keys: F Major (I in F; IV in C), A minor (iii in F; vi in C), C Major (V in F; I in C), and D minor (vi in F; ii in C).

No matter whether you are going to stay in the new key or not, the technique of using the pivot chord works the same way. We are talking about merely the technique of getting from one key into another, so these methods work in both modulation and tonicization.

Example 2b. Look back at the first phrase from Example 2:

Which is the pivot chord? It is the C Major triad, which functions as IV in G and I in C. The pivot chord always immediately precedes the chord that contains the chromatic change needed to form a chord in the new key.

In modulating to a relative key, although the key signatures are the same, in minor, there must be a chromatic alteration to form the leading tone, a note not in the relative major key. The following example shows how this leading tone in a minor key must be cancelled to be solidly in the relative major. The pivot chord is one common to both E minor and G Major: the A minor triad (iv in E minor; ii in G Major).

Example 3. From Sonata in E minor, by Joseph Haydn:

E min: i   V^7 i   i   V/iv iv
G Maj: ii   V   V^7 I

The importance of the pivot chord is emphasized by being preceded by its secondary dominant at the end of the 3rd measure. Then you get A minor, the pivot chord, then you get a major triad built on D. The key of E minor would need a D♯ for a leading tone. Although it would be possible at this point to call it the ♭VII in E minor, you then get its 7th in the top voice and it resolves in the last measure to the chord a P4th above it, making it clear to the ear that you have a V^7 → I progression. Not until this last measure of this excerpt are you firmly now in G Major.

Let's look at one more example of the use of a common chord technique: this time to modulate from A♭ Major to C minor. There is only one flat difference in their key signatures, but we also have to take care of introducing the leading tone for C minor. So, we will need to replace a D♭ with a D♮ as well as change a B♭ to B♮ to give us the leading tone for C minor.

Example 4. From the *Waltz* Op. 39, No. 15 by Johannes Brahms:

Both chromatic changes are done on one chord, V⁷, just before the cadence in C minor. The pivot chord is C minor: functioning as iii in A♭ Major, and i in C minor.

Chromatic Modulation

Chromatic modulation is a process of changing keys by using an ascending or descending chromatic line to introduce a note needed in the new key. The chromatic change in the line provides an opportunity to use a chromatically altered chord, most commonly a secondary dominant or dominant substitute (V or vii in the new key). Following is an example of how this works, showing a change from D Major to E minor, using an <u>ascending</u> chromatic line in the bass.

Example 5. One phrase from the chorale "God the Father, Be Our Stay", by J. S. Bach:

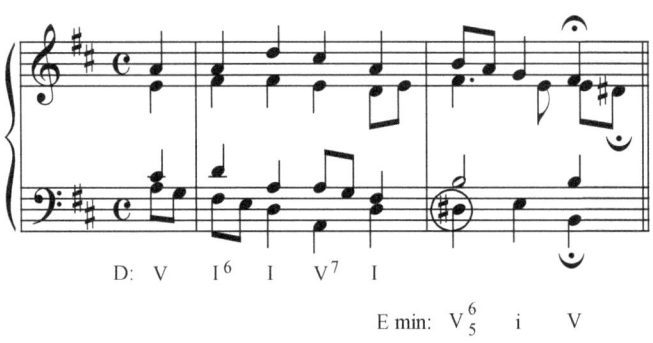

The following excerpt uses a <u>descending</u> chromatic line to change from D Major to G Major.

Example 6. From the *Sonatina in D Major,* by Beethoven:

Notice that the chord used with the chromatic note, C♮, is a dominant substitute, the leading tone diminished triad in G, F♯dim (F♯, A, C♮).

Summary

In this first chapter on modulation, you have studied tonicization, a process of making some scale degree other than ^1 sound like a temporary tonic. Modulation uses the same techniques as tonicization but goes on to stay in the new key for a while after it is established. We then examined two techniques commonly used to change from one key to another closely related key. These two techniques are: (1) common chord modulation and (2) chromatic modulation.

Next

In the next chapter, we continue with modulation by introducing key change techniques that can be used even when the keys are distantly related.

Quiz 31

1. In _____, after changing tonal center focus, the piece goes immediately back to the original key.
   a. modulation
   b. tonicization

2. In the essential process for changing keys, first the original key is established, then a chromatic alteration announces a chord in a different key. The third step is:
   a. go back to the original key.
   b. provide a pivot chord.
   c. confirm the new key with a functional chord progression.
   d. immediately cancel the chromatic change.

3. The keys of G minor and E minor are _____ related.
   a. closely
   b. distantly

4. The keys of G minor and G Major are _____ related.
   a. closely
   b. distantly

5. The keys of A Major and C# minor are _____ related.
   a. closely
   b. distantly

6. Which of the following triads could be a pivot chord between F Major and G minor?
   a. G dim
   b. C Major
   c. E minor
   d. B♭ Major

7. Which of the following triads could be a pivot chord between A Major and E Major?
   a. C# minor
   b. B Major
   c. G# minor
   d. D# dim

8 – 10. Refer to the following passage:

8. Name the original key and the key to which it changes.

9. Beside the abbreviation for each key, write the Roman numeral for the pivot chord. Identify the position of the pivot chord by measure and beat.

10. For the 2nd beat of ms. 2, write the abbreviation for the local key area and the functional designation for the chord (Roman numeral + inversion numbers, if applicable).

CHAPTER 32: MODULATION, PART 2

Objectives:

1. Identify and distinguish among essential techniques and attributes for the following modulation processes:
   a. enharmonic
   b. sequential
   c. common-pitch
   d. phrase
2. Identify which of several chords is enharmonic with a given chord.
3. Specify the change in implied function that results from enharmonically respelling one or more notes of a given chord.
4. Given a short musical passage, identify the type of modulation technique employed.

In this chapter, we continue the study of methods for changing key. These techniques will help in changing to distantly related keys.

Enharmonic Modulation

You already know that an enharmonic note is one that has the same pitch as but different spelling from another note. We look here at how chords can be spelled and named differently through enharmonic changes, and how this can be used in the modulation process. In early music before equal-tempered tuning, composers generally limited modulation to closely related keys. Part of the reason for this was that the further away from a key you got, the less chance that there were any pitches in common. Enharmonic modulations were not used because, for example, an A♭ was not exactly the same pitch as a G♯. Today, however, with our modern tuning system, these enharmonics are usually on the same pitch.

Something extra: Modern keyboard instruments and many other modern instruments are tuned in the equal-tempered system. Doing so allows modulations on such instruments to distantly related keys without some notes sounding "out of key". However, some instruments today do not use this system. If a piece for strings is to remain in closely related keys, the performers may wish to use a tuning system in which enharmonically-spelled notes would not sound exactly the same pitch. Some instruments may be tuned to allow microtones, which are intervals smaller than the equal-tempered half step, for experimenting with the sound of different tunings or to play instruments from cultures that use different tunings.

Assuming 12-tone equal-tempered tuning, here are three different situations that provide the opportunity for using enharmonic notes: (1) respelling a diatonic triad so it is diatonic in a different key; (2) changing a dominant seventh chord to an augmented sixth through enharmonic re-spelling, and (3) changing the functional purpose of a diminished seventh chord through enharmonic re-spelling. First, let's look at how the chords change enharmonically, and then we will see how this is used in modulation.

Altering a chord through enharmonic change

Figure 32-1: Enharmonic re-spelling.

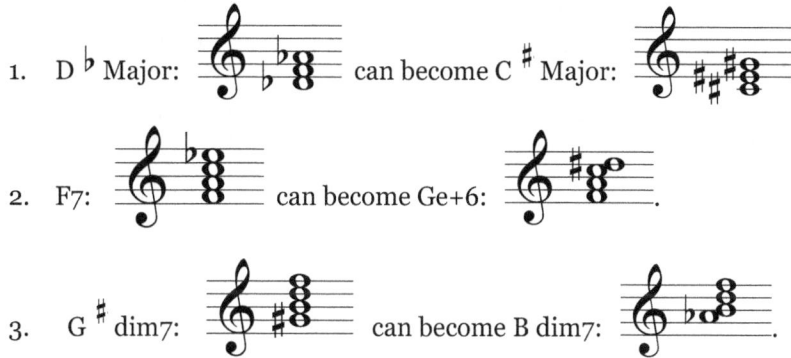

Dual key functions for enharmonic chords

1. The D♭ Major triad functioning as I in the key of D♭ Major could, respelled as C♯ Major, function as V in the key of F♯ minor. Also, the triad C♯ Major functioning as V in the key of F♯ minor could, respelled as D♭ Major, function as the N⁶ chord in C minor.

2. F7 functioning as V7 in the key of B♭ Major could, respelled as a Ge+6 on F, function as a dominant preparation in the key of A (Major or minor).

3. G♯ dim7 functioning as vii°⁷ in the key of A minor could, respelled as B dim7, function as vii°⁷ in the key of C minor.

Examples

In the following piece, the composer gets back to his home key by using a dominant 7th reinterpreted as a Ge+6.

Example 1. From *Waltz*, Op. 9, No. 14, by Franz Schubert:

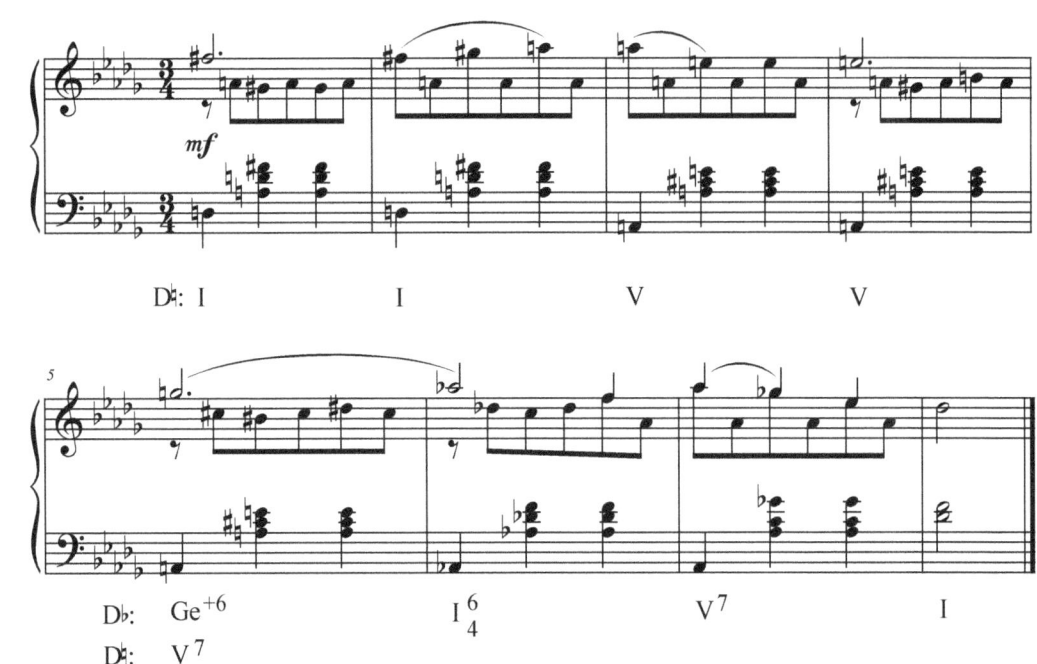

Notice in the fifth measure of the excerpt that the chord is spelled as it had been in previous measures, for the convenience of performance, but it has a dual function and could have been enharmonically spelled in the following way, to clarify its function as the Ge+6 chord in the home key:

Example 1b:

Notice the normal resolution of the +6th chord to tonic 6-4 → dominant 7th → tonic. Next, let's look at an example of using an enharmonic version of a diminished seventh chord to change keys. Look ahead before you listen to this: the last three measures go very fast ("*Allegro molto con brio*" is Italian for "very fast, with brightness").

Example 2. Measures 133-139, Beethoven's *Piano Sonata No. 8*, Op. 13 ("Pathetique"):

The example begins with ms. 133. Look at the spelling of the diminished 7th in ms. 134: F♯, A, C, E♭. This is clearly the vii°7 chord of G minor. Then, on the third beat in the next measure, he respells the chord enharmonically as: D♯, F♯, A, C (D♯ = E♭). Now, it functions as the vii°7 of E minor, smoothly effecting a modulation from G minor to E minor, a distantly related key. You may wonder why there is not a sharp in the key signature when the key changes. This is because in this section, he only starts out in E minor; Beethoven will proceed to change keys several times throughout this section, and the signature of no sharps or flats fit the circumstance of rapid key changes. This process of rapidly changing key centers happens in a section called a "development", something you will study later, when we get to the topic of musical forms.

Sequential Modulation

You already know what a sequence is: the repetition of a passage at a different pitch level. You have seen how this sequence can occur three more times at the same interval and in the same direction. It is also quite common for the passage sequenced to be slightly altered on each repetition. It doesn't have to be exact for the ear to hear the shifting up or down. The next example shows a sequence in a prelude by J. S. Bach in which the result of the sequence is to cause a modulation from A minor to E minor, effecting a return to the home key before ending the piece.

Example 3. Excerpt from *Prelude in E minor*, by J. S. Bach:

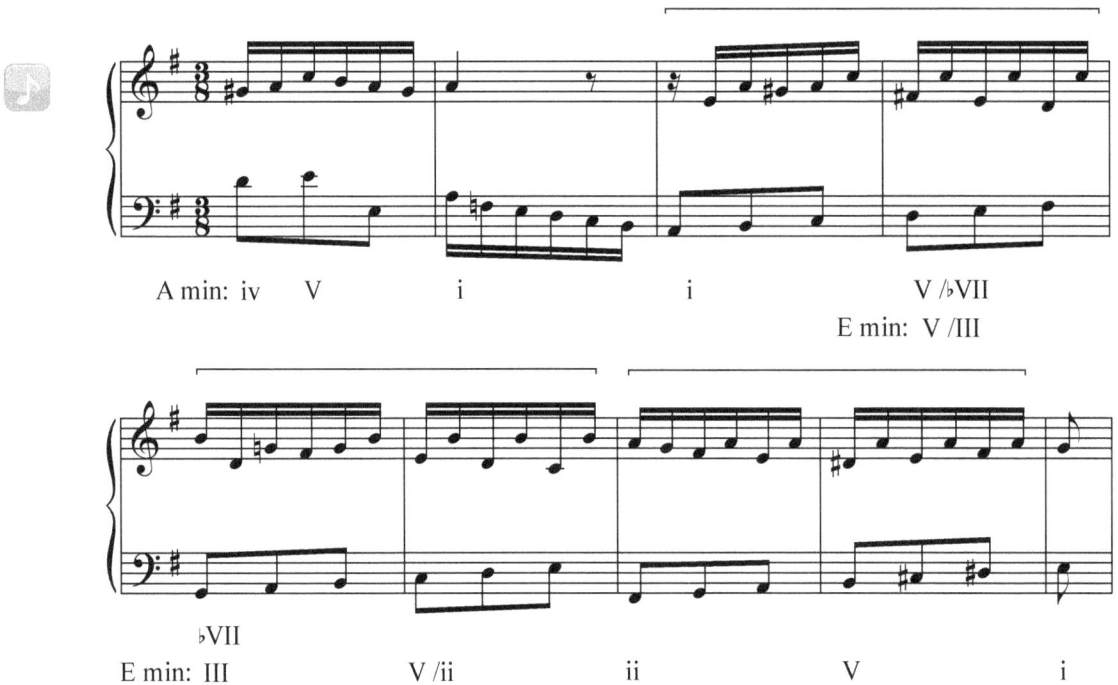

Notice two important features of this sequence:

1. The progression of the chord roots, starting in the third measure, follows a descending "circle of fifths" progression: A → D → G → C → F♯ → B → E.
2. The top line and bottom line in the sequence descend by steps.

    Top line: C → B → A

    Bottom line: A → G → F♯

A descending step progression in melody can always be supported by a circle of fifths chord progression. A composer can just keep going through the circle until she/he reaches the destination key. How the chords in the middle of the sequence are interpreted in the keys is not as important as is the starting key and the destination key. In this case, Bach chose to use notes that were common in both keys, being careful to change the F♮ in A minor to the F♯, in measure 4, needed to help establish E minor. He made a definite move away from A minor in emphasizing G♮ instead of G♯ (the leading-tone in A minor) in measure 5.

Common (Pivot) Pitch Modulation

Common pitch modulation uses a pitch common to both keys to link the two together. This pitch is sustained or repeated, without accompanying chord, to act as a bridge between the two keys, which may be distantly related. In the following example, the pitch D functions in the old key, E minor, as subtonic, and in the new key, B♭ Major, as mediant.

Example 4. from "Tulip", by Heinrich Lichner:

Phrase Modulation

In phrase modulation, one phrase ends with a cadence in the first key; then the next phrase starts in a new key without any transition material linking the two keys. This technique is frequently used in popular music. Many musicians consider this just a key shift, not a modulation, because no modulation procedure is used to transition between the two keys.

If you have a recording of Whitney Houston's version of "I Will Always Love You" (written by Dolly Parton), notice that the song starts out in A Major; then about 2 ½ minutes into the song, it shifts abruptly, at the end of a phrase, up a whole step into B Major. (This song was featured in the movie, *Bodyguard*). In such pieces, this is usually done in order to provide a heightened expression that can be sensed when pitch rises. Another example can be found in "My Heart Will Go On" (by James Horner), the love theme in the movie *Titanic*.

SUMMARY

The following types of modulation were covered in this chapter:

Enharmonic modulation: Using an enharmonic version of a chord in such a way that it has a conventional function in the new key.

Sequential modulation: Using a sequence to shift tonal center to the new key.

Common pitch modulation: Using a pitch that has a conventional function in both keys to pivot from one key to another.

Phrase modulation: After a cadence ends one phrase, the next phrase simply begins in the new key.

NEXT

The next chapter will begin our study of musical forms. We will distinguish the difference between "form" and "genre" and then introduce the first few forms for study.

Quiz 32

1. In _____ modulation, after a cadence, the music simply continues in a different key, with no transition process.
    a. common pitch
    b. enharmonic
    c. phrase
    d. sequential

2. In _____ modulation, the piece uses a sequence to make the transition to the new key.
    a. common pitch
    b. enharmonic
    c. phrase
    d. sequential

3. In _____ modulation, a single note serves as the pivot into a new key.
    a. common pitch
    b. enharmonic
    c. phrase
    d. sequential

4. In _____ modulation, the re-spelled version of a chord leads into the new key.
   a. common pitch
   b. enharmonic
   c. phrase
   d. sequential

5. Which of the following chords is an enharmonic version of C♯dim7?
   a. E, G, B♭, D♭
   b. G, B♭, C♯, E
   c. G, B♭, D♭, F
   d. B♭, D♭, F, A♭

6. If you respell the following chord by changing the F♯ to a G♭, what chord is the result?

   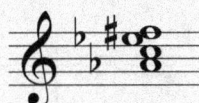

   a. Ge+6 in the key of C.
   b. Ge+6 in the key of G.
   c. V7 in the key of A♭.
   d. V7 in the key of D♭.

7. The following shows an example of _____ modulation.

   a. common pitch
   b. enharmonic
   c. phrase
   d. sequential

8. The following shows an example of _____ modulation.

   a. common pitch
   b. enharmonic
   c. phrase
   d. sequential

9. The following shows an example of _____ modulation.

   a. common pitch
   b. enharmonic
   c. phrase
   d. sequential

10. The following shows an example of _____ modulation.

   a. common pitch
   b. enharmonic
   c. phrase
   d. sequential

CHAPTER 33: MUSICAL FORMS 1

Objectives:

1. Define and distinguish among: structure, genre, and form.
2. Describe or recognize essential features for each of the following forms: simple binary, rounded binary, simple ternary, compound ternary.
3. Sketch or recognize the conventional form diagrams for the following forms: simple binary, rounded binary, simple ternary, compound ternary.
4. Define or describe the following concepts: design, theme, coda.

The first thing to do in this study of musical form is to distinguish among structure, form, and genre.

Structure – how the basic elements of music fit together in relation to one another and to the whole. This concerns the relational patterns created in a composition among the elements of melody, harmony, and rhythm. Functional chord progressions and modulations are topics in the structure of music.

Genre – a distinctive type or category of composition. Examples are: piano sonata, concerto, symphony, opera, mass, popular song.

Form – a broad outline of the design and tonal structure of an entire composition or a complete section of a composition. *Design* is the organization of those elements of music called melody, rhythm, tone color, and tempo.

A single piece that has more than one section can have more than one form because each section can have a different form. A single movement of a piece for violin and piano can have the same form as a movement in a symphony or an act in an opera (which are different genres of music).

There is, of course, an essential relationship between structure and form. How the smaller pieces fit and work together generates the larger form. This is why we study structure before form: structure consists of the pattern of building blocks with which the form is created. To draw on an analogy from narrative technique, structure is how the elements of characters, scenes, linguistic style, and events are related and move and change through the story, while form is the overall plot worked out through these elements.

Relationships among key centers are fundamental to form. Nearly all movements (or single-movement compositions) in the Tonal style unfold in such a way that there is a complete statement in the home key, followed by a digression away from that key, and ending with a move back to "home". This is an integrating principle regardless of the specific form used.

Binary Form

Of course you know that "binary" implies two of something. Pieces in binary form contain two parts: the first begins in the home key and changes to a closely related key by the end of Part 1; the second part begins in the related key and moves back to "home" before the end of the piece, or major section.

Figure 33-1: An outline of the key structure of a piece in binary form.

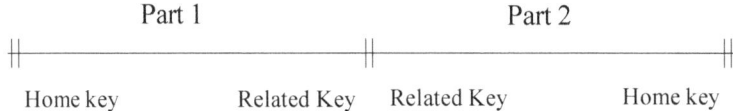

A ***theme*** is a melodic-rhythmic-textural idea that has an important role in the piece. In theoretical discussions, we designate themes with capital letters, starting with "A" for the first theme in the piece. A contrasting theme is given a different letter, but a similar theme – one made from alterations in the first theme but still identifiable as a version of it – is given the same letter with an apostrophe (or with a subscripted number if there will be more than one such variant). Hence, the first theme is always A. If the next theme is a different theme, it would be B. If the next theme after A is a variant of A, it is designated A'. Now we add the thematic information to the outline of the binary form, giving us two possible versions.

Figure 33-2a: Similar theme in 2nd part.

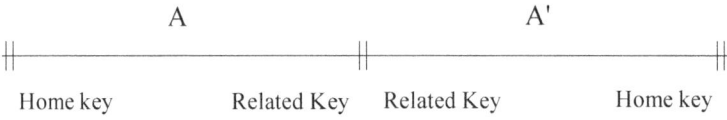

Figure 33-2b: Contrasting theme in 2nd part.

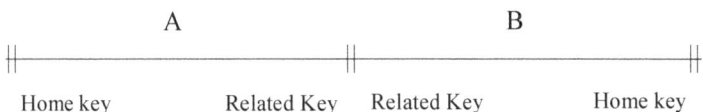

Simple Binary

There are several types of binary form, but we will introduce only two of the most common here: simple binary and rounded binary. Our first example exhibits simple binary form with a contrasting theme.

Example 1. Menuet in D minor, by J. S. Bach:

Figure 33-3: Form chart for this Example 1.

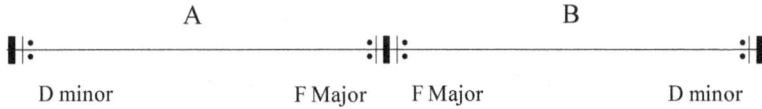

Rounded Binary

In rounded binary, there is a return, in the home key, to the A theme (sometimes varied) after the first theme in the second part.

Exploring Musical Structure

Figure 33-4: *Form chart for rounded binary with contrasting second theme:*

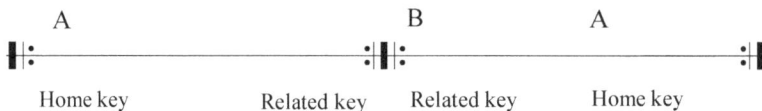

Example 2. Reduction of section from third movement (ms. 37-58) of Mozart's *Symphony* ("Little G Minor"), K. 183:

Notice that the return of the opening theme is altered. The first phrase in this return, measures 49-52, is identical with the first phrase at the beginning of this section, measures 37-40. However, the second phrase, measures 53-58, is altered, but it is still related to the second phrase in the first part, measures 41-44. The alteration facilitates this second phrase staying in G Major instead of modulating as did the second phrase in Part 1.

Example 2b. Look at the first two measures in the second phrase in Part 1:

The V→I progression in D Major is obvious.

Example 2c. The corresponding two measures of the second phrase of A' in Part 2:

While the main chord in measure 53 may be difficult to discern, the V→I in measure 54 clearly keeps the passage in G Major. As if to emphasize that this phrase in the second part is not going to modulate, as did the second phrase in the first part, Mozart repeats these measures (the repetition adding two measures to the phrase). He then ends the section with a perfect authentic cadence in G Major, the home key.

Ternary Form

Simple Ternary

A ternary form looks a bit like the rounded binary with contrasting second theme. There are two noticeable differences: (1) the B theme contrasts from the A theme even more than in the rounded binary; and, (2) the B theme forms a separate full part, with another part for the return to A (or A').

Figure 33-5: Form chart for simple ternary form.

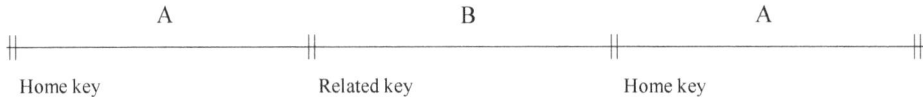

A common practice in songs of the Baroque period (ca. 1600 – 1750) was the "*da capo aria*". This was a song for a soloist accompanied by an ensemble of instruments. It was of simple ternary form. The second (B) part, in a related key, contrasted with the first in mood, musical texture, and sometimes tempo. Since the third part was a literal repetition of the first part, the composer would simply indicate "*da capo*" (D.C.) at the end of the second part, indicating that the performer must repeat from the beginning ("*da capo*" means "to the head"). During part 3, the repetition of the first part, the soloist would often slightly vary the line by adding subtle variations and ornaments. A good example of the *da capo aria* is the first air, for alto, in Part II of Handel's *Messiah*: "He Was Despised".

Example 3. Outline of form for "He Was Despised", Part II, *Messiah*, by Georg Friedrich Händel:

After a brief, eight measure orchestral introduction, the alto begins her solo, in E♭ Major:

Example 3a.

The end of the first part has the following line in the solo:

Example 3b.

The orchestra then has an additional six bars to end this first part, still in E♭ Major. The accompaniment up to this point has been a very smoothly flowing legato. Here is how the contrasting part begins, with a different melodic theme in the solo and a very different accompaniment – the key is now the relative minor, C minor:

Example 3c.

The middle section continues in this manner, ending on a G minor triad, which cancels the leading tone (B-natural), using the subtonic (B-flat) instead. This helps get back to the home key: E-flat Major. Then the score shows "D.C." So, everything starts back at the beginning of the aria. How do they know when to stop? In the score, there is a "*Fine*" at the end of the first part. The first time through, the players ignore this Fine and continue on to the second part; after the repeat, they stop at *Fine*. Here is an outline of the form of this aria:

Figure 33-6: Form chart for Example 3.

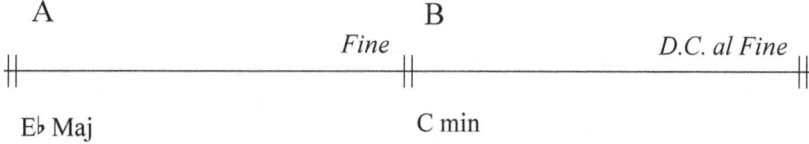

Compound Ternary (Minuet & Trio)

Another form of ternary is a three-part form that contains another form inside of it, usually binary. In the Classic and Romantic periods of music history, the minuet & trio was a particular type of compound ternary form in which each section of the overall ternary form was in binary form, often rounded binary.

Figure 33-7: Form chart for compound ternary.

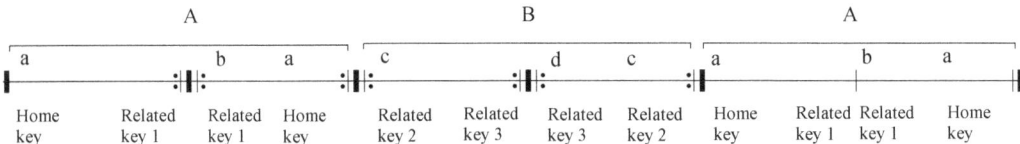

The A sections are the Minuet, and the B, the Trio. Notice that the A section begins and ends in the home key, and that neither of the keys in the contrasting B section is "home". Note also that upon the repeat of the minuet after going through the trio, the repeats of the two parts within the minuet are not usually taken.

For an example, we will look at the minuet and trio form in an early Beethoven piano sonata, *Piano Sonata No. 1*, Op. 2, Nr. 1.

Figure 33-8: Form chart for Example 4.

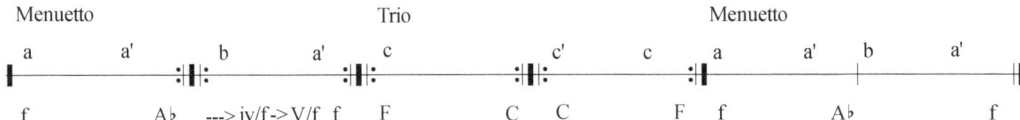

However, we will see that Beethoven inserts some interesting twists in how he weaves the various elements to create this form, making it unique.

The movement begins with a single interval: C, A♭. If this is meant to be part of a triad, then it could be either A♭ Major or F minor, either of which would be tonic for the written key signature of four flats. Therefore, we have to look at the first phrase to see what key is implied by the functional chord progression:

Example 4a.

The E♮ is the leading tone to F, and it is part of the C Major triad, which is dominant to F, so the key is F minor. This first phrase also provides us with the first theme for the minuet part. The minuet is in binary form, with the first part ending with a short "tag" onto the theme, so we have indicated a' to indicate a modified version of the theme. Also, this passage is in the relative Major, A♭:

Example 4b.

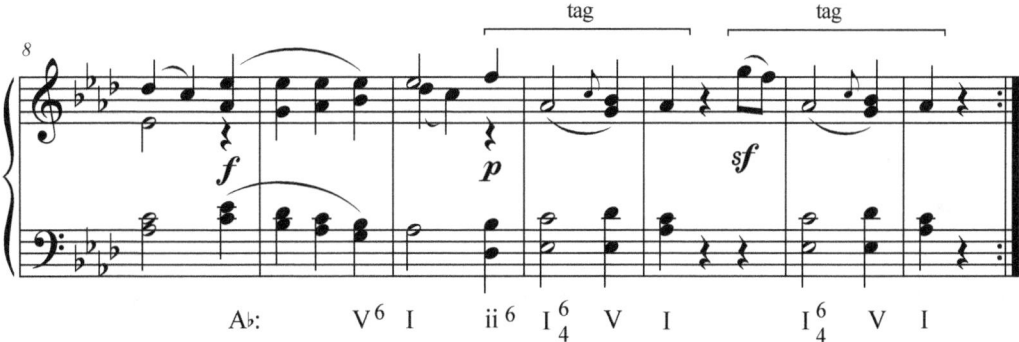

Even as far back as measure 4, the E♮ was replaced with E♭.

Now we are into the second part of the minuet, and it is difficult to tell what key this part is in until you get to the first cadence, which gives you a V of B♭ going to B♭ minor:

Example 4c.

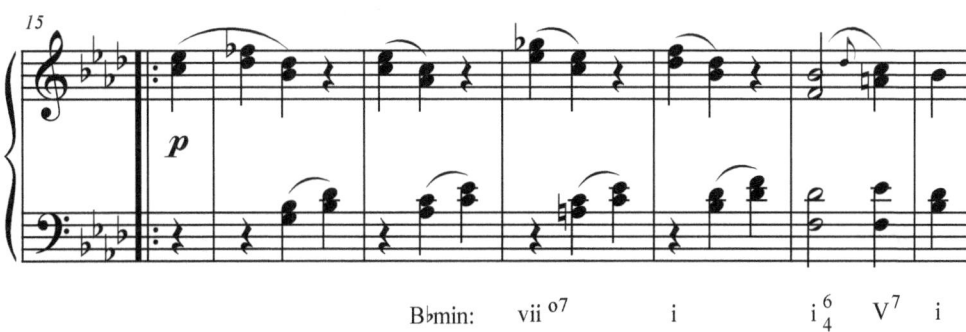

As if to emphasize the importance of B♭, Beethoven then repeats the cadence several times:

Example 4d.

In the form chart, we call B♭ a tonal area, as the iv of F minor. This is because he moves off of the B♭ right after this, as we will see after we look at the theme at this point in the piece.

Now let's look at the theme. Theme "b" is made up of the beginning motive of theme "a", with the last part of it inverted in the left hand and overlapping the right hand motive. Here is the opening motive from theme "a":

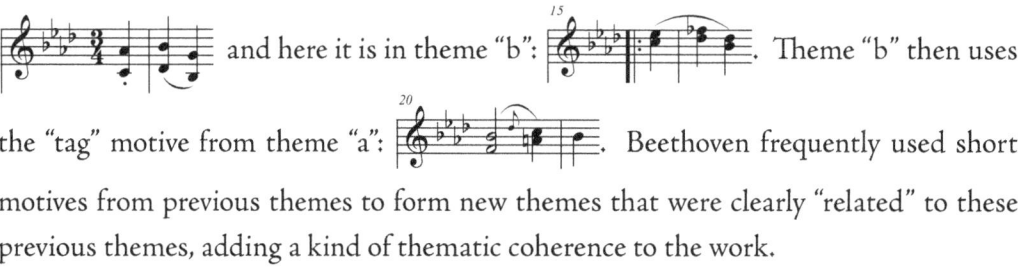

Beethoven frequently used short motives from previous themes to form new themes that were clearly "related" to these previous themes, adding a kind of thematic coherence to the work.

Next, he has a short run in 8th notes that links us back to the opening of theme "a". This is just a transitional passage:

Example 4e.

theme "a"? ---

Notice that the A ♮, which was the leading tone for B♭, has been replaced with A♭. However, he has tonicized C by introducing B♮ (leading tone for C). It is significant that C is the dominant note in F.

Next, notice he uses a sequence to get back to F minor:

Example 4f.

Using the B diminished chord in measure 35 is a way to avoid stating F minor until he is ready to do so with an authentic cadence, which follows, ending the minuet part:

Example 4g.

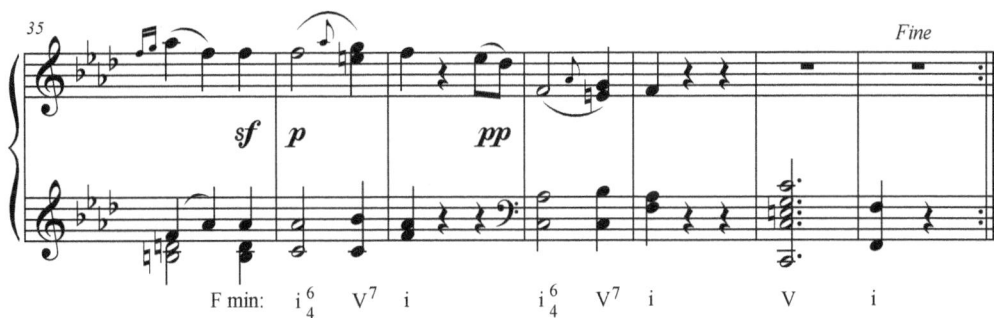

Notice the use of the "tag" motive at the cadence.

Now we will point out only the essential elements of the structure of the trio. At its beginning is theme "c", in the key of F Major, the parallel key to the tonic for the minuet.

Example 4h.

It continues with this theme all the way through the first part of the trio, changing key center to C Major (dominant of F):

Example 4j.

C: I^6_4 V^7 I

The second section of the trio presents a variation of the "c" theme, starting out in C Major:

Example 4k.

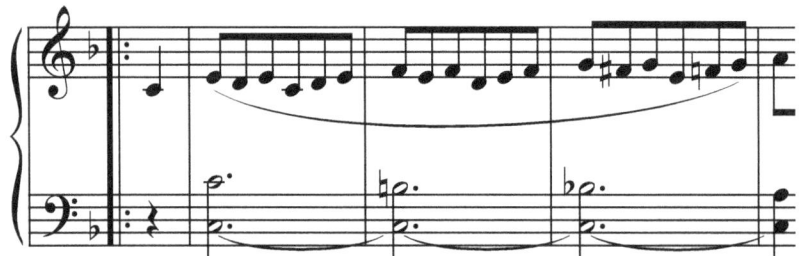

Then he returns to theme "c" in F Major to drive to the end of the trio:

Example 4m.

When the trio ends, there is a *D.C. al Fine* direction, telling the player to go back to the beginning and play the minuet – straight through without the repeats – until getting to the *"Fine"* marking.

Now listen to the entire minuet and trio and see if you can follow the themes, key changes, and overall form. Don't forget at the *D.C. al Fine* to go back to the beginning of the minuet.

Example 5. "Minuet & Trio", *Piano Sonata No. 1*, Op. 2, No. 1, by Beethoven.

Beethoven also wrote movements called "Scherzos", which were in compound ternary form. A *"scherzo"*, in Italian, means *"joke"*. Such compositions are light and usually in a moderately quick tempo. Sometimes the middle section is called a "trio", but often it is named for a shift in mode – from major to minor or *vice versa*. If the first section is in a major key, the middle section could be called *Minore* if in a minor key; if the first section is in a minor key with the middle section in major, it could be called *Maggiore*. For example, in Beethoven's *Piano Sonata* Op. 2 Nr. 2, the first section of the Scherzo is in A Major and is named by its tempo marking, "Allegretto". The second part, the middle section, is in A minor and is called "Minore". As in the minuet & trio, the first section of the scherzo is repeated "*da capo*" and without the inner section repeats.

One more practice should be mentioned. Any of these forms could have a part called a *"coda"* added onto the ending. The word *"coda"* is Italian for "tail". The **coda** extends some ideas (motives or complete themes) that have already been introduced and given some treatment in the main body of the movement, and brings the movement to a satisfactory close. A coda can be quite short – for example, only sixteen measures in Beethoven's *Piano Sonata* Op 14, Nr. 1, 2nd movement. It can also be very long, as in the first movement of Beethoven's *Eroica* Symphony.

Summary

We started with a distinction among three concepts:

Structure – how the basic elements of music fit together in relation to one another and to the whole.

Genre – a distinctive type or category of composition.

Form – a broad outline of the design and tonal structure of an entire composition or a complete section of a composition.

Following are the forms examined in this section:

Binary form – two-part form; two sub-categories:

Simple binary – Part 1 contains only theme A; part 2 contains only theme B (or A'). Conventional form diagram:

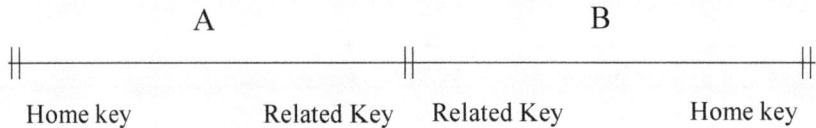

Rounded binary – There is a return to theme A before the ending of the second part. Conventional form diagram:

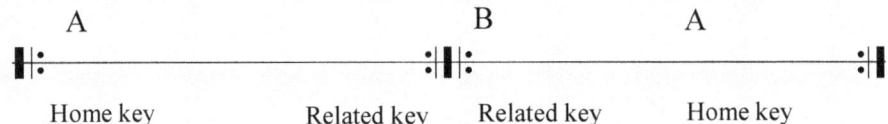

(The repeats are not mandatory, but are common practice.)

Ternary form – three-part form; two sub-categories:

Simple ternary – There are three distinct parts. The middle part contrasts from the first and third parts in both theme and key. Conventional form diagram:

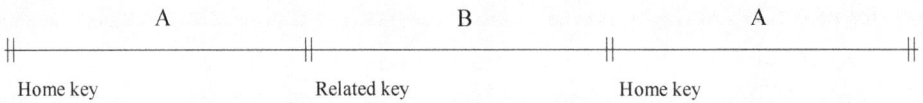

Compound ternary – Each of the three parts is a sub-part, conventionally in binary form. Conventional form diagram:

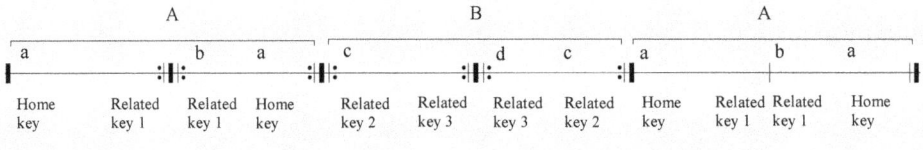

Additional terms defined:

Design is the organization of those elements of music called melody, rhythm, tone color, and tempo.

A *theme* is a melodic-rhythmic-textural idea that has an important role in the piece.

A *coda* is a passage at the end of a piece or movement that extends some ideas (motives or complete themes) that have already been introduced and given some treatment in the main body of the movement, and brings the movement to a satisfactory close.

Next

Our next task will be to study two more forms: Theme & Variation, and Rondo.

Quiz 33

1. _____ shows how the basic elements of music fit together in relation to one another and to the whole.
   a. Form
   b. Genre
   c. Shape
   d. Structure

2. _____ is a broad outline of the design and tonal structure of a piece.
   a. Form
   b. Genre
   c. Shape
   d. Structure

3. _____ is a distinctive type or category of composition.
   a. Form
   b. Genre
   c. Shape
   d. Structure

4. In _____ form, there are three distinct parts and no sub-parts within them.
   a. simple binary
   b. rounded binary
   c. simple ternary
   d. compound ternary

5. In _____ form, there are two parts and each contains only one theme.
   a. simple binary
   b. rounded binary
   c. simple ternary
   d. compound ternary

6. In _____ form, there are three main parts, each being usually a two-part form.
   a. simple binary
   b. rounded binary
   c. simple ternary
   d. compound ternary

7. In _____ form, there are two parts and the second part contains a return to the opening theme of the first part.
   a. simple binary
   b. rounded binary
   c. simple ternary
   d. compound ternary

8. A passage at the end of a movement that extends ideas and ends the piece.
   a. coda
   b. da capo
   c. design
   d. theme

9. A melodic-rhythmic-textural idea that has an important role in the piece:
   a. coda
   b. da capo
   c. design
   d. theme

10. The organization of those elements of music called melody, rhythm, tone color, and tempo:
    a. coda
    b. da capo
    c. design
    d. theme

CHAPTER 34: MUSICAL FORMS 2

Objectives:

1. Identify theme patterns for Theme & Variations form and for Rondo form.
2. Identify common key relationships for the sections of the Theme & Variations or the Rondo form.
3. For a rondo form, report how the episodes differ from the theme.
4. Report what is and what is not typically varied in the theme & variations form.
5. Report what are the earlier names for the theme and episodes of the rondo form.

In this chapter, we will examine two traditional forms: Theme & Variations, and Rondo. It is important to understand that forms are not molds into which a composer pours content. Theoretical ideas are formed after practice and serve to aid understanding. Of course all composers study musical structures and forms, so they do not create work in a vacuum. However, one of the purposes of the composer is to express unique ideas or express ideas in unique ways. Therefore, they know what is expected and can creatively play with listener expectations to generate artistic and individual expression. How one breaks a rule – or an expectation – can be clever or expressive only if she/he knows the expectation very well.

Theme and Variations

In the theme and variations form, the composer first presents a theme in a simple and straight-forward manner: no elaborations, diversions, or complications. Even though this first statement of the theme might contain tonicization of one or more scale degrees in the key, there will be no modulations within it. We will examine a single work to demonstrate essential features of this form.

Example 1. *Piano Sonata No. 11*, K. 331, 1st movement, by W. A. Mozart.
Following is the theme. Notice that it is in two parts. Unlike other two-part forms, there is only one theme, although it is slightly varied in the first half of the second part, and there are no key changes. This is conventional practice for the first section of a theme & variations form.

(The Italian word *"grazioso"* means "graceful".)

The first variation is in the same key and meter as is the theme. Even the chord progressions and bottom bass line are identical. So, what is different? In the case of this first variation, only the rhythm and texture are different. Texture is how many notes are sounding at the same time and in what registers. We will look at only the first part of selected variations; the second part is varied in exactly the same way that is the first part.

Example 1b. The first part of the first variation

Even the texture is similar, so the rhythm is the main variant.

How else is a theme conventionally varied? One way is to change not only the rhythm and texture, but also the mode: in this case, changing major to parallel minor, in the third variation:

Example 1c. Variation III.

Again, if you do a harmonic analysis, you will find basically the same functional chord progression as in the first part of the original theme, even though this is in minor instead of major.

Tempo can also be changed. Variation V is at tempo "adagio". Look at the first eight bars of Variation VI. It is in a different tempo: "allegro". It is also in a different meter, 4/4.

Example 1d. Variation VI:

One more point, the theme & variations form, as is the case with any form, also can have a coda.

Rondo

A *rondo form* is one in which a main theme, called the *rondo theme* or the "refrain", keeps coming back after each diversion to another theme. The contrasting themes are called *episodes*. The general form is: A→B→A→C→A → ... → N → A (N being the last episode). Most common were five-part (A→B→A→C→A) and seven-part (A→B→A→C→A→B→A) forms. The next-to-last part in the seven-part form could be a statement of B, or B', or D. Also, each time A returns, it normally is varied at least slightly from the original statement of A at the beginning of the rondo. In fact, variations in the refrain can give the movement the character of being a combination of a rondo and a theme & variations. In a later section, we will see how the rondo can be combined with yet another form.

In terms of the tonality, the rondo theme is always in the home key each time it returns, and each of the episodes is in a different key or key area. Early rondos in the Baroque period were called *rondeau* (the French name). For an example, we will study an early *rondeau* by Purcell.

We will examine the "Festival Rondeau", from *Abdelazer*, by Henry Purcell. The refrain from this *rondeau* was later used by Benjamin Britten in a set of variations in the *Young Person's Guide to the Orchestra*.

Example 2a. Purcell's refrain:

This is a five-part rondo (A-B-A-C-A), which means that this theme (A) is played three times. Each time it returns, it is played without alterations and always in the home key of D minor. This was typical of the Baroque *rondeau*.

The first episode, called a **couplet** in these early rondeaux (plural for *rondeau*), is in the relative Major key, F Major:

Example 2b. First couplet:

After an exact repeat of the **refrain** (the theme) comes the second couplet (part C), in A minor, including a statement of the V (dominant) of D, preparing the work to return to D minor.

Example 2c. Second couplet:

The terms "refrain" and "couplet" come from their use in poetic works of the Medieval and Renaissance periods in which a refrain alternated with a pair of successive lines of verse called "couplets".

Now follow the (reduced) score for this *rondeau* while listening to it.

Example 2. "Festival Rondeau", from *Abdelazer*, by Henry Purcell:

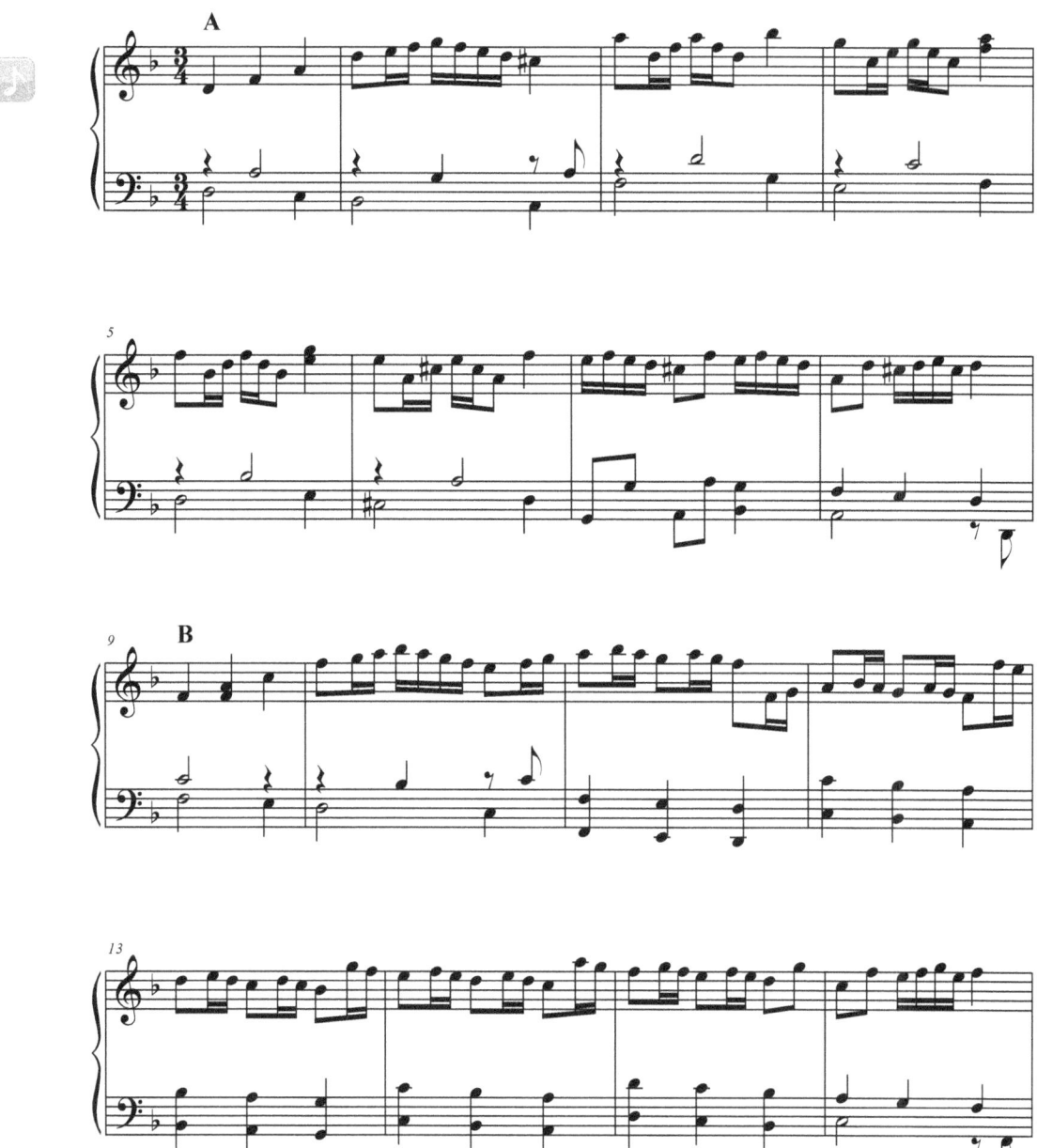

Chapter 34: Musical Forms 2

Summary

Two more forms were studied in this chapter: the Theme & Variations and the Rondo.

Form for theme & variations:

Theme→Variation 1→Variation 2→ … →Variation n (sometimes → coda)
Ways in which theme is typically varied: rhythm, texture, meter, mode (Maj to min, or min to Maj).

Two standard forms for rondo:

Five-part: A→B→A→C→A

Seven-part: A→B→A→C→A→B (or D)→A

The main theme, A, will always be in the home key; the episodes (B, C, etc.) will be in other keys.

Next

We will conclude the study of common musical forms in the next chapter, where we will examine the "sonata form".

Quiz 34

1. Which of the following theme patterns could reflect the theme and variations form?

    a. A-A-B-A'-A

    b. A-B-A-C-A

    c. A-A^1-A^2-A^3-A^4-A^5-A^6

    d. A-B-A-C-A-B-A

2. Which of the following theme patterns could reflect the five-part rondo form?

    a. A-A-B-A'-A

    b. A-B-A-C-A

    c. A-A^1-A^2-A^3-A^4-A^5-A^6

    d. A-B-A-C-A-B-A

3. Which of the following theme patterns could reflect the seven-part rondo form?
   a. A-A-B-A'-A
   b. A-B-A-C-A
   c. A-A^1-A^2-A^3-A^4-A^5-A^6
   d. A-B-A-C-A-B-A

4. In a theme & variations form, each variation is usually in a different key or mode.
   a. true
   b. false

5. In a rondo form, each episode is usually in a different key or mode.
   a. true
   b. false

6. Which of the following is **typically NOT** varied in a theme and variations form?
   a. basic chord progression
   b. rhythm
   c. texture
   d. mode

7. Which of the following **is** common in a theme and variations form?
   a. new basic chord progression in each variation
   b. change of tonal center in the last variation
   c. modulation to distant keys
   d. change in meter in one or more variations

8. In rondo form what is another name for "episode" (used in music of the Renaissance and Baroque periods)?

9. What was an earlier name for the main theme of a rondo?

10. If such existed, a three-part rondo would, in form, look like a _____ form:
    a. binary
    b. rounded binary
    c. ternary
    d. theme and variations

CHAPTER 35: MUSICAL FORMS 3

Objectives:

1. Write the names of the three parts of the sonata form, in the order in which they appear in the piece.
2. Identify design characteristics of the sonata form.
3. Sketch or identify the conventional diagram that shows design details for the sonata form.
4. Describe how each of the following function in the sonata form: development, exposition, recapitulation, transition, coda.
5. Report how many theme groups are normally in a sonata form movement and describe how they are treated in the different parts of the form.
6. Explain or identify the overall key scheme of a sonata form.

Sonata Form

The term "sonata" has been used in two very different ways: as a genre, a *sonata* is a multi-movement composition for solo instrument or solo with keyboard accompaniment. Each movement of such a piece can be in a different form. The *sonata form* is a particular musical form that generally applied to one movement of a musical work. A movement of a sonata, a symphony, a quartet, or any of many other genre, may be in "sonata form". An important design feature of sonata form is the practice of going away from "home base" and then getting back to "home". Of course, several forms such as rounded binary and ternary forms have this as an organizational feature, but the sonata form is the most dramatic and extended of the traditional ways in which this was conventionally accomplished. The second important feature of sonata form is the statement and relationship between two contrasting themes. In many pieces, the two themes can be identified as masculine (strong, angular) and feminine (delicate, flowing). Regardless of how these two themes may be describable in extra-musical terms, they are definitely contrasting in character. The sonata form builds upon and takes advantage of contrasts in themes, key centers, textures, and timing.

The overall form for "sonata form" may be shown as follows:

Figure 35-1: Form chart for sonata form.

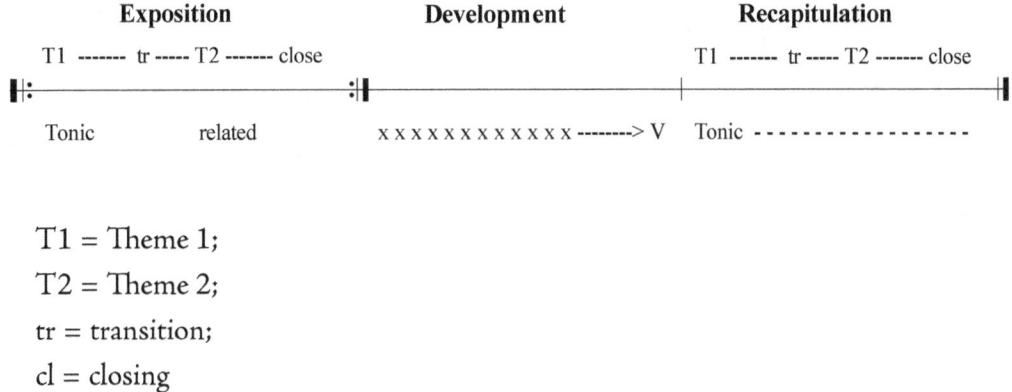

T1 = Theme 1;
T2 = Theme 2;
tr = transition;
cl = closing

There are three parts and two sections in a sonata form. The first part contains the "exposition", in which the ideas (themes) are introduced (or "exposed"). The second part contains a departure from the exposition and then a return. The departure, called the development, works with motives from the thematic material presented in the exposition and takes such material through a number of modulations until it makes a move back toward the home key. The return, called the recapitulation, returns to the two main themes and the home key. Notice that the recap stays in the home key when the second theme is restated instead of modulating. This is done by altering the transition passage between the two main themes. The closing in the recap often is extended into a coda. Sometimes, the restatement of the first theme in the recapitulation is in a key closely related to home base and then modulates back to the home key for the restatement of the second theme. Most frequently the exposition section is repeated, but not always; also, sometimes the second section – development and recapitulation – is repeated. In some cases, neither section is repeated. The themes themselves are much longer than in most other forms and may consist of more than one melody. In those cases where a theme contains more than one melodic idea, it may be clearer to describe it as a "theme group". So, if after the first melody, there is another melody presented, how do you know if it still belongs to the same "theme group" or if it has changed to the second theme? If you have changed to the second theme, the piece will have modulated to a different key and the theme will be clearly a contrast to the first theme or theme group. Also, there will usually be a transitional passage that effects the modulation to connect to the new thematic idea. Those are the basics of sonata form; now we need to look at a typical example. Because these movements are so long, we will show just main ideas with tonal design.

Example 1. *Piano Sonata No. 5, K. 283,* by W. A. Mozart.

Here is a skeletal outline of the overall form:

Figure 35-2: Form chart for Example 1.

	Exposition			Development	Recapitulation		
Measure #:	1	16	23	54	72	83	90
Themes:	Th1	tr~~~ Th2	closing	(mix)	Th1'	tr~~~ Th2	closing
Keys:	G	D	D	--> V/G	G		

Consistent with sonata form, it contains three parts: exposition (expo), development, and recapitulation (recap). The expo takes up the first section, which is repeated. The second section, also notated as repeated, contains the development and the recap.

Let's first look at relative durations. The development is only 18 measures in length, relatively short for this form. Notice also that the statement of Th1 initially takes 15 measures, but in the recap, it is only 11 measures in duration. The piece ends on measure 120. If you do the arithmetic, you will find that the duration from the transition through the end of the expo is the same as from the transition in the second section to the end of the recap (and the end of the piece). This gives us two interesting questions to answer: (1) What happened to the statement of Theme 1 to shorten it in the recap, and what effect does this change have on the piece? (2) Just how similar is the material from the transition through the second theme in each of the two sections, and how is this material different? One difference apparent from the diagram is that Theme 2 is in G Major, the home key, in the recap, whereas it is in the dominant key, D Major, in the expo.

Now let's examine the key scheme. Home key is G Major: the piece begins and ends in this key. The only other main key area is D Major, the dominant of the home key. The statement of Theme 2 in the expo and the material in the development are in D Major; everything else is in G Major. Even though there is some tonicization of other scale degrees, G and D are the only main key areas.

Now review the themes: Th1 opens the expo, then there is a transition (tr) into Th2. The "closing" is made up entirely of material from Theme 2, so it is an extension of the theme to drive the piece to the end of the section. The development section contains pieces made up from ideas from both main themes and the transition. The themes in the recap look just like those in the expo except that Th1 has been modified and shortened. Next, we will examine each section in more detail and take a look at material from the score.

Exposition

Following are the thematic ideas (shown above the staff) and functional chord progressions (below the staff) for the first theme, as it appears in the exposition:

Figure 35-3: First theme group in exposition.

Thematic idea 1b may be heard as a sort of "tag" onto the main idea for Theme 1, which is stated in 1a. The two together make up the entire theme. The harmonic rhythm is basically one chord per measure, but it is speeded up in a bit in 1b. There are two phrases, with a perfect authentic cadence in measures 9-10 and 15-16. The only chord other than tonic and dominant is the subdominant, which carries its conventional role as a dominant preparation. Notice that even though I immediately follows IV, it is inverted in each case, which makes it merely an effective connection between IV and V.

Then we get a transition passage that ends on D. This could imply V in G or I in D. It will depend upon what follows.

Figure 35-4: Transition between themes in exposition.

What follows is Theme 2, and it is in D Major. Here is the opening idea for Th2:

Figure 35-5: Theme 2a.

Next comes a restatement of 2a with some melodic embellishment:

Figure 35-6: Theme 2a embellished.

The chord progression is the same.

Then comes two more melodic ideas still under theme group 2: 2b and 2c:

Figure 35-7: Themes 2b and 2c.

Conventional chord progressions lead to a perfect authentic cadence at measure 38. However, the resolution of the top line is delayed off the beat, which propels the piece onward to repeat the material between measures 33 and 38 (in 38 – 43).

The closing consists of the opening motive from the transition, followed by melody 2a, then 2a embellished (slightly differently from before), and finally the opening motive from melody 2b.

Figure 35-8: Closing the exposition.

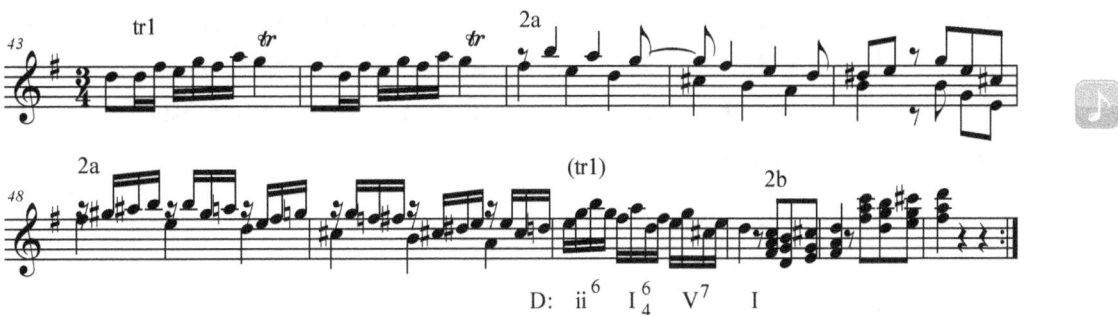

In measure 50 is that very familiar Beethoven authentic cadence: ii (or IV)→I^6_4→V^7→I. However, let's look at the full texture (both hands) for the last four measures:

Figure 35-9: Last 4 measures of exposition.

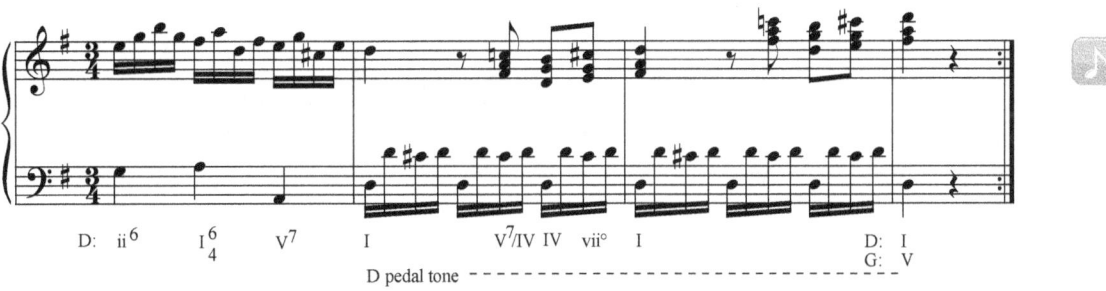

The bass defines the harmony in the first of these measures, but then it sustains the note D through the last three measures. On top of this sustained D there is a functional progression toward the D major triad (in the third to last measure, repeated an octave higher in the next to last measure). When the bass repeats a note, and the chords change over that one single note, the bass is called a **pedal tone**. Notice that the last chord has two possible functions: tonic (I) in D Major or dominant (V) in G Major. Why? Because when the piece takes the repeat, it goes back to G Major at the beginning of the piece, so this D functions as V; after the repeat, the piece goes on into the development section, which begins in D Major, so the D functions then as I. It is very common practice in the Classical period for the last chord in a repeated section to have one harmonic function when the passage repeats and a different harmonic function when it continues on to the next section.

That is the exposition: the two main thematic ideas have been introduced, along with some transitional material.

Recapitulation

We'll take a look at the recap next and then later look at how the development connects the exposition with the recapitulation. The recap starts with the pick-up to measure 72. The piece is back in G Major at this point. Let's see what Mozart does to shorten Theme 1. The opening of this theme through the second beat of the fourth measure is identical with the opening of the expo:

Figure 35-10: Recall theme 1.

In the exposition, this is how the theme continues from this point:

Figure 35-11: Themes 1a and 1b in exposition.

In the recap, it is altered as follows, only hinting at theme 1b in ms. 82:

Figure 35-12: Theme 1 compressed in recap.

Examine what the entire Theme 1 up to the transition looked like in the exposition:

Figure 35-13a: Entire theme 1 group in expo.

Now compare this with the shortened theme in the recapitulation:

Figure 35-13b: Entire theme 1 in recap.

Notice that the expo passage ends with a perfect authentic cadence, but the cadence at the end of theme 1 in the recap is plagal and the tonic triad is inverted, which, being a much less stable progression, propels the piece forward.

What follows for the rest of the recapitulation is a repeat of the corresponding material in the exposition, with only one difference: Starting after the transition passage, theme 2 on through the rest of the recap is transposed to G Major instead of D Major. All passagework from the start of theme 2 is identical with that in the exposition except it is written either down a P5th or up a P4th so it is expressed in the key of G instead of D. The transition is exactly as before, ending on the D. In the exposition, this D functioned as tonic in D, the key of the second theme group in the expo; this time, the same D functions as V in the key of G.

Figure 35-14a: Compare the opening of Theme 2a in the expo:

Figure 35-14b: with the same theme in the recap:

It's the same thing, just down a P5th.

Now compare the ornamented versions of 2a.

Figure 35-15a: Ornamented theme 2a from the expo:

Figure 35-15b: Ornamented theme 2a from the recap:

The rest of the changes are treated the same way: either down a P5th or up a P4th in order for it to be in G Major instead of D major.

Development

The exposition ended with a satisfactory cadence on the D Major triad. At this point, this chord could function as V for the repeat to G Major or as I in the key of D Major. Look at the first four measures of the development, and listen to it.

Figure 35-16a: Opening of development.

It might not look familiar, but it should sound familiar.

Figure 35-16b: Compare it with theme 1a:

Of particular importance in identifying the theme is the interval between the opening D followed by the low F♯ (minor 6th), and then between the high A and the B (minor 7th). Now look at corresponding intervals in the opening theme of the development:

Figure 35-16c: Intervals in opening theme of development.

With the timing being approximately the same, this is enough for the ear to hear this as a variant of theme 1a. Then this same passage is elaborated and repeated (along with the same chord progression) in the next four measures. After this comes a sequence within which is a change back to G Major – and here is a pedal tone on D again:

Figure 35-17: Continuing passage with sequence → back to G Major.

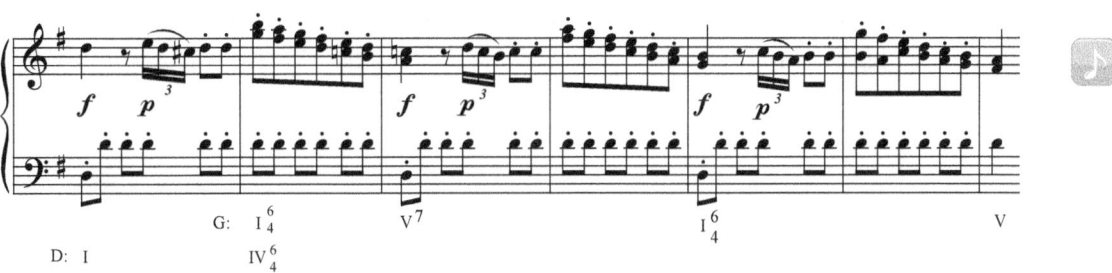

The introduction of the C♮ in place of the C♯ is the clue that you have cancelled D Major. The G Major triad in second inversion in the second measure is the pivot chord. This phrase ends on a half cadence on the dominant (V) of G Major. Thematically, the first measure above is just an ornamented note D; the second measure is a time-compressed version of theme 2a (8th notes instead of quarter notes).

Then we get an interesting, and brief, transition to take us into the recapitulation:

Figure 35-18: Transition at end of development.

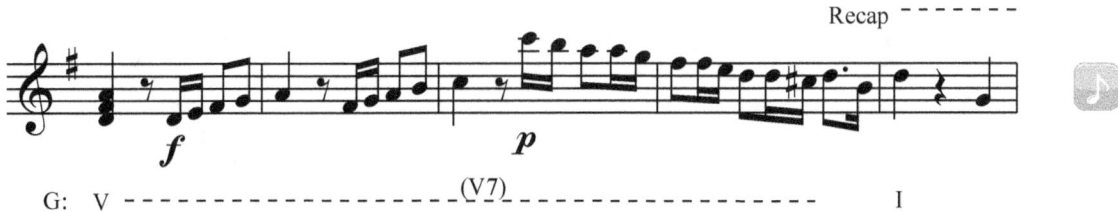

Okay, now go back and review the themes and form of the piece. Then listen to the entire first movement and see if you can follow the form:

Figure 35-19: Form chart for this example.

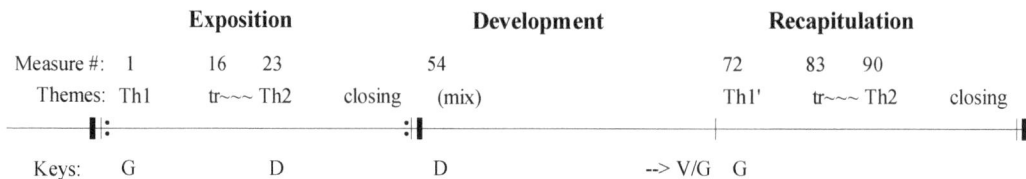

[Note: Most music stores and audio sections of public libraries will have this piece: Piano Sonata in G Major, K. 283, by Mozart.]

Summary

In this last chapter on musical form, you have studied what is perhaps the most dramatic and interesting form in Classical music, the sonata form. It consists of three parts in two sections. The general scheme for this form is given in the following graphic:

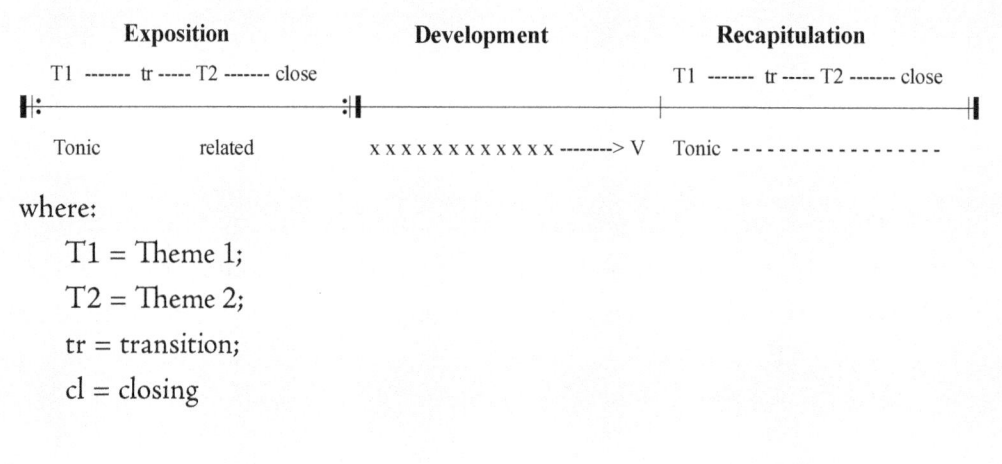

where:

T1 = Theme 1;
T2 = Theme 2;
tr = transition;
cl = closing

Next

In the final chapter, we will take a look at some aspects of music after the traditional tonal music of the 18th and 19th centuries.

Quiz 35

1. In the overall form of "sonata form", the _____ part comes first.
    a. development
    b. exposition
    c. recapitulation

2. In the overall form of "sonata form", the _____ part comes second.
    a. development
    b. exposition
    c. recapitulation

3. The last part in "sonata form" is the _____ .
    a. development
    b. exposition
    c. recapitulation

4. How many "sections" are there in a movement in sonata form?

5. How many "theme groups" are normally found in a sonata form movement?

6. The second theme group in the exposition is normally in the home key.
    a. true
    b. false

7. The second theme group in the recapitulation is normally in the home key.
    a. true
    b. false

8. Which part of the sonata form could, as standard practice, modulate to several (more than two) keys or key areas?
    a. development
    b. exposition
    c. recapitulation

9. The material that connects Theme 1 to Theme 2 is conventionally called a _____ .
   a. closing
   b. coda
   c. codetta
   d. transition

10. Of the tasks to be accomplished in the _____ part, one of these is a modulation to prpare the piece to return to the home key (after having left it for a while).
    a. development
    b. exposition
    c. recapitulation

CHAPTER 36: BEYOND TRADITIONAL TONALITY

Objectives:

1. Name and briefly describe the five means discussed in this chapter by which composers have extended, abandoned, and reinterpreted tonal style.
2. Identify characteristics or examples of each of the following: serial technique, polytonality, ostinato.
3. Define or recognize definitions for: symmetric scale, polytonality, bitonality, ostinato, atonal, tone row.

Western Tonal music through the 19th century emphasized, in each piece or movement of a piece, a tonal goal centered on a single home key. This home tone was established, moved away from, and then finally the piece would focus back on "home". Such structure has been challenged in a number of ways in late Romantic period (19th century to about 1910) pieces, early 20th century experiments with atonality, and in contemporary works that exhibit a new freedom with regard to tonal organization. We will examine some of these main ways that tonality was stretched, abandoned, and reinterpreted.

Late Romantic Music Extensions

There are several 19th century and early 20th century composers whose works, though clearly tonal, seemed to push the envelope of what had been done in Tonal styles. Among these were Frederic Chopin (1810-1849), Richard Wagner (1813-1883), Gustav Mahler (1860-1911), and Richard Strauss (1864-1949) – to name just a few.

We begin with a fairly early example of stretching tonal limits and still returning "home".

Example 1. Chopin, *Prelude in E Major*, Op. 28, No. 9. First, just listen to it and follow the score, paying special attention to the bass (L.H.) part. The entire piece is only twelve measures long, but the tempo is very slow.

Exploring Musical Structure

This is clearly a monothematic piece, which focuses our attention on the harmony. If you examine the opening idea in the first measure, you will notice it returning again in measure 5 and measure 9. The chord progression at measure 5 is identical with the opening for only two beats before it digresses; the one at measure 9 repeats the opening progression for three beats. The progression in the first two measures, though there is not yet a cadence, clearly identifies the home key of E Major: I→V→I→IV→ii→V. The piece actually ends with a perfect authentic cadence in E Major.

Examine the measure just before the first return of the opening idea. We had a progression to V, which resolved deceptively to vi at the end of ms. 3, then back to V and another deceptive resolution to vi at the beginning of ms. 4. Then on the second beat of ms. 4, there is a chord that looks like V⁷/V, if we hear the D♯ as a non-harmonic note. The fact that the F♯ is in the bass and there is an A♯ in the upper voices, provides strong support for hearing this as a secondary dominant function.

Example 1b. Ms. 4-5:

However, it does not resolve in the most expected way. Instead of moving immediately to V, we get a progression to the dominant substitute, vii⁷. Only at the very last note in ms. 4 does the C♯ on top move to a B so we get a dominant chord, after which is the first return to E Major and an exact repetition of the first two beats of the beginning of the piece. So, you have deceptive resolutions of dominant and a secondary dominant that resolves to a dominant substitute. The top voice in these measures also indicates a stretch in traditional tonality in that you have non-harmonic notes that stretch through several chord changes. Look at the top line from the last beat of ms. 3 through the first beat of ms. 5:

Example 1c. Ms. 3-5:

The D♯ is consonant with the bass at the V chord, then it is suspended over into the next measure where it is dissonant with the C♯ in the bass. It obviously is not a member of the secondary dominant chord on the second beat, so we are still looking for its

373

resolution. Then it moves by step down to C♯ on the third beat, but at the point where it moves, this note forms a seventh with the D♯ in the bass. While this may sound like a member of a seventh chord, it still is not a resolution that is consonant with the bass. Sevenths in Tonal style still want to move on down by step. Well, the C♯ does finally resolve to B at the beginning of the next measure exactly where we have the return to E Major and the opening passage. Notice that the D♯ remained non-harmonic through two changes of chords, which further delayed our anticipation of resolution; then the resolution was not consonant. Such are typical Romantic period techniques that are used to prolong harmonic and melodic stress in such pieces.

There are many interesting features of this piece that stretch traditional tonality, such as tonicization of key centers that are distant to E Major, but let's look at just one more place. In measure 8, Chopin uses enharmonic respelling to pivot the listener rather abruptly back into E Major. Let's see how this is done.

Example 1d. Ms. 8-9:

There is a strong progression in A♭ through the third beat; then follows the same strong progression in E. How did he get so quickly from A♭ to E? Look at the chord in the upper voices on the third beat: E♭, A♭, C: an A♭ Major triad. Then the C changes to C♭, giving us the minor triad on A♭. Now let's respell these notes: E♭→D♯, A♭→G♯, and C♭→B. The result on the next beat is the triad G♯, B, D♯, which is the diatonic iii chord in E Major. However, it immediately is transformed into V very easily: since iii has two notes in common with V, he just moves the G♯ up to A to form the 7th of V⁷ in E and then moves to I at the beginning of measure 9, where the opening of the piece returns again. Because of the enharmonic change, the rather abrupt tonal shift occurs quite smoothly.

Another way in which late Romanticists differed from Classical style was in frequently using wider registration and greater variety in rhythms in melodic material.

Example 2. Check out the melodic theme in the first 13 measures of *Ein Heldenleben* (A Hero's Life), Op. 40, by Richard Strauss:

Notice how quickly the pitches move through different pitch ranges. Also, notice the variety of rhythms. Tonally, it begins on tonic (E♭). Then we notice chromatic notes in measures 7 and 10 through 12, finally ending on the dominant note (B♭) at the end of the melody in measure 13. Notice that in measures 11 and 12, Strauss wrote all five of the chromatic pitches not found in the E♭ major scale of the home key (in E♭ scale: E♭, F, G, A♭, B♭, C, D; outside of E♭: B♮, A♮, F♯, E♮, and C♯). Experiments with using all twelve pitch classes were very common in music from late 19th century onward (but occasionally could be found even before then).

Impressionistic Style

In the early 20th century, some composers experimented with sets of pitch-class material that were quite different from major and minor scales. We introduced these when covering sections on non-diatonic, modal, and non-Western scales. There was much experimenting with the exotic sounds of non-Western tonal materials, such as modal and pentatonic scales used in traditional folk music from a variety of cultures. Another characteristic of Impressionistic music was the frequent, rather long stretches during which tonal center was abandoned, suspending the attention of the listener on the sonority of a particular sound created by a collection of notes. This worked best when using scales that were symmetric in nature. In a ***symmetric scale***, there is a repetition of a single interval or a set of intervals. Common examples are:

    the 12-note chromatic scale (all half steps);

    the 6-note whole-tone scales; and

    the 8-note octatonic scales (succession of half- + whole-step pattern).

During this period in music history, musicians, authors, painters, and sculptors all exchanged ideas. In several cases, a composer would write a piece based upon creating a sound that could link to the style of visual art, or would write a piece to evoke a visual impression (such as Debussy's *La Mer* – The Sea).

There is much to study in this music, but let's focus on techniques used by the Impressionists to cause the listener to lose track of pitch center and focus on the qualities of chords, colorful textures and melodic ideas. There are many composers during this period who practiced such techniques. Central to the movement were Claude Debussy, Maurice Ravel, and Charles Griffes. Let's demonstrate this style with a couple of passages from Debussy.

Example 3a. Consider the following passage from *1st Arabesque* by Debussy, ms. 6-9:

The bass clearly emphasizes E, which, if you looked at the end of the piece, turns out to be the key, but it does not sound tonal. For one thing, the progression of triads in the left hand would be I→vi⁶→I→vi⁶, not exactly a conventional progression in Classical style. If you put all of the notes together in the same octave except the D♯, you get the following:

Figure 36-1: Pentatonic scale in Example 3.

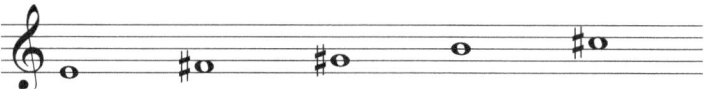

This pentatonic scale sets the tone of the piece until the D♯ arrives. When it does, it sounds non-harmonic for two reasons: (1) it is out of the sound of the pentatonic collection; (2) it forms a harsh dissonance of a major 7th against the bass. It sounds "non-harmonic" not because it is outside of a prevailing triad but because it is outside of a prevailing scale.

Example 3b. Later in the same piece – measures 15-16 – we hear the following:

Well, if your ear is by now tuned to scale qualities, this should sound whole-tone-**ish**. What's the "ish"? the C♯. However, this note does not, in this case, sound like it does not belong. So what is the scale?

Figure 36-2: Another scale in Example 3:

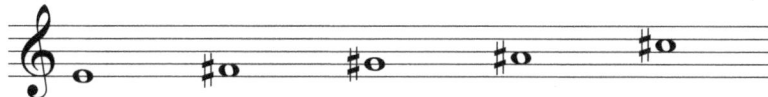

a whole-tone-ish pentatonic! (perhaps Debussy's own invention)

Bitonality and Polytonality

Another excursion in the early 20th century was into **polytonality**: sounding more than one key at the same time usually separated in register (pitch range). **Bitonality** is the use of <u>two</u> keys simultaneously. Early examples of writing in more than one key simultaneously can be found in some works by Maurice Ravel, Igor Stravinsky, Bela Bartok, and Charles Ives. In Stravinsky's ballet Petrushka, one clarinet plays a C Major triad while another clarinet plays an F♯ Major triad under it:

Figure 36-3: C Major + F♯ Major.

Bartok's Mikrokosmos No. 125, "Boating", ms. 1-14, is bimodal, has a pentatonic collection on E♭ in the right hand:

Figure 36-4a: Pentatonic scale in "Boating":

and a six-note scale that could be either G Mixolydian (missing 3rd) or G Dorian (missing 3rd) in the left:

Figure 36-4b: Six-note scale in "Boating":

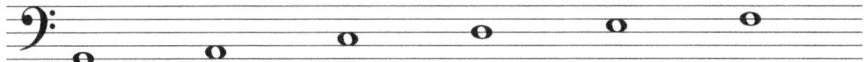

Listen to a short excerpt from this piece. Can you hear different modal sounds in different parts?

Example 4. Mikrokosmos #125, "Boating", by Bela Bartok, first 14 measures:

The repeating pattern in the left hand is called an ***ostinato***, a very common feature in music since the early 20th C.

One of the most interesting examples of a piece containing polytonality is "Putnam's Camp", the second movement of *Three Places in New England*, by American composer Charles Ives.

Atonality and Serial Music

The most severe departure from Tonal style came through a revolution spearheaded by Arnold Schoenberg. He proposed eliminating the influence of traditional tonality by constructing pieces in such a way that all 12 tones in the octave were used, so that no one tone was the focus of the structure. In fact, no two or three tones should have a traditionally tonal focus in his 12-tone technique. Other composers before him had used all twelve tones of the equal-tempered tuning system in order to experiment with this tonal resource in single pieces. One of the earliest examples is found in the 18th century in the fugue section of the "Prelude and Fugue in B minor" from the *Well Tempered Clavier, Book I*, by J. S. Bach. Following is the main theme from this piece, showing the first appearance of each of the twelve notes. We simply count the first pitch class as 1, the second as 2, the third as 3, etc. until we reach the 12th. Repetitions of a pitch class already sounded are not counted again.

Figure 36-5: All 12 pitch classes in J. S. Bach theme.

So, all twelve pitch classes are sounded in the course of this single melody, but the piece is still in B minor. (Caution: We are counting pitch classes, not just notes. So, the B♯ in the last measure is not counted because it is in the same pitch class as C♮, which has already been played.)

Later, in the music of Richard Strauss, we find all twelve pitch classes in a theme from *Also Sprach Zarathustra*. We count the pitch classes of the twelve tones in the same manner as above:

Figure 36-6: All 12 pitch classes in R. Strauss theme.

Still, the passage emphasizes an overall focus on C and G and maintains its tonal context.

However, the above excursions, though interesting extensions of pitch resources, were not done to eliminate tonal centering. Works in which tonal centering has been avoided, through the way pitch resources are structured, are called **atonal** works. Arnold Schoenberg proposed a system of structuring in which a fixed succession of tones would comprise the pitch-class material for the piece. This succession has been called a **tone row**, or a **series** (hence the term "serial music"). Such tone row would have to go through all of the twelve pitch classes before going back to a previously sounded pitch except that there can be immediate repetitions of single pitches or short motives. Harmonic content would likewise be derived from sequences of pitches within the row. The row can appear in the four structures we discussed earlier for variations of a motive: prime, inversion, retrograde, and retrograde inversion. For inverted forms, one would follow the exact succession of intervals except to invert them.

Figure 36-7: The four forms of the tone row in Schoenberg's Suite, Op. 25:

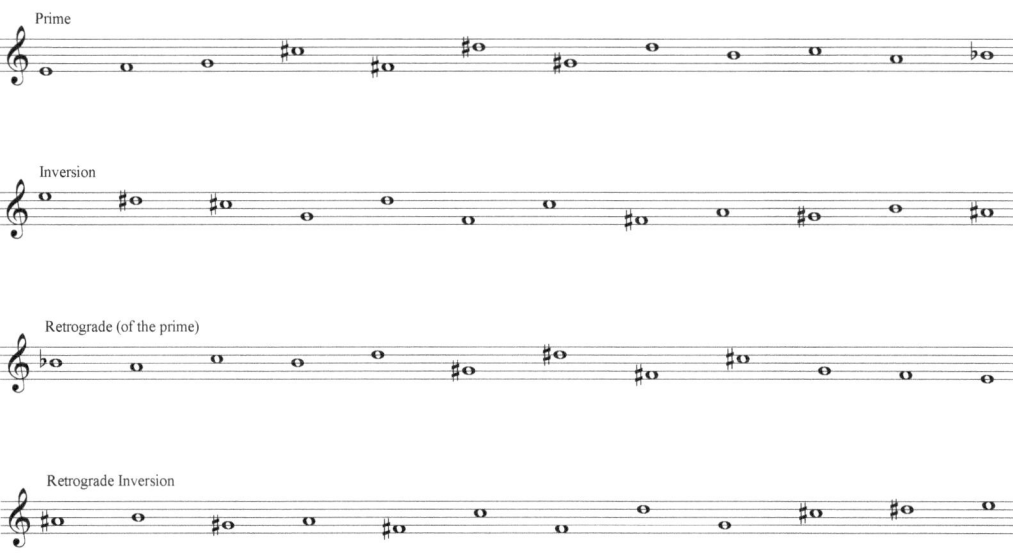

In addition, you can have transpositions of each of these. This provides 48 varieties of possible rows.

Example 5. Here is the beginning of the Prelude from the *Suite for Piano*, Op. 25, by Arnold Schoenberg:

While going into detail about how the row technique is used melodically and harmonically is beyond the scope of this explanation, one can certainly hear that tonal centering is not supported. Notice, however, the expression generated by very precise and sensitive control of rhythm and dynamics.

One of the most dramatic and expressive uses of atonal serial technique can be found in *Igor Stravinsky's In Memoriam Dylan Thomas*. Dylan Thomas had written a poem for his father, upon his father's death, "Do not go gentle into that good night". Igor Stravinsky had approached Dylan Thomas about doing an opera together with him. (Can you imagine?) However, before they could discuss the project face-to-face, Dylan Thomas died while in New York. Upon hearing of Thomas' death, Stravinsky set the "Do not go gentle" poem to music. The piece is based upon a five-tone row, used in various transformations.

Example 6. Excerpt from "In Memoriam Dylan Thomas", by Igor Stravinsky. Listen to the opening melody of the song for this piece.

The opening gesture sounds like a 7-tone row, but it is really two 5-tone rows which overlap by sharing pitches:

Figure 36-8: Tone row structure from Example 6.

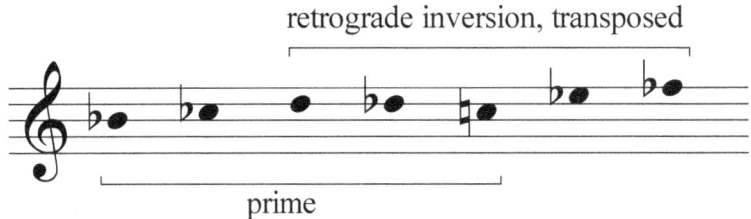

Some atonal music may sound bland and lifeless to you, but do not discount the expressive possibilities of this technique until you hear this piece. There is a very important lesson here: Technique does not have to master the composer; the composer can master the technique.

Contemporary Experiments with Tonality

Since the middle to late 20th century, some composers have made a move to re-establish tonal centering as an organizational feature of their works. In some cases, they simply have returned to an extended form of tonality similar to what was used in works of the early part of the 20th century or even earlier. Such works may be described as "neo-" ("new") – for example, neo-romanticism or neo-classicism (more in regard to classical forms than structure). In other cases, there may be an attempt to produce tonal centering while avoiding or extending the traditional harmonic relations and progressions.

Let's look at a contemporary tonal piece that creates a tonal context in non-traditional ways.

Example 7. We will examine some features of "Anna's Theme" by John Corigliano, from the movie *The Red Violin*.

Example 7a. It opens with a motive that returns four more times in the piece:

This is not enough to establish anything except a melodic idea that is central to the piece. So, let's look at and listen to the first phrase:

Example 7b. First phrase of "Anna's Theme".

The note D is the first, highest, and lowest note and is articulated more times than is any other note in the phrase. The ear is naturally going to hear D as an important note. However, we still don't have enough information to say for sure what key or mode we are in; only that it could be D Dorian. It is easy to hear that the G at the end of the phrase does not sound like a "home base", so the melodic cadence has the sound of a progressive cadence at the end of an eight-measure phrase. Well, we do actually get a repeat of the idea with a different ending, providing a second phrase that has the character of a consequent to the first phrase.

Example 7c. Second phrase of "Anna's Theme".

Now this second phrase ends with a terminal melodic cadence with the G♯ sounding like a leading tone. We can thus easily hear that the opening period of antecedent and consequent phrases have, by the end of the second phrase, established A minor as the (at least temporary) key. What are some non-traditional features of this opening passage?

- Each phrase begins on the subdominant relative to the key established at the end of the period.
- The opening definitely emphasizes D Dorian instead of a key.
- The first phrase ends on G♮ the subdominant of D Dorian, or the subtonic of A minor. (A half cadence on the dominant in the prevailing key would have been the most common ending of a Classical antecedent phrase.)

Now let's examine a place where there is a non-traditional – but very musically effective – progression back to the opening motive.

Example 7d.

We get a diminished seventh chord, which could be the vii⌀⁷ of D, but the 7ᵗʰ of the chord does not resolve downward by step, as it would conventionally move in a traditional tonal work. This chord does actually move to a D, but the 7ᵗʰ of the chord moves up a step to C♮ and then up another step to D. Also, the C♮ forms an unusual, highly dissonant diminished 8ᵗʰ with the C♯ bass, adding to the tension that needs resolution. Now let's look at how the piece ends:

Example 7e.

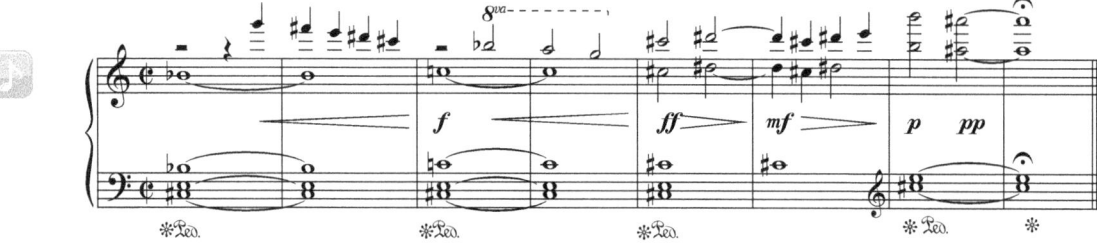

The opening motive, transposed, is played one more time. There is no need to continue. What is left unstated (which would likely include a motion of the A♯ in the top line on down to G♯) purposefully leaves the listener hanging at the end, an effect that is part of the sound and purposeful effect of the piece. So, we have a piece that starts by emphasizing D Dorian, with an early cadence emphasizing A minor, but then ends emphasizing D-sharp (perhaps Dorian) – certainly not a "home" key, as we would expect in traditional tonality.

There is much more one could say about such a piece, but the above observations give you a glimpse into non-traditional ways that tonality can be utilized in today's music.

Summary

Since the early 20th century, many composers have extended, abandoned, and reinterpreted tonal style. These include:

- **Romantic period** extensions of chords and chord functions, but maintaining tonality and home key.
- **Impressionism** in music: In these pieces, tonal center is obscured or suspended by passages in which non-diatonic scales, including symmetric scales, are used, and tonal chord functions are avoided, creating more emphasis on the "color of sound" than upon tonal direction.
- **Polytonality** has been employed to have passages playing in different keys at the same time.
- **Atonal, serial** compositions have used tone rows to create new rules for organizing pitches so that migration toward a tonal goal is abandoned.
- A **new kind of tonality?** Contemporary composers are experimenting with creating tonal focusing without using traditional chord functions.

Quiz 36

1. Which of the following would you commonly find in Romantic period pieces?
    a. use of a chromatic tone row
    b. enharmonic modulation
    c. polytonality
    d. serial composition

2. Having different parts in a piece simultaneously sounding in different keys is called:
    a. serial technique
    b. mixed keys
    c. polytonality
    d. ostinato

3. A short passage that is repeated several times, without change, in one part while the rest of the music varies is called:
   a. serial technique
   b. mixed keys
   c. polytonality
   d. ostinato

4. A scale in which an interval or short sequence of intervals is repeated is called a _____ scale.
   a. symmetric
   b. diatonic
   c. pentatonic
   d. modal

5. Use of non-diatonic scales was most frequent in which of the following styles?
   a. Baroque
   b. Classical
   c. Romantic
   d. Impressionistic

6. Serial technique was most commonly practiced in _____ music.
   a. Classical
   b. Romantic
   c. atonal
   d. modal

APPENDICES

Appendix A ♦   Recommended Listening Exercises
Appendix B ♦   Instrument Transpositions and Ranges
Appendix C ♦   Quiz Answer Keys

APPENDIX A: RECOMMENDED LISTENING EXERCISES

These comprise recommended listening to full songs or movements of larger works with suggestions of theoretical principles to track during listening.

Chapter 7

Ludwig van Beethoven, *Piano Concerto No. 1*, 1st movement
Listen for very rapid runs through the major scale.

Chapter 9

Scott Joplin, "The Entertainer" (or any ragtime piece)
Count beats and listen for where notes are held over the beat.

John Philip Sousa, "The Stars and Stripes Forever" (or nearly any Sousa march)
Tap the beat and listen for the dotted rhythms.

Chapter 12

Ignace Paderewski, *Minuet in G*
Listen for the many occurrences of quintuplets and triplets in this piece.

Franz Schubert, *Moments Musicale*, Op. 93, No. 3
There are lots of grace notes in this piece.

Chapter 13

Claude Debussy, *La Mer*, 1st movement
Listen for several whole-tone passages. When you think you hear one, pause the piece and see if you can pick out the scale on your instrument (or sing it).

Charles T. Griffes, *Roman Sketches*, "The Fountain of the Aqua Paola"
Several passages emphasize pentatonic scales or are entirely pentatonic. The colors of sound, due to use of pitch resources and texture are amazing, even though it is for only one instrument (the piano).

Chapter 15

Richard Rogers, "My Funny Valentine"
Good song for listening to the sound of seventh chords.

Appendix A: Recommended Listening Exercises

Chapter 19

Scott Joplin, "Maple Leaf Rag" (or any ragtime piece)
The sound of syncopated rhythms.

Wolfgang Amadeus Mozart, *Symphony No. 40*, 3rd movement
Very interesting early example of what was called "hemiola", and gave the sense of shifting meters (but without a change in meter signatures).

Dave Brubeck, "Blue Rondo a la Turk"; and Paul Desmond, "Take Five"
Both on the album *Take Five*, these are examples of unequal beats and unequal subdivisions of a measure.

Leonard Bernstein, *West Side Story*, "America"
Listen for the shifting meter.

Chapter 20

Art Simon and Paul Garfunkel, "Are You Going to Scarborough Fair?"
This is an example of a song in Dorian mode. It is also interesting to listen to the war protest verse that is going on against the poetic love song.

Chapter 21

Wolfgang Amadeus Mozart, *Piano Sonata No. 2*, K. 280, 2nd movement (Adagio)
Excellent example of effective use of non-harmonic notes in a solidly tonal piece.

Chapter 24

Ludwig van Beethoven, Piano Sonata No. 14 ("Moonlight"), Op. 27. No. 2, 1st movement
Good example for aurally studying chromatically altered chords.

Chapter 26

J. S. Bach, "Two-Part Invention in D Minor"
Listen for different ways a motive is altered and to how the two voices expressively move against one another.

Chapter 29

Benjamin Britton, *The Young Person's Guide to the Orchestra*
Excellent for being introduced to the different instruments of an orchestra; how they sound individually and in groups.

Chapter 31

Johannes Brahms, *Waltz*, Op. 39, No. 15
Listen for modulations. There are several in this piece. After going away from the home key, how does he get back before the end?

Chapter 33

Ludwig van Beethoven, *Piano Sonata No. 1*, Op. 2, No. 1, 3rd movement ("Menuetto")
For an example of the minuet & trio form, listen to this entire movement while following the score in the book.

Chapter 34

W.A. Mozart, *Piano Sonata No. 11*, K. 331, 1st movement
Good example of theme and variations form.

Henry Purcell, *Abdelazer*, "Festival Rondeau"
Listen to this rondo form piece while following the score in the book.

Chapter 35

W. A. Mozart, *Piano Sonata in G Major*, K. 283, 1st movement
Listen to this piece while following the sonata form chart in the book (Section 4-8, just before the summary).

Chapter 36

Bela Bartok, Mikrokosmos #125 ("Boating")
Listen for two different scales or keys being played at the same time.

Igor Stravinsky, *In Memoriam Dylan Thomas* (Dirge-Canons and Song)
A very expressive and dramatic piece in the early atonal serial style.

John Corigliano, "Anna's Theme" (from the movie, The Red Violin)
Example of a contemporary piece in a modern tonal style.

APPENDIX B: INSTRUMENT TRANSPOSITIONS AND RANGES

Notes:
- Only the most common band and orchestra instruments are included.
- All ranges shown are practical ranges.
- For instruments that sound where written, the "Concert range" column is blank.
- Instruments are listed in conventional orchestral score order.
- Remember how the C clef is interpreted.
- A clef with an "8" above or below it indicates all pitches are an octave higher or lower than they are without the 8.

Instrument	Sounds	Concert range	Written range
Piccolo	8ve higher	(treble clef, with 8va: low D to high C)	(treble clef: low D to high C)
Flute	as written		(treble clef: middle C to high C)
Oboe	as written		(treble clef: Bb below middle C to high D)
English Horn	P5th lower	(treble clef: E below middle C to A above treble staff)	(treble clef: B below middle C to high E)

Appendix B: Instrument Transpositions and Ranges

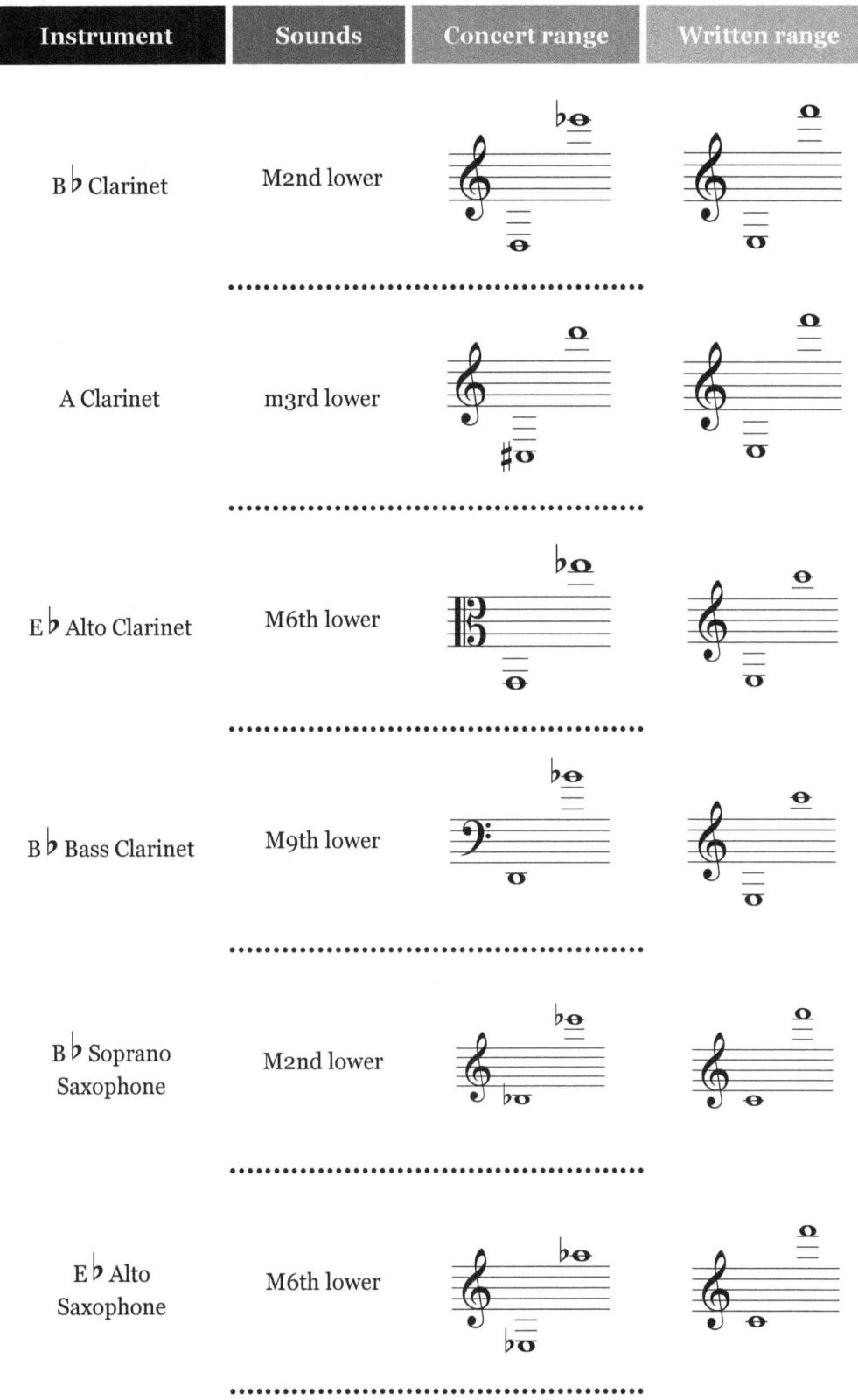

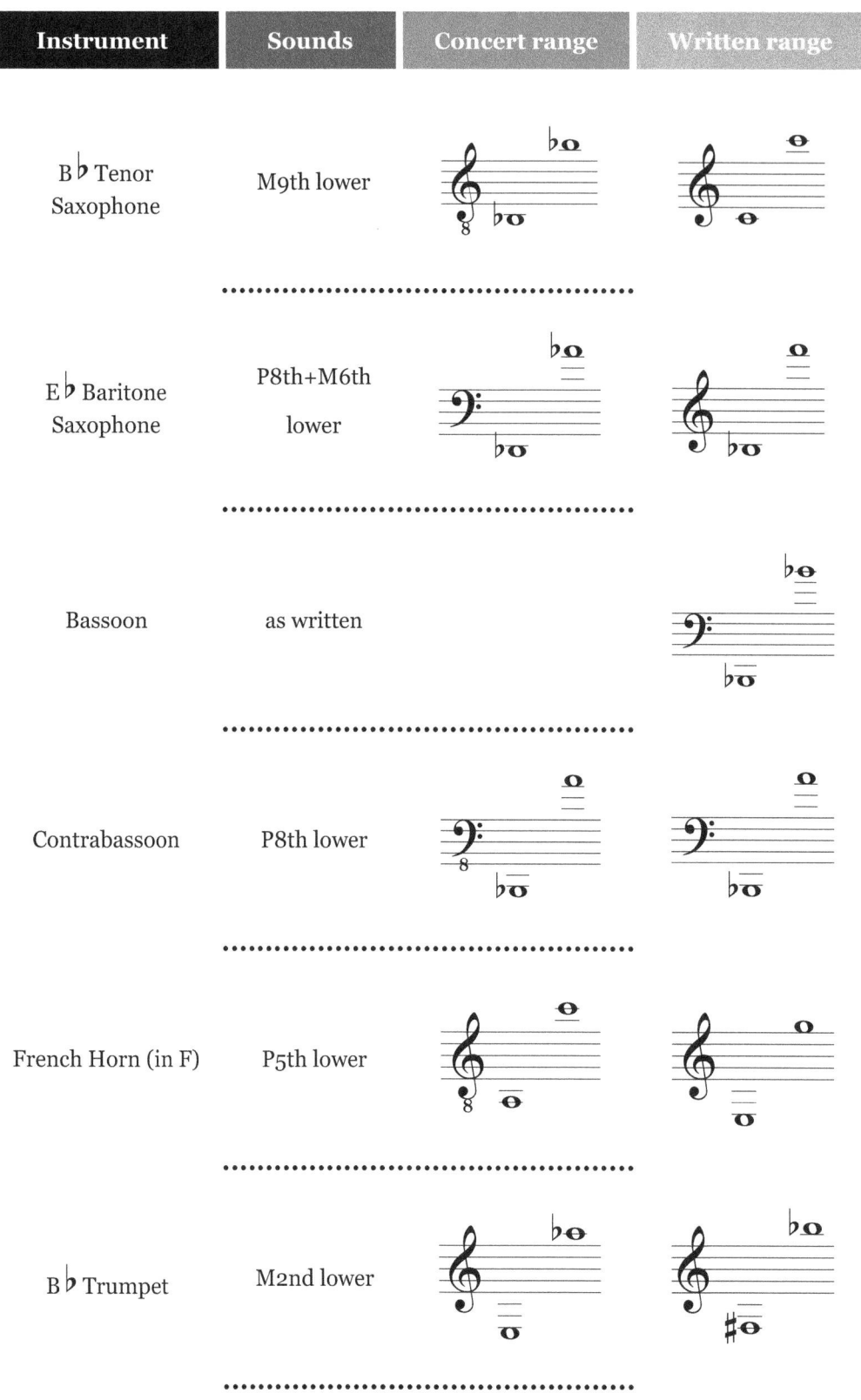

Appendix B: Instrument Transpositions and Ranges

Instrument	Sounds	Concert range	Written range
Euphonium	M9th lower		
Tenor Trombone	as written		
Bass Trombone	as written		
Tuba	as written		
Timpani 26-25"	as written		
Timpani 29-28"	as written		

397

Exploring Musical Structure

Instrument	Sounds	Concert range	Written range

Instrument	Sounds
Timpani 32-30"	as written
Xylophone	P8th higher
Marimba	as written
Vibraphone	as written
Bells (Chimes)	as written
Celesta	P8th higher

Appendix B: Instrument Transpositions and Ranges

Instrument	Sounds	Concert range	Written range
Harp	as written		
Piano	as written		
Violin	as written		
Viola	as written		
Cello	as written		
Double Bass	P8th lower		

399

APPENDIX C: QUIZ ANSWER KEYS

Quiz 1

1. a
2. f
3. b
4. c
5. d
6. k
7. g
8. m
9. j
10. e
11. c
12. j
13. d
14. e
15. f
16. g
17. k
18. h
19. b
20. a

Quiz 2

1. c
2. e
3. b
4. d
5. d
6. a
7. c
8. b
9. b
10. c

Quiz 3

1. G
2. F
3. G
4. D
5. F
6. A
7. D
8. F
9. left
10. right

Quiz 4

1. E
2. A
3. D
4. G
5. F
6. B
7. C
8. a
9. a
10. c
11. b
12. d
13. a
14. c
15. d

Quiz 5

1. a
2. b
3. a
4. c
5. a
6. b
7. b
8. a
9. c
10. b

Quiz 6

1. b
2. d
3. e
4. a
5. c
6. a
7. b
8. c
9. b
10. b

Quiz 7

1. 3 and 7
2. G Major
3. F Major
4. F♯ Major
5. mi
6. B♭
7. A♭
8. D
9. C
10. F♯
11. dominant
12. tonic

Quiz 8

1. sharp; flat
2. 4th; 5th
3. C
4. B♭
5. E
6. F♯
7. E♭
8. F
9. G
10. A♭

Quiz 9

1. d
2. c
3. c
4. a
5. b
6. d
7. b
8. a
9. b
10. a

Quiz 10

1. m3
2. dim5
3. P4
4. m7
5. M2
6. aug2
7. m6
8. P8
9. aug4
10. M3
11. M6
12. P5
13. aug6
14. dim7
15. dim5
16. b (minor)
17. e (augmented)
18. perfect 4th
19. major 2nd
20. minor 3rd

Quiz 11

1. a
2. a
3. b
4. c
5. F♯
6. F
7. E♭
8. E♭
9. E
10. a

Quiz 12

1. b
2. c
3. d
4. c
5. b
6. a
7. a
8. e
9. d
10. b

Quiz 13

1. d
2. b
3. a
4. c
5. b
6. c
7. b
8. d
9. c
10. a

Quiz 14

1. D
2. E♭
3. D
4. E♭
5. B
6. F Major, root pos.
7. G♯ dim, 1st inv.
8. E minor, root pos.
9. D aug, 1st inv.
10. E♭ minor, 2nd inv.
11. F minor triad
12. E diminished triad

Quiz 15

1. c
2. a
3. b
4. a
5. d
6. b
7. d
8. a
9. minor-minor
10. Major-minor
11. Augmented-Major
12. diminished-minor
13. Major-Major
14. c
15. b
16. a

Quiz 16

1. IV
2. ii6
3. I_4^6
4. V
5. iii$_6$
6. period
7. b
8. a
9. d
10. c

Quiz 17

1. b
2. a
3. d
4. c
5. d
6. 7th
7. b
8. V^7
9. iv^6
10. ii°$_6$

Quiz 18

1. b
2. d
3. c
4. a
5. 1
6. 3
7. 4
8. b
9. a
10. c

Quiz 19

1. d
2. c
3. $\frac{3}{8} + \frac{2}{4}$
4. written accents off the normal beat locations; rests inserted at weak beats or off of beat positions; ties hold notes through beat positions.
5. $\frac{2}{4} + \frac{6}{8}$
6. $\frac{3}{8} + \frac{3}{4}$
7. ♪♫♫♪♫♫♪
8. ♪♫♫♪♫♫♪
9. composite meter
10. syncopation

Quiz 20

1. b
2. d
3. c
4. Lydian
5. Dorian
6. Mixolydian
7. Phrygian
8. a
9. d
10. d

Quiz 21

1. c
2. d
3. a
4. e
5. b
6. d
7. a
8. c
9. b
10. e
11. d
12. c

Quiz 22

1. b
2. c
3. a
4. d
5. 5: leaps in both voices in same direction to a P5th
6. 2: overlap in pitch range
7. 3: voices too close together low in bass staff
8. 4: parallel octaves
9. 6: similar motion leaps in both voices twice in succession
10. 7: all leaps in upper voice; steps in bass. This is backwards from normal.

Quiz 23

1. Parallel P5ths between bass and alto.
2. First chord: wrong note doubled.
3. Overlapping voices: alto B overlaps tenor C.
4. Leading tone doubled in second chord.
5. The 7th of the dominant 7th chord does not resolve downward by step; it resolves upward. Also, the common note, G, was not maintained in the tenor part.
6. Leading tone in soprano does not resolve up to tonic. This also forces doubling the wrong note in the second chord.
7. First chord is a primary triad in 1st inversion (IV6): the soprano note should be doubled.
8. Leap in same direction to a P8 (the C) in alto and bass.
9. Parallel motion from dim 5th to P5th in soprano and alto.
10. Bass and tenor voices cross.

Quiz 24

1. Ge+6
2. B (actually the ii°)
3. III+
4. It+6
5. Tr+6
6. N6
7. V+
8. Fr+6
9. i^6_4 or V
10. i^6_4 ; V

Quiz 25

1. V^7 / IV
2. Fr^{+6}
3. V+
4. N^6

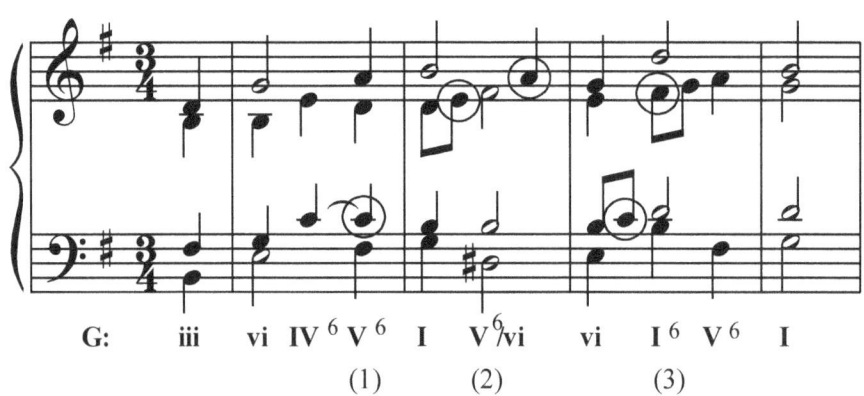

Correct alternative answers:

(1) could be V 6-5 with no non-harmonic note in the tenor voice;

(2) could be V 6-5 / vi with no non-harmonic note in soprano;

(3) could be iii with the G in the alto circled as a non-harmonic note instead of the F; or the student could label two chords here: iii followed by I⁶ and no non-harmonic notes in the alto voice.

Quiz 26

1. Phrases: Two four-measure phrases: antecedent-consequent.
   Cadences: both are progressive.
2. Motive 1 begins each phrase, up a step in the second phrase.
3. Sequence: The melody of the fist phrase is repeated a step up in the second phrase, forming a sequence.
4. Arpeggios are marked with a dotted slur in the example above, with the chords outlined written below these slurs.
5. The first shape is the rising and falling line of the first two measures. The last part of this shape is then repeated in the next measure. The entire phrase has a shape that rises and then falls just slightly at the end of the phrase. Each phrase is identical in shape.
6. Most likely harmonic rhythm is two chords per measure; also accept one chord per measure. Also accept a judgment that the harmonic rhythm may be irregular (static through most of the phrase and then moving at the end).
7. Notes specially emphasized are marked with asterisks. These are the minimum; the student may identify others – e.g., the high E♭ in ms. 2-3 and the high F in ms. 6-7.

Quiz 27

HINT: For motive 1 in the second phrase, try using the same chord progression used for this motive in the first phrase but up one diatonic step, even though in B♭ some of the chords will not seem to follow the conventional progression of chords (in C minor, they will be the same progression as in the first phrase).

The following is a model solution, but the student may choose many other options. This assignment will have to be sent in to an instructor for individual evaluation and suggestions.

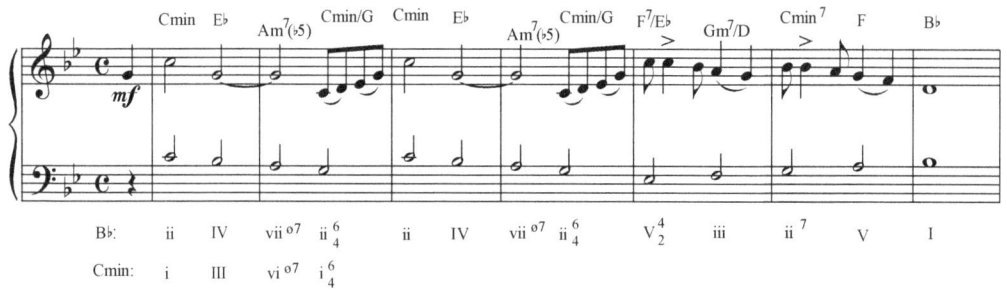

Quiz 28

Model solution (by J.S. Bach):

Quiz 29

1. c
2. a
3. d
4. b
5. a
6. a
7. c
8. d
9. b
10. c
11. a
12. d

Quiz 30

1. Root progression expectations are the same; and the bass line is the foundation for the harmony.

2. In jazz, the 7ths in 7th chords are usually treated as chord notes; in classical style as non-harmonic tones. In jazz, parallel motion is very common, with parallel 5ths and 8th common; in classical style, frequent contrary motion is important to help independence of voices. In jazz, musicians frequently improvise; in classical style, solo lines are written out.

3. a. chord note
4. D, F♯, A, B
5. b
6. c
7. a
8. b
9. d
10. c

Quiz 31

1. b
2. c
3. b
4. b
5. a
6. d
7. a
8. A min à D min
9. Am: iv; Dm: i
10. Dm: ii$^4_2$

Complete solution for 8-10 example:

A min: i   iv   V   i   iv
                D min: i   ii$^4_2$ V^7 i

Exploring Musical Structure

Quiz 32

1. c
2. d
3. a
4. b
5. a
6. d
7. c
8. a
9. d
10. b

Quiz 33

1. d
2. a
3. b
4. c
5. a
6. d
7. b
8. a
9. d
10. c

Quiz 34

1. c
2. b
3. d
4. b
5. a
6. a
7. d
8. couplet
9. refrain
10. c

Quiz 35

1. b
2. a
3. c
4. 2
5. 2
6. b
7. a
8. a
9. d
10. a

Quiz 36

1. b
2. c
3. d
4. a
5. d
6. c

www.ingramcontent.com/pod-product-compliance
Lightning Source LLC
Chambersburg PA
CBHW080723230426
43665CB00020B/2589